The
Nature
of
Space

A book in the series Latin America in
Translation / En Traducción / Em tradução
Sponsored by the Duke–University of North
Carolina Program in Latin American Studies

The Nature of Space

Milton Santos

TRANSLATED BY BRENDA BALETTI
WITH AN INTRODUCTION BY SUSANNA HECHT

DUKE UNIVERSITY PRESS   DURHAM AND LONDON   2021

A Natureza do Espaço: Técnica e Tempo, Razão e Emoção

Dados Internacionais de Catalogação na Publicação (CIP)
(Câmara Brasileira do Livro, SP, Brasil)
Santos, Milton, 1926–2001
A Natureza do Espaço: Técnica e Tempo, Razão e Emoção
/ Milton Santos.—4. ed. 2. reimpr.—São Paulo: Editora
da Universidade de São Paulo, 2006.—(Coleção Milton
Santos; 1)
Bibliografia.
ISBN 85–314–0713–3
1. Espaço e tempo 2. Geografia 3. Geografia—Filosofia
4. Geografia humana I. Título. II. Série.
02–3478 CDD-910.01
Índices para catálogo sistemático:
1. Espaço e tempo: Geografia: Teoria 910.01
2. Tempo e espaço: Geografia: Teoria 910.01

Designed by Matthew Tauch
Typeset in Garamond Premier Pro by Westchester
Publishing Services

Library of Congress Cataloging-in-Publication Data
Names: Santos, Milton, author. | Baletti, Brenda C., [date] translator.
Title: The nature of space / Milton Santos ; translated by Brenda Baletti.
Other titles: Natureza do espaço. English | Latin America in
translation/en traducción/em tradução.
Description: Durham : Duke University Press, 2021. | Series: Latin
America in translation/en traducción/em tradução | Includes
bibliographical references and index.
Identifiers:LCCN 2021000786 (print) | LCCN 2021000787 (ebook)
ISBN 9781478013488 (hardcover)
ISBN 9781478014409 (paperback)
ISBN 9781478021704 (ebook)
Subjects: LCSH: Space and time. | Geography.
Classification:LCC BD621 .S2613 2021 (print) | LCC BD621 (ebook) |
DDC 114—dc23
LC recordavailableathttps:// lccn.loc.gov/2021000786
LC ebook recordavailableathttps:// lccn.loc.gov/2021000787

Cover art: Photograph of Milton Santos, 1977.

Contents

Introduction to the
English-Language Edition

Milton Santos
Rebel of the Backlands, Insurgent Academic, Prescient Scholar

SUSANNA HECHT

Milton Santos was a Brazilian geographer, development ana-
lyst, and activist. Born into a family of teachers descended from
slaves, he was among the most prominent public intellectuals of
his generation. His intellectual ties to French analyses of regional
development and American critical geography did much to transform those fields, from their somewhat parochial perspectives to
perspectives more engaged in both theory and practice "from the
South." Santos helped transform the understandings of development and provided a robust critique of development planning as
it unfolded in the 1960s and 1970s, while simultaneously forging
new methods and practices for the transformation of communities, as well as new understandings of how nature, history, and the
complexities of lived life produced citizenship, rights, and the formations of urban and rural life.

Milton Santos's writings are enjoying new prominence as his work is finally more widely translated. Appreciations of his intellectual contributions have recently appeared in special issues of journals such as *Antipode* (in 2017) and in volumes such as the collection edited by Luis Melgaço and Carolyn Prouse, *Milton Santos: A Pioneer in Critical Geography from the Global South.* Such belated acclaim is appearing now, in part, because his letters and archive are now available at the Institute for Brazilian Studies (IEB) in São Paulo, which materials have helped chart his complex international trajectory. The extent and influence that Santos had on his international networks in France, the United States, and Brazil has become better known as this archive has become accessible. Santos's status in research in critical and integrative geography has advanced as these areas have grown in prestige and as Latin American and especially Brazilian scholars have assessed his legacy.[1] This intellectual inheritance is deeply cosmopolitan and multilingual, and it reflects his engagement with French geographers and regional development thinkers as well as his dedication to reconsidering and nourishing Brazilian geography, helping it evolve from what had been a kind of descriptive and cartographic slumber into a discipline focused on tracking and analyzing the complexity of the forces and outcomes of Brazil's aggressive modernist planning, warp-speed urbanization, and environmental change. In his highly itinerant life, Santos also expanded relationships with Marxist and development geographers in the United States, such as Richard Peet and Neil Smith, on the problematics of development as discourse and practice, and he later interacted geographer and planning scholar (and Henri Lefebvre acolyte) Edward Soja on the constructions of spatiality and postmodern geographies.

Santos built upon the long-standing "French connection" maintained by Brazilian intellectuals with their continental counterparts, although historically this had been expressed primarily through the consumption of continental fashions. In contrast to what had been a kind of imitative affinity, Santos contributed actively to Third World decolonial analytics and a strong critique of Third World development—especially the dominant growth pole models—to the French geographic community, whose members included such thinkers as Jean Tricart and development geographer Yves Lacoste. He questioned whether such models could easily fit with the tropical realities they were meant to transform and what, really, these places were supposed to transform into, once one looked at the realities a bit more closely. Diasporic intellectuals from Brazil were, as Ferretti points out, part of "international, cosmopolitan and multilingual scholarly and activist networks on geography and development, where they interacted with scholars from the 'Global North' and exerted an important influence in these radical circuits, especially in the 1960s and 1970s."[2] As an Afro-Brazilian from the interior of the Brazilian Northeast, Santos was part of a broader community of political exiles that included physician (and geographer) Josué de Castro (who worked at institutes with Michel Foucault and Gilles Deleuze) and economist and regional planner Celso Furtado, both of whom had participated in the attempts to transform the Northeast under the new ideas of regional planning and had left under duress during the military dictatorship (1964–1985). Santos, like his exiled colleagues, had held important political and activist positions as a planner and advisor in the Northeast development agencies, and indeed in the highest realms of national politics. The Northeast was a hot spot of national poverty, the apotheosis of uneven development, and a laboratory for the politics and practices of development—and was a brutal realm for development models to fail in. Santos was a close advisor of President João Goulart during an especially tumultuous and radical phase in Brazilian history. Santos traveled with him to Cuba in 1961 and dreamed of an international career. Santos had in mind the world of diplomacy rather than that of exile.

Like Josué de Castro (*The Geography of Hunger*) and the economist Celso Furtado (*Obstacles to Development in Latin America*), the critiques developed by this exile cohort were informed by significant experience in the bureaucracies and realities of tropical development politics and practices. These, in the end, did little to change the approach to, or the reality of, the economic structures of the Northeast, especially once the military took over in 1964. These exiles, however, were collectively able to begin critical and substantive rethinking of development discourses and practices through their ideas, which were rooted in the history, landscapes, repeated climate catastrophes, and vast social inequalities of the Northeast. It is in this context that Santos's work can be seen as shaping and updating the nature of the debates on development through theory, but also tying these questions to the material processes, including (and especially) those of the environment, that produced the poverty, wealth and instabilities in the socio-economies of the perennially insurgent Northeast. Santos's work shaped the nature of the debates on development through modifying classic geographic "man and nature" thematics with modern political economic ideas, while De Castro worked from the medical and historical perspectives, and Furtado from the development economics framings of Henri Perroux's growth pole development ideas, and Raul Prebisch's import substitution macropolitics. This intellectual dynamic contextualized the more rooted "totalizing" approach embraced by Santos, and his strong critique of the planning practices of the time.

Historians of science and scholars of cultural studies and politics have made the mobility of ideas a focus in the construction of cosmopolitan cultures. This approach ranges from the long history of indigenous guides informing the work of Von Humboldt and European enlightenment sciences to today's remote sensing experts, historians, and development analysts.[3] What is surprising is how late critical geography and critical development studies were in really understanding and embracing the work of Latin American scholars, especially geographers such as Milton Santos, who were years if not decades ahead of the curve when their ideas and insights— the Latin American origins of which were certainly underappreciated— became all the rage in Euro-American academic circles and seminar rooms. Partly this has to do with the Anglophone dominance of postwar geography and the poor understanding in the US of how integral Latin American thinkers were to the creation of critical studies of development, especially as it evolved in France.[4] These circuits were not exactly unknown but were certainly appreciated to a lesser extent than "dependista" scholars such as the sociologist (and later president of Brazil) Fernando Henrique Cardoso.

During the period of the decolonization of the Third World after World War II, as well as of what one might call the "golden age of planning" in Brazil (of which the city of Brasilia is probably the best known result), a series of showcase projects were being implemented in the Brazilian Northeast for managing watershed basin development under the more general influence of French regional economists, the CEPAL (United Nations Center for Economic Policy for Latin America) school of macroeconomics, and Tennessee Valley Authority (TVA) intellectuals and technocrats.[5] This combination of development paradigms, as well as the aggressive *ex nihilo* high modernist (and authoritarian) urban planning, was to become the hallmark of Brazilian planners and their advisors throughout most of the postwar period, especially during the dictatorship, and was widely used as the operative model for regional planning throughout South America.[6]

The conditions of possibility for activist scholars at this time were primarily as participants in a fragile progressive moment from the mid-1950s to the early 1960s, as critics and public intellectuals, and, with the arrival of the military regime, finally as exiles. Santos's collaboration in and commitment to critical analytic circuits in geography, development studies, and theories of globalization were fueled in part by the features of his own biography, and despite the early appearance of his published work (beginning in the 1960s and continuing through the early 1980s), Santos's ideas are especially insightful because he came to them as a very dark "preto," even in the expansive Brazilian lexicon of race, and as a person from "the interior"— the poverty-wracked hinterlands of the Brazilian Northeast, shaped by the legacy of slavery, indigenous death, millenarianism, revolt, and poetry.

EARLY TIMES IN THE BAHIAN SERTÃO

Santos was born in the village of Brotas de Macaúbas—a place named after a local palm which slaver settlers drove to extinction. Macaúbas is now mostly known for its beautiful white quartzite, currently mined for its popularity as kitchen countertops. Santos was the child of a poor family of elementary school teachers, descendants of slaves, who taught him how to read at an early age even though he would not formally begin study until the age of ten. He exhibited great intellectual talent, and although he came from exceedingly humble origins, he would go on to have an exalted career. Initially trained in law at the University of Bahia, he received his doctorate in geography from the University of Strasbourg. While he did not overlap at Strasbourg with another seminal spatial thinker of the later twentieth century, Henri Lefebvre, clearly the ambiance was conducive to critical thought and integrative ways of understanding place. Writing in a clear and powerful style, Santos would become one of the intellectual progenitors of critical geography and critical development studies, publishing numerous books and winning a number of prizes, including the Vautrin Lud award, considered the "Nobel" of geography for outstanding achievement.

The great Brazilian writer Euclides da Cunha made his reputation with his description of life in the Bahian backlands, *Os Sertões* (1902), the region that was the landscape of Santos's youth.[7] Da Cunha described how the newly minted Republic of the 1890s waged war against a millenarian uprising based in a tropical utopia called Canudos, in the arid forests of the Caatinga.[8] The settlement was basically a Kilombola community, or slave refuge. It also served as a sanctuary for women whose men had been coffled and shunted to labor in the coffee fields of Brazil during the twilight days of slavery, as the delicious tropical beverage exploded into Brazil's southern forests and into global markets. Canudos was a liberational space at the far margins of Brazilian history. The backlands, Milton Santos's homeland, was a region of forgotten villages whose culture was formed from the syncretic amalgam of black, indigenous, and European lineages and cultures, which produced what da Cunha called the "bedrock of our race." These cultures fueled creativity and adaptability in the face of extreme poverty, an unforgiving nature, and an indifferent social world. But this place, for both da Cunha and for Milton Santos, provided an excellent locale for thinking through questions of history, power, economics, nature, and geography. What is so striking is the historical, environmental, and social sense of place evoked by da Cunha, which is echoed in the approach to the reality of place and the creation of extended spaces of meaning and action that Santos insisted on in his writing. Human life was not just some disarticulated way of being, divorced from the planet and its places. Space and place were essential to the creation of ontologies and epistemologies (framings) and were structured by both human and nonhuman forces interacting with and through each other, what Bruno Latour would later term "actants."[9] In the terminology of political ecology, spatial studies, and science and technology studies, these places are "coproduced" by the interaction of nonhuman and human agents. These landscapes and urban systems materialized as outcomes of histories, economies, cultures, imaginaries, and symbolic meanings.[10] As austere and unforgiving as these Bahian landscapes seemed, they were also something else, and for both da Cunha and Santos, the backlands served as a wellspring, a way of using the periphery (and the *periferias*, Brazil's favelas) as a way to understand central processes of nature, culture, economy, and power in shaping the human habitats and lives—and particularly how these processes had unfolded in Third World development, urbanization, and general contexts of capacities and capabilities. The method would later become known as "decentering."

The Bahian backlands—scourged by drought and penury—was the early heartland and incubator of Brazilian slavery, but it also produced its opposite, what the Brazilian historian João José Reis has called "the invention of freedom."[11] These were the kilombos, the runaway slave refuges which constituted a significant part of the occupation of the Brazilian interior at the time and which occupied both daily folklore and heroic mythologies. Kilombos became enduring emblems of the resilience, power, and potential of the alternatives shaped by interior inhabitants and interior lands, and a symbol of transgressions against power. Kilombos were also testimony to the powers of creativity and reinvention wielded by Northeasterners, da Cunha's "bronzed titans," whether they reconstituted themselves in Amazonia or in the vast "urban jungles" of southern Brazil.[12] They were, in a fundamental sense, the desperate labor reserve army for whichever development program was on offer, but they also could offer different imaginaries of the future.[13] Attentiveness to the liberational energies that could emerge from the most dire of circumstances is part of what gave Santos his immense humanism—his "reason and emotion."

ITINERANT INTELLECTUALS

As has already been mentioned, Santos was a member of a diaspora of activist intellectuals from the Brazilian Northeast. They had all been engaged with regional development programs and their massive associated planning apparatus—a keystone enterprise of the "Alliance for Progress" as part of a Cold War counterweight to radical movements in Latin America. Various programs, but especially the state-coordinated SUDENE (Superintendency for the Development of the Northeast), focused on this constellation of very poor states, which were periodically ravaged by El Niño droughts, were mired in a class system resembling feudalism, and which had some of the highest indices of inequality and lowest indicators of human welfare in South America. Not surprisingly, its populace was given to insurrection, millenarianism, banditry, and agrarian reforms movements.[14] These were all understood, framed by the Cold War ideology of the military regime that came to power in 1964, as communist and subversive activities.[15]

Santos was a close advisor to the progressive president João Goulart. Santos had been highly critical of the autocratic processes and outcomes of regional planning regimes in the Northeast, and this put him at odds with both the national and regional development coteries and the local elites who continued to structure policy and programs.[16] Santos's experience as a person working as a practitioner in the "high modernist" projects of development was important in forming his critical and also emotional perspectives on the nature of development and change within the brutal politics of modernization, the legacies of which—despite being mostly invisible to outsiders—were still largely in place. It also made him a tireless critic of modern planning, as his manifesto "Planning Underdevelopment" clearly lays out.[17]

Santos was arrested and subsequently spent three months in jail, and was then released from prison only on the condition that he be deported. The Brazilian military regime was generous to some in its expansive view of banishment, rather than simple torture or death, as a means of cleansing the body politic. Santos then spent much of his professional life as an exiled nomad—and for thirteen years was unable to return to Brazil. In this time he became a deeply cosmopolitan intellectual, juggling posts in Europe, Africa, and the United States.

SANTOS, CRITICAL DEVELOPMENT, AND CRITICAL GEOGRAPHIC STUDIES: THE NATURE OF SPACE

Santos's contributions can be considered part of a more general movement diverting critical geography away from simple Marxist critiques and infusing them with more cultural and environmental content. Santos's concern with the nature of power relations, technologies, and economies—and how these together constructed spatial regimes—incorporated questions of nature that set him apart from more doctrinaire Marxist thinkers whose approaches at the time had very little environmental content. Santos's concern was more generally to move away from deterministic, reductionist, or descriptive models (which had affected a lot of Latin American development analytics) and instead toward explanatory ones, which he used to address the larger question, "What is geography?" Santos's focus was less on the form of geographies than on their formation, and how in the end geographic methods had to be explicatory. His concerns were not the self-indulgent outpourings that came to characterize much of the later cultural turn in critical geography, where, given his background, he could have had an adulating audience. Rather, Santos soundly rejected the language and posturing of the cultural turn even as he explored cultural questions through his work on epistemology and on what would appear as an early harbinger of Bruno Latour's idea of networked "actants" in the construction of place.[18] Santos never abandoned empiricism as part of his method, and he linked empiricism to questions of landscape, territorial configurations (systems of governance over place), divisions of labor, citizenship, and questions of region, network, and scale. Santos would frame these within the historical systems that produced them, both in their ontological and local configurations, as well as in their broader external formation through the dynamics of regional economies and globalization, woven together through meta-epistemologies and methods. The initial works in which Santos develops these ideas were written in the 1970s and 1980s, most seminally in the work "Toward a New Geography" (1978). His studies of "socio-spatial dialectics" form an integral part of his work, one in which expressions of power are never distant, where the idea of insurgent citizenship is always present and, perhaps less noticed, the physical environment also influences. His realism and humanism help explains his concern over questions of citizenship and urban rights, as well as his significant role in the Peace and Reconciliation Council—modeled on those of South Africa—of the Archdiocese of São Paulo at the end of the military dictatorship. He very much believed in transformation, and he also imagined a globalization of rights, dignity, responsibilities, and care. His deep internationalism—developed first as an exile and later as an illustrious visiting professor in Europe, Tanzania, and the United States—helped him clarify the articulations of social formations at multiple scales.

In addition to his experiences in the Bahia of his youth and early training, and his disillusionment with the modernist planning project, Santos's research and writing were influenced both by the Brazilian dependent development analytics and by the widely influential French spatial philosopher and sociologist Henri Lefebvre.[19] Although Santos and Lefebvre did not overlap at the University of Strasbourg, the critical mentalities in the emergent social sciences there exerted a strong influence and he engaged Lefebvre's ideas throughout his life—although Santos was far less doctrinaire than his spatial "muse" and his work more environmentally inflected. It could certainly be argued that the practical and biographical experience of Santos and the other exiles suffused French thought in critical geography and in the more radical critiques of development, and that the global movement and maturation of these ideas relied heavily on the informed experiences of the small group of Northeastern exiles.[20]

Santos's work is also characterized by the clarity of his prose. In a time of turgid, jargon-laden articles on spatiality, his luminous sentences reveal his mastery of the ideas and the depth of his scholarship. He is also a scholar of multiple intellectual lineages, especially those that fall outside the Anglophone realm, who brings earlier thinkers—including geographers as well as development thinkers—together in a larger narrative. What Santos's work shows is the complexity of modernity, how multiple modernities can be usefully engaged in more concrete ways. While many Brazilian analysts melt into air, either with very small case studies or with hyperabstraction, Santos actually tacks very effectively and illuminatingly between the theoretical and the concrete.

Santos's point of departure in *The Nature of Space* is the question, "What is Geography?" Although the discipline has fragmented into disparate elements, and has ranged and reinvented itself widely, it remains one of the few disciplines that maintains a nineteenth-century interest in the meaning and the unveiling of the whole human-environment planetary exercise. It is here where Santos's positioning as part of a search for operational and constitutive rather than simple descriptive reality is most salient. Santos focuses on ontology and fluently integrates the actor-network framework into his explanatory framework, emphasizing how nonhuman elements form part of the shaping of everyday enterprise as well as the cumulative structuring of lives, economies, cultures, and environments. In Santos's rejection of the simple dichotomies of socioculture/economics or socioculture/nature, his work seeks a tripartite linkage of socioculture, economics, and nature in a holistic way, an approach which is completely recognizable today as political ecology—though few political ecologists are aware of this legacy. Santos further frames these ideas within historical sensibilities in the evolution of place, and thus in a way prefigures a kind of environmental history that evokes and integrates humanized landscapes as well as nonhuman forces. He is not a determinist, but his insights in many ways prefigure how climate and history are increasingly used in understanding how powerful interactions of human forces are materialized in places. Thus, writers like Dipesh Chakrabarty, Mike Davis, and Gillen Wood, among others, have now operationalized the kind of approach that Santos advocated, in which nonhuman actors are also part of the action and the narrative.[21] Santos most explicitly speaks to multidisciplinarity, but speaks perhaps more importantly to *metadisciplinarity*, that is, the engagement of analytics of different disciplines through the apprehension of their varied epistemologies or framing paradigms. The poverty-stricken Northeast of Brazil had been a kind of development planning laboratory, a key site for the implementation of TVA planning exercises, intended as a showcase for development approaches that were supposed to define the Alliance for Progress.[22] Santos's role in Northeastern planning under Goulart had given him up-close experience with the complexity and contradictions of development as both idea and practice, and this not only led him to reframe his geographical thinking, but shaped his formation of critical development studies. Santos's approach remains remarkable for his time, especially given the triumphalist contemporary language about the "dreamscapes of development"

Santos's discussion of metadisciplinary thinking is a crucial element of his geographic analytics and catalytics. He relies significantly on Latourian ideas to argue that such concepts and places have constitutive force in the shaping of the world. The questions of spaces, regions, scales, and environments emerge through a *technosphere*—a kind of epistemology of practices—infused with symbolic ideas and incarnations of historical ideological forms that infuse the physical and social processes that structure the world. Because Santos engages both large-scale as well as nonhegemonic local rationalities, he is able to stimulate the construction of different epistemologies within the context of geographical inquiry. This was especially important in the 1960s and 1970s, when geography was turning away from its "people and places" roots toward a more quantitative empirical discipline. Santos's style of integrative and explicatory geography is now becoming more visible through new approaches such as political ecology, critical urbanism, global studies, and the social studies of sciences. Santos gives us in many ways the "deep background" and intellectual roots that underpin these contemporary empirical and social frameworks. While critical geography may have had its day and run aground on its language, dissociation, and over-heated constructionism, critical development studies and political ecology remain vibrant and active in multiple disciplines. The final section of *The Nature of Space* attends to globalization writ large and to the how local and global orders intersect in the construction of space. While this hardly appears novel now, at the time the sense of the overpowering ability of external forces to obliterate the local required the articulation of a counterargument, what might be called "the taming power of the small." Such global forces appear irresistible, but they confront local orders that may point forward to a different future. This is to some degree the deep lesson of da Cunha as well as of Santos.

The Nature of Space captures the generosity of spirit of Santos's work. This volume, twenty-five years in the making, provides a useful stratigraphy and genealogy to current geographical thought in development thinking. Much is made these days of postcoloniality, and there is much interest in scholars whose mentalities were not colonized, not always referential (and to a degree deferential) to fashionable Global North academics on both sides of the Atlantic—but they are few. For the most part, scholars from the non-Anglophone Global South, and especially from its peripheries, such as the backlands of Bahia, almost never break away from or break through their circumstances. In this way Santos is all the more remarkable, and what is especially impressive is that he reads as fresh as ever. International ideas have caught up with him, especially through his insights on the profound influences of natures and spaces in the interaction and shaping of human conditions, through the triple forces of environment, globalization, and urbanization in the developing world. What is geography? For Santos it was the scale of history as it unfolds in active places. While *The Nature of Space* is a product of its era, its insights continue their relevance today.

Introduction

MILTON SANTOS

This book is the product of many years of research. The task that I initially took up grew over time, as did my uncertainty regarding where exactly the project was headed. The technical-scientific period in human history that this book seeks to interrogate has been taking shape little by little since World War II, and a systematic understanding of its central characteristics could therefore only emerge gradually. Since the 1980s its development has accelerated significantly, and my timidity and hesitation intensified accordingly, delaying the completion of this project.

When Jean Brunhes published *Human Geography* in 1914, he apologized to his public and his editor for the book's ten-year delay. In this case my responsibility is greater, because my delay has been even longer. I can echo him in saying that my delay is due to care, rather than to negligence.

The research that forms the basis of this book, along with a few other related publications, spans nearly a quarter of a century and has all of the limitations typical of such an endeavor. In trying to interpret the present moment, the sheer multitude of events can seem to accelerate time and, in doing so, challenge established truths and dismantle existing knowledge. But even a tremendous groundswell of new commentaries cannot obviate the importance of philosophical debates whose lessons are not merely conjunctural. Perhaps it is this insight that has allowed me to overcome the same fear that Maximilien Sorre expressed in the introduction to his *Treatise,* where he noted that certain pages of his book would be outdated before the book was even printed. He wrote, "I will accept this catastrophe and I will not be devastated by it, as long as I still am able to provide the reader with an orientation and a method."

My explicit goal in writing this book is to produce a system of ideas that can serve as a point of departure for a descriptive and interpretive system of geography. Geography has always aspired to present itself as a description of land, its inhabitants, and the products emerging from their relations, which effectively includes all human action on the planet. This aspiration begs the question, what is a good description? Description and explication are inseparable. The desire to explicate should be the basis of good description, and good description itself presupposes the existence of a system. When such a system is lacking, the resulting descriptions are merely isolated fragments that move us further from the goal of producing a coherent branch of knowledge and an indissoluble object of study.

This book emerges from my long-term dissatisfaction with conversations around a few key questions in geography. The first is regarding the question of what constitutes geography's proper object of study. This question often gives rise to an interminable discussion about what geography is, and the commentaries tend to be extremely contradictory, rarely allowing us to move beyond tautological formulations. This is due in part to the fact that some geographers explicitly argue, and many practice, the idea that we can define geography by what each geographer does. Following from this perspective, we have as many geographies as geographers. Thus, with the pretense of openness, asking the question—"What is geography?"— becomes an exercise in futility. In other words, even an exhaustive discussion of the discipline cannot substitute for what is actually required to answer such a question, which is the discussion of the object of the discipline.

In reality, the *corpus* of a discipline should be subordinated to its object and not vice versa. In other words, our primary concern must be with space rather than with the nature of the practice of geography. A discussion of space necessarily presupposes an approach to method; to speak of an object without speaking of method is simply to state a problem without truly understanding it. An ontological approach—i.e., an interpretive effort *from within* the object—is therefore imperative, because it allows us to identify the nature of space and articulate the categories of study through which we can properly analyze it.

Such a task assumes that we encounter concepts drawn from reality, which fertilize one another through their compulsory association and which can be used to grasp that same reality in movement. We might call this method the search for operationality, the search for a constitutive rather than descriptive force, which can only be found through historical analysis—an analysis of a reality in movement.

My second point of dissatisfaction is around the much-discussed unity of time and space, which we will address here by exploring the inseparability of these two categories. In practice most research begins by stating its commitment to affirm the unity of these concepts, but then proceeds to treat them separately. There have been a few advances made toward thinking this unity. For example, the concepts of period and periodization do this, as does Torsten Hägerstrand's work, which allows us to think about the spatial order created by time. Nevertheless, much work remains to be done in this area.

A third theme taken up in this work interrogates the Anglophone expression, "Place matters," which is to say that place is important—something that we had previously argued in our 1978 book *Por uma geografia nova*. Yet the literature that followed that book demonstrated that in the absence of a clear definition of space, even an abundance of examples can only amount to a description, and never an explication, of the role of space and place in social processes. Perhaps this limitation helps to explain why this discussion was exhausted so quickly.

Our fourth point of dissatisfaction is in the way that geography has approached an analysis of the contemporary moment. As if caught up in a fad, geography has succumbed to the weaknesses of postmodernism, the most popular version of which can only offer metaphor and description, and which remains incapable of producing a system of thought. That is to say that it is only in this spirit of developing a systemic analysis that we might encounter the key concepts that would constitute the foundations of an object and of a discipline. Take, for example, Georges Gurvitch (1971: 250), who insists that "there is no rigorous parallelism between the spheres of the real and the sciences that study them." This is similar to William James's (1950) discussion of the reality of all that is conceived. In another example, Schutz's idea of "the limited provinces of meaning" (1987c: 128) parallels James's idea of "sub-universes." Drawing from these authors we might argue that fields of study should correspond to areas of social life or, following the geographer Carl Sauer (1963: 316), parts of reality.

The challenge is therefore to separate out a particular field from the whole of reality so that this field can appear autonomous while remaining integrated into the whole. This raises the important problem of defining an object for a discipline and ensuring that the delimitation and relevance of that discipline necessarily passes through metadisciplinarity and not the reverse. That is, constructing the object of a discipline and constructing that discipline's metadiscipline are simultaneous, linked processes. There is only one world. It is seen through a given prism, through a given discipline, although, for a set of disciplines, the constitutive materials are the same. This is what brings the different disciplines together and what, for each, should guarantee, as a sort of control, the criteria of total reality. A discipline is one autonomous, though not independent, piece of general knowledge. Through metadisciplinarity we can transcend truncated realities and partial truths without trying to philosophize or theorize our way around them. However, to transcend is not to escape. To avoid the illusion of escaping, we must also adopt the opposite course of action [*démarche*]: in seeking transcendence, the rule of the metadiscipline is the discipline itself. To transcend without transgressing depends on knowing the appearance of the real that we are addressing or, in other words, knowing our object.

This raises the question of geography's disciplinary relevance. In order for space to be an independent analytic entity within the social sciences, its concepts and instruments of analysis must have a sense of coherence and operationality. This is the only way that we may we demonstrate the legitimacy and indispensability of the object of study. Analytic categories and instruments are the heart of method within the various disciplines. When we lack coherence and operationality, that which becomes residual is often considered "given" and, as such, it gets eliminated from the central system of analysis. For example, each time that a geographer does their research without first concerning themselves with their object, they are acting as if that object is "given," and they end up engaging in a blind exercise without providing adequate explanation for the procedures adopted, and without establishing consistent, adequate, or appropriate rules for implementing those procedures. This practice is quite common, and this points to the need for the methodological construction of a field of knowledge that has both internal and external coherence. Externally, such coherence is developed through the possibility of a given field being distinct and yet at the same time completing and complementing other knowledges in the common process of knowing the totality of the real. Internal coherence is formed by separating analytic categories that on the one hand account for the particular appearance of the real within a given field's own partial knowledge and, on the other hand, allow for the production of instruments of analysis that are removed from historical processes. These concepts should, by definition, be internal to the object that they correspond to—in this case, space—and simultaneously be constitutive of and operational to it.

As a point of departure, we propose that space be defined as an indissoluble set of systems of objects and systems of actions. To systematize our analysis, we seek to construct a unitary analytic framework that would allow us to overcome ambiguities and tautologies. In doing so, we would be able, following Canguilhem (1955), both to formulate problems and to see concepts appear. Our secret objective, following the example laid out by Bruno Latour in his book *Aramis, ou, L'amour des techniques* (1992), is for these concepts, notions, and instruments of analysis to appear as real actors in a novel, seen within their own shared history. Should science not, as Neil Postman (1992: 154) proposed, be "a way to tell stories?" To do this, the researcher facilitates a process by which some actors take center stage, while others are made secondary or are tossed out. Method in social sciences then becomes the production of an "artificial device" in which the actors are what Schutz (1987c: 157–58) calls marionettes or homunculi. The one who ultimately gives them life is the author, which is why they are called "homunculi," and their presence in the plot is subordinated to the actual qualitative modeling—which is why we might think of them as marionettes. But the text should also make it possible for the puppets to surprise the ventriloquists and take on lives of their own, writing an unanticipated story—ensuring that the analysis conforms to concrete history.

In this case, we seek a precise and simple characterization of geographic space that does not risk dependence on mere analogies or metaphors. As Dominique Lecourt (1974: 79) wrote, "metaphors and analogies should be analyzed and referenced within their terrain of origin," which is to say that comparisons might be brilliant in a literary sense, but such brilliance is not always synonymous with conceptual richness.

If we begin from the idea of space as indissoluble systems of objects and systems of actions, then we can recognize its internal analytic categories, including landscape, territorial organization, the territorial division of labor, produced or productive space, roughness [*rugosidade*], and content-form. Similarly, and also as a point of departure, we encounter the problem of defining spatial areas and the corresponding debates around region, place, networks, and scales. We must also attend to the question of the environment, with its diverse human-made content, as well as to the question of complementarity between the technosphere and a psychosphere. We can simultaneously propose that the question of the rationality of space is both an actual historical concept and the result of the emergence of networks and the process of globalization. The geographic content of the everyday is also included among these constitutive and operational concepts that belong to the reality of geographic space, alongside the questions of both a world order and a local order.

The dynamic study of the internal categories of space requires that we recognize certain basic processes originally external to space, including: technique, action, objects, norms, events, universality, particularity, totality, totalization, temporalization, temporality, idealization, objectivization, symbols, and ideology.

The internal coherence of a theoretical construct depends on the extent to which the analytic elements of that construct can adequately represent the object of study. In other words, a system's categories of analysis should reveal its existential content. They should reflect the very ontology of space, beginning with its internal structures. A construct's external coherence emerges from the exterior structures in which it is located, and which define society and the planet. For example, the understanding of the internal categories of space would be impossible without history and the sciences as common knowledge.

A focus on technique brings these internal and external categories together and allows for internal and external coherence to be empirically integrated. This focus should be seen as having a triple function: revealing the historic production of reality; inspiring a unitary method (distancing us from dualisms and ambiguities); and, finally, guaranteeing that we can apprehend the future, in that it does not allow us to become mired in a concern with the particulars of any given specific technique. Rather, we should be guided, in our method, by technical phenomenon seen philosophically, that is, as a whole.

Based on these premises this book seeks to provide a geographic contribution to the production of a critical social theory. In building this contribution, I privilege four moments. In the first moment, I attempt to work with the concepts that constitute the being of space in order to encounter its ontology: technique, time, and intentionality, as materialized in objects and actions. In the second moment, I take up the ontological question again, considering space as a content-form. In the third moment, I revisit the ideas established above in the context of present history in order to understand the contemporary constitution of space and to be surprised by the concepts—whose system is open and dialectic—that are emerging in the contemporary world, and that are located both in hegemonic and nonhegemonic rationalities. In the fourth moment, the recognition that concurrent rationalities exist in the face of the dominant rationality provides new perspectives on method and action, which allow for shifting perspectives on spatial and social evolution and suggest changes in the very epistemology of geography and the social sciences as a whole.

These four moments are the basis for the four major sections of the book, which provide the structure for its fifteen chapters.

The first part, "An Ontology of Space: Founding Ideas," addresses the nature and role of techniques (chapter 1) and the movement of production and of life, through objects and actions (chapter 2). I examine techniques, which function as systems that define different eras, through their own histories and in terms of their material and immaterial characteristics. I argue that the concept of technique allows us to make time empirical and able to be understood through the idea of a geographic milieu. In this analysis, it is important to understand technique as something where the "human" and the "nonhuman" are inseparable. Otherwise, it would be impossible to overcome the dichotomies, so persistent in geography and the social sciences, that oppose the natural and the cultural, the objective and subjective, the global and the local, and so on. In the second chapter, I consider the movement of production and life around objects and actions, where technique again plays a central role. In other words, I argue that both natural and man-made objects can be analyzed according to their respective contents, or, put differently, according to their technical conditions. The same can be said for actions, which can be distinguished according to their varying degrees of intentionality and rationality.

The second part of the book takes up the question of the ontology of space; however, rather than foregrounding the foundational concepts, I examine historical outcomes. I analyze space in terms of its existence as a content-form. In other words, I explore it as a form that has no empirical or philosophical existence separate from its content; or in still other words: content cannot exist without the form that houses it. Given the inseparability of objects and actions discussed earlier, the notion of intentionality is fundamental here for understanding the process by which actions and objects become merged through the permanent movement of the dissolution and recreation of meaning. The production and reproduction of this hybrid—space—with the interminable succession of content-forms, is the central dynamic trait of its ontology and the focus of chapter three. The category of totality is key for understanding this movement (chapter 4), because we understand it to exist within a permanent process of totalization that is simultaneously one of unification, fragmentation, and individuation.

Places are created, recreated, and reworked with each movement of society. The division of labor is the motor of this movement (chapter 5), and in every scission of totality, it imbues places with new content—a thousand new meanings and one entirely new sensibility. Events (chapter 6) are the vectors of this metamorphosis, uniting objects and actions. They do not represent some unnamed time but an empiricized, concrete one that is produced precisely as the bearer of a historic action. According to this formulation, the union between space and time that we are seeking is more likely to be treated systematically in geography than elsewhere.

The third part of the book offers a discussion of the present moment and the conditions that exist for the realization and transformation of space. Addressing these issues implies understanding what constitutes the existing technical system (chapter 7), and how, from the conditions of this contemporary—informational—technical formation, material and political conditions are created that allow for the production of a planetary intelligence (chapter 8). These dynamics of contemporary history allow us to return to one of the central discussions of the book, which pertains to how contemporary objects and actions create and intensify norms (chapter 9). This same data allows us to characterize the current geographic environment as a technical-scientific-informational one (chapter 10). Chapter 11 explores the existence of networks as the product of contemporary techniques, along with the problems and ambiguities that they produce. In the functioning of these networks we can examine the production of verticalities (the "space" of flows formed by points) which serve a regulatory function at all geographic scales, even while horizontalities (the spaces of contiguity) renew and recreate themselves (chapter 12). The idea of the rationality of space (chapter 13) also emerges from the contemporary conditions of the world, and demonstrates how the development of capitalism makes possible the diffusion of the hegemonic rationality into different aspects of economic, social, political, and cultural life, and also establishes that rationality through construction of territory.

Although the fourth part of the book might appear to be a conclusion, it should not be thought of as one. This part of the book addresses what we are calling the power of place. Chapter 14 seeks to demonstrate the relationship between place and the everyday, revealing the ways that the same place can be used in contradictory ways according to the different perspectives held by different actors. This chapter moves toward an epistemological rupture, given the surprising evidence of the effectiveness of counter- and parallel rationalities that make themselves realities in the face of the hegemonic rationality and that point toward new and unsuspected paths of thought and action. The same idea inspires the final chapter, entitled "Universal Order, Local Order." Although the universal order may be frequently presented as irresistible, it is nevertheless faced and confronted, in practice, by a local order, which is a source of meaning and which points toward a different future.

AN
ONTOLOGY
OF SPACE
FOUNDING
IDEAS

1

Techniques, Time, and Geographic Space

INTRODUCTION

It is well known that techniques are what primarily set the terms for the relationship between humans and nature or, better stated, between humans and environment.[1] Techniques are the group of instrumental and social means that people utilize in order to realize their lives, to produce and simultaneously to create space. This understanding of technique has not yet been fully explored.

THE NEGLECT OF TECHNIQUES

In the existing literature, technique is often analyzed as if it were separate from territory, rather than as a fundamental element in territory's constitution and transformation. A few examples illustrate this point. Mackenzie and Wajcman (1985), for example, do not mention space at all in the discussion at the end of their book on issues in the study of technology. In fact, space does not even appear as a secondary area of study in their chapters on "other themes."

In another example, Adam Schaff (1992) describes the social consequences of the technical-scientific revolution, delineating four types of changes—economic, political, cultural, and social—but does not mention geographic change. He is not the first wide-ranging thinker to disregard space as a separate category of historical thought. Pinch and Bijker (1987), historians of technology, divide that field's literature into three areas—studies of innovations, the history of technology, and the sociology of technology—and also disregard the question of space.

Similarly, in Barre and Papon's (1993) work on economy and the politics of science and technology, in which territory does take on a significant role, the treatment of science and technology still remains to some extent external to space, as neither subject appears substantively integrated with it. For example, one of their chapters, "The Geography of Science and Technology" (1993: 52–89), describes the spatial distribution of scientists and technologies in different areas and countries of the world, but leaves open the particularly geographic question of how science and technology actually form the content of space. In his discussion of "scientific potentials," Denis-Clair Lambert (1979: 64–76) has used the expression *scientific space* to signify the density, or lack thereof, of researchers, research activities, and scientific production in different countries. However even this idea of space is merely metaphorical; it fails to address the constituent reality of territory and the technical content of territory that would allow us to identify and distinguish it.

Historians of science and technical specialists like Bernward Joerges (1988: 16) lament the fact that in historical studies, technical systems appear as given, lacking conceptualization. Joerges also criticizes economists who discuss companies or firms without analyzing the objects that they work with. He critiques sociologists and political scientists for failing to consider, for example, dams, pipes, generators, reactors, and transformers, and so on, as if the technologies embedded in objects were not important material for sociological analysis. In other words, for Joerges, it is insufficient to treat technology as merely a metaphor for other social phenomena.

This critique, however, is not new. In the journal *L'homme sociologique*, Marcel Mauss, a follower of Émile Durkheim, notes that Durkheim himself did not give due importance to technical phenomena. Armand Cuvillier (1973: 189) shared this critique in his discussion of three groups of scholars who "became aware" of the importance of technique: prehistorians and archeologists; ethnographers (who write the history of people "without history"); and technologists themselves. Indeed Mauss (1947: 19) went so far as to propose the creation of a form of knowledge—*technomorphology*—concerned with the relationships between techniques and the earth and vice versa, arguing that "through techniques we observe the geographical basis of social life: the ocean, the mountain, the river, and the lagoon."

If this advice had been taken up, later critiques of both archaeology and geography might have been avoided. Olivier Buchsenschutz (1987) lamented the fact that archaeologists rarely concerned themselves with technological problems, arguing that they seldom approach questions of the technical processes of the "material traces left by human societies" head on. Although François Sigaud (1981) noted some exceptions to this fail- ure, he also questioned why "geographers systematically avoid the study of the techniques at the center of society-environment relations (Sigaud 1991: 67–79)." Begag, Claisse, and Moreau also express this same frustration with respect to "the spatial economy." They write, "The spatial economy continu- ally changes the focus of questions related to the development of commu- nications technology, reducing them to questions of distance" (1990: 187).

In contrast, Bertrand Gille (1981: 22–23), in his research on "industrial archeology," proposed to study the organization of territory [*aménagement du territoire*] alongside the exploitation of nature and the transformation of the products and objects of everyday life. This category includes high- ways, railways, canals, bridges, tunnels, locks and their associated buildings, ports, electric lines, gas lines, pipelines, and storage for liquid fuel, as well as construction, urban development, and the evolution of landscape. It is therefore not surprising that in his major work *Histoire des techniques* (1978), published in *The Encyclopedia of the Pléiade,* that there is a chapter on "geography and techniques" written by André Fel.

While geographic articles and books, especially empirical case studies, have often addressed techniques, there has rarely been any generalized ef- fort toward the production of a geographic theory and method of tech- niques. Historians and, later, geographers have paid some attention to things like railways and later to highways. Both Vidal de la Blanche and Lucien Febvre used the idea of technical progress in their research, and as a result they are considered among the pioneers of a geography linked to technique. Albert Demangeon (1942) also made this link in his work on international commerce.

A more explicit concern with technique appears in work such as that of Anglo-Saxon geographer Philip Wagner (1960), who argued that "neither human ecology nor regional geography can progress very far without pay- ing due attention to the particular role of the artificial environment in man's biology and nature's schema." S. H. Beaver (1961) also made contributions in this area in his work on the relationship between geography and tech- nology. J. F. Kolars and J. D. Nysten (1974: 113) discuss, from the point of view of planning, the way that society operates in geographic space through transportation and communication systems, demonstrating the possible problems linked to the movement of things and of ideas.

In *Vere des techniques: Constructions on destructions* (1974: 13), geographer Pierre George argues that "technique's influence over space is exercised in two different manners and scales: through the occupation of land by the infrastructure of modern techniques (factories, mines, *carrieres*, spaces reserved for circulation) on the one hand, and through generalized transformations imposed by the use of machines and the implementation of new methods of production and of existence, on the other."

In a concrete analysis, George (1974: 82) also distinguishes the contemporary city from previous cities, arguing that in the mid-nineteenth century, the city was a *cultural product*, whereas today the city "is on the path to very quickly become, all across the world, a *technical product*," adding that, "culture was national or regional; technique is universal."

For geographer Pierre Gourou (1973: 17), "man, this maker of landscapes, only exists because he is a member of a group that itself is a fabrication of techniques." The human facts of space must be examined in terms of a set of techniques. He divided techniques into two major groups: techniques for production and techniques for creating "frameworks."[2]

While for Gourou (1973: 10) the level of progress of a civilization could be measured by its techniques, others, such as M. Bruneau (1989), P.-J. Roca (1989), and especially D. Dory (1989) have critiqued this position as an *a priori* quantitative assessment of civilizations that places some people on top of and others at the base of an unequal cultural pyramid. They further argue that this analysis lacks analytical clarity on the role of social and political dynamics in any given society. Gourou also introduced the notion of "landscape effectiveness" (1973: 17, 30–31). Given that landscape and space are not the same thing, one might ask in which of the two "effectiveness" resides.

Maximilien Sorre was the first geographer to consider technical phenomena in all of their magnitude. For him "this word 'technique' should be considered in its broadest sense rather than in its strict one, [which is] limited to mechanical applications." For Sorre, the concept of technique "extends to everything that belongs to the realm of industry and art, all domains of human action" (1948: 5). The idea of technique as system is already present in his work, as are the ideas of technology's self-expansion and rapid diffusion (11–12). He was convinced that an understanding of the relationship between technological and geographic change was fundamental, and he argued that geographic studies must therefore simultaneously consider the techniques of social life, of energy, of the conquest of space and the relations of life, and of the production and the transformation of primary materials (66–67). According to Anne Buttimer (1976: 66–67), however, "French geographers paid little attention to Sorre; they tended to see him as orthodox, verbose, and perhaps even inclined to confuse science with philosophy."

In his article, mentioned above, on geography and techniques, Fel (another geographer) assesses the multiple relations between techniques and geographic fact, arguing that "if technical objects are installed on the surface of the earth, they are put there to respond to people's fundamental material needs: to eat, to have a place to live, to move around, and to surround themselves with useful objects" (1978: 1062–1110). He also recognizes the lack of a true geographical science of techniques that clearly defined its objects and methods, and he actually suggests the creation of a discipline called *geotecnica,* that would take up this task (1062).

Geographers have not been indifferent to the current technological revolution in which information technologies predominate. This is clear in the work of Gunnar Tornqvist (1968; 1970; 1973; 1990), Henry Bakis (1984; 1987; 1990), and Suzanne Paré (1982), whose book *Informatique et geógraphie* that contains an inventory of French computer equipment, by region and city, but that ultimately fails to make an analysis from *within* space—rather than from the outside of this social reality—that would allow us to interpret how new technical presences act and transform territory. Such an analysis would need to go beyond pure informatics and would require an assessment of the past and present techniques that exist within the form of a given territory through the process of unequal and combined development. It is also worth noting the distinction between the particular techniques examined individually and *technique*—that is, the technical phenomenon—understood in its totality.[3]

When geographers argue that society operates in geographic space through systems of communication and transportation, they are correct; however, the relation between space and technical phenomena that must be investigated actually encompasses all technical manifestations, including the techniques of action itself. We should not only consider techniques of production, or what some call "industrial techniques," which are specific techniques meant to realize one or another particular outcome and which might lead us to focus, for example, on ideas of agricultural space, industrial space (Y. Cohen 1994: 95), or economic space. Only by investigating the entire scope of technical phenomena can we arrive at the concept of geographic space. In his book *Espacio, economia y sociedad*, Spanish geographer Joan-Eugeni Sánchez (1991: 263–319), took a major step in this direction, especially in the chapter "El espacio y la innovación tecnológica," as did Brazilian geographer Ruy Moreira (1995).

For P.-J. Roca (1989: 119), geographic discourse on technique has had three principle foci, which in his view constitute three different schemas. The first schema relates Vidal de la Blanche's concept of a "way of life," in which, as André Fel (1978; 1062–1110) explains, techniques, the societies that use them, and their geographic environment form a coherent whole. The second schema, which Roca attributes to Cresswell, focuses on a study of techniques that begins with the instruments of work. For Cresswell, technique is "a whole series of actions that comprise an agent, a material, and an instrument of work or a means of action on a material, whose inter-action allows for the fabrication of an object or a product" (Roca 1989: 119). A third schema, according to Roca (1989: 120), places three entities into relation: society, techniques, and environment. According to Roca, because they lack the necessary methods, in taking up this schema geographers run the risk of concentrating their efforts only on man-environment or society-environment relations (119).

TECHNIQUE, ITSELF, IS A MILIEU

How can we approach the question of technique such that it might serve as the basis for geographic explanation? We believe that a first step would be to consider technique itself as a milieu. This approach builds on the work of thinkers such as Jacques Ellul (1977), who argues that technique creates an order that places people into a completely new "natural" environment. Böhme (1987) makes a similar proposition with his concept of the "techno-structure," a product of the fundamental interactions of a system of techni-cal objects with social and ecological structures, a conceptualization that Joerges (1988: 17) argues effectively eliminated ambiguities from the con-cepts of the technique and technology in the social sciences.

In this section, we will explore the question of the technical object, beginning with J.-P. Séris's (1994: 24) question of whether every artificial object constitutes a technical object. Would, he asked, a grain of flour or a newspaper be considered technical objects? For the sake of our analysis, even supposedly "natural" objects could be understood as technical objects if our criterion for classifying them as such is whether they might serve some potential use. To accept Séris's (1994: 35) proposition that "any object that could function as the means for or the result of a technical activity is a technical object" would be to subject technical objects to a sort of Darwinian process of natural selection—whether or not they are adopted for societal use determines their technical value.

In her analysis of technical objects, Madeleine Akrich (1987: 51) argues that a technical object constantly vacillates between its "interior" (internal structure) and its relation to the "exterior" (social structure). The diffusion of technical objects is, however, never uniform or homogenous because they occur unequally in history, territory, time, and space.

Thus, Jacques Prades (1992: 18) argues, "technology acquires a presence and creates a milieu." In her analysis of the sociotechnical networks that develop when technical objects are introduced, Akrich (1987) also provides us with a key for understanding the production and transformation of a geographic environment based in technological phenomena, and also for understanding the conditions of social and geographic organization necessary for introducing a new technology. Through her study of the diffusion of the electricity network on the Ivory Coast and her assessment of its role in producing a forced solidarity among individuals, she argues that any technological object is defined simultaneously with the actors and the space involved.

Usher's (1954: 64) observation that, "in any given moment the available options are limited by the geographic and social surroundings," inspired Stiegler (1994) to argue that these mechanisms limit what Simondon (1989) called the "hypertely" (*hipertilia*) of a technical object. The progress of science and technology, however, has made it possible to increase the production of objects with overdetermined functional possibilities (i.e., hypertelic objects). These concrete objects tend to be exceedingly specialized and to have an extremely particular intentionality.

For Simondon, these "technical concrete objects" are distinct from the "abstract objects" typical of the early phases of human history (1989: 36). Thierry Gaudin (1978: 31) explains that "abstract objects" are formed through the juxtaposition of different components that each exercise a single abstract function. In the "concrete object," on the other hand, each element fits into the whole and as an object becomes more concrete, each one of its parts collaborates more closely with the others such that they tend to become united within a single form. For Simondon, the closer to nature that an object is, the more imperfect; and the more technologized it is, the more perfect, because people can more effectively control it. The "technical concrete object" is therefore ultimately even more perfect than nature itself.

But each time that the object is inserted into a group of objects and its operation incorporated into a series of operations—all of this constituting a system—the potential for the hypertely of that object itself becomes limited.

We might say, following Georges Balandier (1991: 6), that it is impossible to separate the concepts of technology and milieu, given that we understand the term *milieu* as "having a broader meaning that goes well beyond that of the natural environment." According to L. Winner (1980: 374), technical objects must be analyzed along with their surroundings. We can therefore argue that each new object is appropriated in a manner specific to the preexisting space.

Undoubtedly, space is made up of objects, but objects do not determine objects. *Space* determines objects: space understood as a group of objects organized according to a logic and utilized (operated) according to a logic. Such a logic of establishing things and realizing actions can be easily confused with the logic of history, for which space ensures continuity. We would tend to agree with Rotenstreich (1985: 58) who argues that history itself is a milieu (an *environment* [English in original]) and that the synthesis that happens through space does not imply a preexisting harmony. Every time a new synthesis is produced, a new unity is also produced.

Space itself redefines technical objects, regardless of what their original vocations may have been, by incorporating them into a coherent whole where their contiguity forces them to act together and in solidarity. We should think this process through Simondon's conception of the *naturalization of concrete objects*, which is an object's full integration with the environment that contains it, or what he calls the process of adaptation-concretization. This is how his concept of the "techno-geographical milieu" is created—a milieu that is only possible, he argues, with the help of human intelligence and whose existence indicates the presence of an inventive function of anticipation which is not found, he argues, in nature, or in already constituted technical objects (1989: 56).

For Simondon, this techno-geographical milieu is not simply the addition of the technical milieu to the natural one. Rather it is the production of something else, where the technical object appears as the conditions for the existence of a mixed milieu that is simultaneously technical and geographic. He calls this the "associated milieu." Simondon's proposal should help us to build a concept adequate to the geographic milieu, which used to be technical and is now technical-scientific-informational. The irony is that this idea, recently revisited by Stiegler (1994: 94), still remains incomplete precisely because it tends to reproduce the dualism and ambiguities of geography's traditional epistemological premise. For example, when Simondon (1989: 52) explains that "the technical object is the point of encounter between two milieus, *the technical and the geographic*," and that it "must be incorporated into them; it is a compromise between these two worlds" (quoted in Stiegler 1994: 92). His analysis begs the question: Why unite them through a separation rather than treating them as the foundation for producing a geographic milieu? I would argue that, in fact, there is no such thing as a geographic milieu on the one hand and a technical milieu on the other. Or, that the geographic milieu has always been produced by this fusion of the technical and the geographic. For millennia, the geographic milieu was a natural or pretechnical one; it was then called technical or mechanic for two or three centuries; and today we are proposing that it be understood as a technical-scientific-informational milieu. But Simondon's flawed proposal is certainly a legacy of geography's own position vis-à-vis its particular slice of reality, which this discipline insistently continues to see in a dualist manner. It is as if geography sought to reinforce the opposition between a natural and technical milieu, refusing to see technique integrated into the milieu as part of a single reality. Is that not exactly also how technical and geographic milieus are often described and explained? Even Stiegler's (1994: 94) allusion to a human environment, a human (not physical) geography "integrated in the process of realization," demonstrates this fundamental limitation. In reality, however, space is a mixture, a hybrid, a complex of content-forms.

THE NEED FOR A COMPREHENSIVE APPROACH

To understand the relations between technique and space, we must be attentive to the unequal diffusion of technologies. Jean-Louis Lespes (1980: 56–75) describes an important debate that has emerged around the diffusion of technologies and their selective implantation throughout space. Technical subsystems developed in different time periods can coexist within the same piece of territory.

When Jacques Perrin (1988) wrote, "A technological system can absorb, if there is a technological *compatibility*, structures belonging to a previous system," he was commenting on the strictly technical problem of efficiency, because the full efficiency of a technical system depends on the articulation between its various parts.

From a geographic standpoint, we would pose the question differently—beginning with the premise that these different technical systems form a situation and exist in a given place—in order to try to understand how human actions are realized within this (technical) substrate. How technical systems of different ages interact in place has consequences for the forms of life possible there. From the standpoint of the dominant technique, the question would be even different; it would be a question of how the residues of the past create obstacles to the diffusion of new technologies or whether together they can allow for simultaneous actions.

Tom Hughes's (1980: 73) idea of a "reverse salient" [English in original] provides an example of this historical contingency. He defines a salient as a protrusion resulting from the differential expansion of technological systems. Reverse salients are remnant components of a previous system. Joerges (1988) describes them as technical or organizational anomalies resulting from the unequal evolution of a whole such that, as one part of it progresses, another drags behind. This is similar to my concept of roughness, or *rugosidade* (Santos 1978: 136–40), which attempts to capture the role of the "dynamic inertia" of these inherited forms.

There are, however, differences in these two conceptualizations. For one, rugosidades cannot only be seen as a physical territorial legacy but also as socioterritorial or sociogeographic. Also, the reverse salient is thought to have an inherent technical content regardless of the particular situation in which it occurs. The geographical concept of rugosidade has no inherent value, because the value of a given element of space, whether it be a more concrete technical object or more performative element, comes from society and is expressed through the reality of the space that it is embedded within.

Understanding the diffuse and unequal use of technique also allows us to distinguish what has happened in the past from the present moment, when technique has become universal, directly or indirectly present everywhere. Looking historically, we can see that the acceptance of new techniques was always relative and incomplete. Even in the countries responsible for the greatest technological advances, such advances were never implemented homogeneously. For example, the United States does not have the best railroad in the world, nor the fastest mail. We could extend a similar analysis across any group of countries. For example, at the end of the last century, when many countries industrialized, new techniques allowed the world to enter into an imperialist phase, but the available technologies were not universally utilized.

If technique were an absolute, it would be impossible to imagine the permanence—for such a long period—of the imperialist system that was defined by the coexistence of colonial empires (those of England, France, Belgium, Holland, and Portugal), despite their sometimes glaring inequality of technological power. Political factors made possible the simultaneous, relatively harmonious functioning of these empires with vastly different levels of technological development in the center and on the periphery. The command unit, headquartered in each metropole, imposed rigid norms of commerce on the colonies, along with a closed circuit of regulation that generated a certain equilibrium. These norms ranged from the creation of monopolies to the establishment of prices and quotas for import and export and were maintained through colonial pacts. In a savvy political use of technological inequality, they compensated for productive disequilibrium with commercial equilibrium. This system lasted for practically a century, but finally entered a crisis when it became necessary for the countries that had new technologies but no colonies to penetrate these closed loops, which they did either by making their participation enticing or by encouraging the open implosion of empires.

When the United States was ready to enter and to use its new informational technologies and corresponding productive systems to gain a comparative advantage, they understood that first they needed to dismantle the socioeconomic and sociopolitical systems that presented an obstacle to their market expansion. The United States thus encouraged and supported the development of a psychological and intellectual climate for decolonization across the world, which ultimately precipitated a crisis within each empire. The struggles for national independence, and the subsequent creation of new countries, dismantled the scaffolding that had allowed the old empires to survive and often expand without the important and necessary contribution of new technologies. Unlike the empires that preceded it, the postwar American empire is not based on the possession of colonies but rather on the control of the productive apparatus of science and technology and the link between this apparatus and economic and military activity, which together opened the door to the triumph of a new system.

The current phase of globalization is marked by a move to establish world domination by connecting large organizations through the blind use of technology. But the lived reality of territories and the contingencies of their "associated milieus" present an impossible obstacle to globalization's desired homogenization.

This raises the question, on the one hand, of the degree to which a concept of space can contribute to the interpretation of technical phenomenon and, on the other, of what role technical phenomena play in the production and transformation of geographic space.

In *La vocation actuelle de la sociologie* (1950), Georges Gurvitch critiques the nineteenth-century technological school of sociological thought, which, he argues, interpreted the movement of social reality exclusively using the study of technological milieus, attributing a principal role to tools without properly accounting for the social frameworks within which those tools and their associated technologies emerged and functioned. He directs this critique toward thinkers such as Daniel Burnham and his idea of technocracy, and also toward others perhaps more debatable, such as Thorstein Veblen, William Fielding Ogburn, André Leroi-Gourhan, and Lewis Mumford, although he did express some reservations about critiquing Mumford. Daniel Bell (1976: x) also criticizes the discipline's tendency to emphasize technology as the determinant of all other social change. Henri Lefebvre (1949) also cautions against conjuring up a "technological illusion," critiquing Proudhon's assumption of "the history of the machine or of technology as an independent given." Clearly technology is an important explicative element for society and for places, but technology alone does not explain anything. Relative value is only identified within a system of reality and within a system of references elaborated to understand it, that is, a system that removes isolated facts from their loneliness and silence.

How can the category of space be useful in developing a systemic framework for technique? The philosopher J.-P. Séris (1994: 90) uses the concepts of "extension" and "succession" to argue that geography and history are particular constraining conditions. However, whenever a given problem requires explanation rather than simply empirical observation, the discipline of history, and not geography, tends to dominate in Séris's analysis. Séris does reference geography, and even makes particular reference to the technologies of space present during the Neolithic period (60), but he appears to limit such observations to the dawn of history, begging the question: Do technologies of space cease to exist over the long term? Séris's conception of space—as a space-receptacle, something that only takes form as a reflection of the actor—lends itself to this type of disappearance. He is equally dismissive of both space and time in his discussion of "normalization," in which he sees both as simply based in dominant norms—and therefore as irrelevant because they are domesticated and essentially annulled. I would argue that this interpretation, based in a static view of the geographical phenomenon, is mistaken, in that it misses the fact that the technical content of space is, necessarily, a content that exists within time—the time of things—upon which other manifestations of time, such as time-as-action and time-as-norms, come to act. This does not mean that space and time are negated, but that that their texture is changed.

As a key example, Séris (1994: 50) describes "the space of the automobile": as "the perfect symbol of autonomy, the private automobile only materializes within the set of technical relations or relations technically established in space and time . . . and it does not remain concrete itself, rather the relationships maintain it." He insists on the importance of this relationship between technique and history, explaining, "Technique is necessarily history" (91). While this may be true, we would also insist that technique is geography.

Within space, "node problems" and "generalized mediation" indisputably manifest (Séris 1994: 53). That "systematic unity" integrated into the "social totality" (the totality of resources at a given moment in history over a common cultural area), occurs very specifically over a space, and that space, evolving and changing, assures "historic continuity" (95). Space, however, does not participate in history as one of these *grands sacies imobiles et muets* from Foucault's allegory in *The Archeology of Knowledge*, which Séris cites, but rather as something active whose role in orientations, choices, actions, and results expands throughout history.

Is this lack of geographic analysis Séris's fault? Is it geographers'? I would argue that the response to the first question is no and to the second is yes. Lacking a clear epistemology, geography has generally had a difficult time participating in philosophical and interdisciplinary debates. In my view, this is why specialists from other disciplines, not exactly knowing what geographers do, fail to include them in their debates. What is needed is a metadiscipline of geography inspired by technique that is, by the technical phenomenon, and not by the techniques or technologies themselves.

The fact that geographers frequently overlook technique in their methodological formulations, or consider it to be an external given rather than as constitutive of their theoretical-empirical *démarche,* has implications for the way that other specialists treat the question of space. As discussed earlier, Simondon, for example, proposes the ideas of the associated milieu and the technogeographic milieu to explain the association between technique and milieu that emerged historically, rather than considering the technical milieu as a natural evolution of the geographic milieu. As a sort of revenge, geographers ignore the importance of Simondon's work. The result has been a loss both for geography, because its own development has been slowed, and also a loss for the philosophy of technique, because it has not benefitted from a parallel geographic approach.

Geography's ambiguous epistemological status, today still timid and hesitant, has also contributed to this problem.

When Anne Buttimer (1976: 249) observes, "the organization of space and time are among the central concerns of modern geography," her purpose is not explicitly to discover the totality of human experience, but rather the totality of technical experience, or the rational use of space-time in order to ensure economic effectiveness in the administration of investments. I would argue that geography should not be concerned primarily with investments but with all forms of existence. It should privilege an analysis that takes all aspects of a given situation into account. Every situation should be understood as a real construct that coincides with a logical construct, which can be understood through its history of production. A focus on technique would allow us to identify and classify all of the elements that constitute a given situation. These elements are historical, because all technique includes history. Moreover, all technique is actually embedded history. In other words, when we examine a technological object we see that technique becomes history at the moment of its creation and in every place, it reveals the encounter of the historic conditions (economic, political, geographic) that allowed for its emergence and structure its operation. In other words, technique is time congealed and reveals a history.

The use of objects through time demonstrates successive histories that have developed in and out of place. Each object is utilized according to relations of force that may originate at different scales but that intersect and manifest in place, where they change over the course of time. The nature of this merging of space and time can be understood through the history of technique—a general and a local history—and geographic epistemology should take this into account. Technique helps us to historicize, that is, to consider space as a historical phenomenon of geo-graphing, of producing a geography as a historical science. This approach allows for the construction of a heuristic and genetic geographic epistemology rather than merely the historicist and analytic one that Edward Soja (1993) so feared.

An analytic epistemology (Escolar 1996) allows for logical constructions, an elegant and perhaps even coherent discourse in and of itself, but one that is often located outside of reality. With this approach, we risk constructing a metaphysical discourse of geography that does not allow for the production of operational concepts. Through a focus that instead takes the premises laid out here into consideration, geography should, at minimum, be seen as a case study for the philosophy of technique, if not as a specific contribution toward producing a philosophy of techniques. Geography's epistemological problem is to find a path adequate to systematize techniques' relationship with time and space.

A focus on techniques is particularly critical for addressing the slippery question of the relationship between time and space in geography. Commenting on this neglected analysis, David Harvey (1967) acerbically commented:

> Just as Marshall considered the spatial dimension to be relatively unimportant in the formulation of his economic systems, and just like what Isard (1956: 24) called the "Anglo-Saxon bias," geographers neglect the temporal dimension, a defect for which Sauer firmly blamed Hartshorne (Sauer 1963: 352).

So many people implicated! For Richard Morrill (1965) geographers are people who critique economists for creating a "wonderland without space" but who themselves seem unconcerned with the fact that geography is constructed within a space that is situated outside of time.

Edward Ullman (1973: 138) described his "economist friends" as retaliating when they complain about the absence of action or normative goals in the work of geographers. He concluded, "an explicit recognition of time would help to guide geographers sensibly and objectively in this interesting direction." But what would this "explicit recognition of time" consist of? Would it be the study of modernization and the diffusion of innovations, the delimitation of historic periods according to geographic scales? Or, would it simply be the recognition of the inseparability of time and space?

Addressing the question of time in geographic studies is no longer taboo, but it does continue to be mired in a certain conceptual sloppiness. The analyses that do exist are often circumlocutory and tautological, notwithstanding a few recent solid advances, such as Torsten Hägerstrand's notion of a "geography of time."

How can we move beyond the narrative that preaches the need to treat time and space equally, beyond the critiques by other specialists who are opposed to doing so, and also beyond the internal critiques by geographers, all of which are at fault here? How do we move beyond the oversimplified and gratuitous statements about the union of time and space that simply relativizes them? How do we translate the idea that space is also time, and vice versa, into analytic categories?

Reaffirming the relations between geography and history is, to be sure, the most simple and also the most naïve of approaches. Certainly, we would agree that Élisée Reclus's century-old argument—that geography is history in space and history is geography in time—is true. The endless repetition of this truism, however, was never meant to be a guide for method.

To some extent, historical geography tried to invert this idea in seeking to make a geography located in time by reconstructing the geographies of the past. As H. C. Darby (1957: 6) argued, however, we cannot trace a dividing line between geography and history "because there is only one process of becoming." Maybe historical geographers would have disagreed with Darby's statement that "all geography is historical geography, either real or potential." Historical geography seeks to retrace the past, but it does so while located in the present. How could it be possible to reveal that which is arbitrarily called "the past" when, instead of explicating the simultaneous spatial and temporal coherence of a given moment, they simply bring together disparate and distant moments within the arrow of time? Here we encounter the difficulty of discerning, through a retrospective geography, what was, at a given moment in the past, the present. This question continues to be a nightmare for geographers.

The 1960s and 1970s saw major progress in the search for geographic explanations that included a concept of time. And most of the questions that we are facing today have their basis, directly or indirectly, in this debate.

Parkes and Thrift (1980: 279) argued that, "with movement, space and time become coextensive as space-time," which is certainly valid as a principle of physics. What is less certain, or completely uncertain, is whether we can simply transpose this reasoning into a historical discipline like geography. In a geography of movement, we must first recognize the encounter of a real time and a real space. This is not always the case.

Historical geography is also concerned with the question of periodization. C. T. Smith (1965: 133), among others, considered the study of the relations between period and place to be fundamental and argued that it might be useful to think about space in terms of time. Of course, within each temporal system, space changes. How then can we move from this general idea to analyze particular cases? We might begin by constructing a periodization not only on the world scale but also at smaller scales, which themselves act on smaller spaces. Our proposal for a *spatial time* (Santos 1971) was based on such an approach. We found, however, that it did not resolve the problem at hand because while periodizations do provide us with a time, it is only an *external time* for each subspace and thus fails to resolve the question of *internal time*. Bailly and Bégion's (1992) proposal to judiciously, but separately, analyze the relations of space and time with society is thus a promising advance, but to what extent is this still a time-space approach?

Studies devoted to innovation and modernization have been useful for understanding the genesis of these phenomena and their geographic forms. Research by Hägerstrand and the Lund school, along with studies of modernization by Barry Ridell (1970), Peter Gould (1970), Edward Soja (1968), and others, still hold value today. The limitation of these approaches is that by focusing on the arrival of new things, a particular date, a given place, makes it appear as if "time" was crossed by "space," by objects and actions, passing through but not mixing with place. They were unable to provide a method for understanding the fusion of space and time.

Since writing that "asking for a record of events that takes the unification of time and space into consideration is asking a lot," Hägerstrand (1973) made a major advance in thinking on this topic. In his *Geography of Time,* he proposed to map the times of a reality in movement by "freezing" events in geographic patterns so that their contents could be analyzed. More recently (Hägerstrand 1985; 1989; 1991a), he has explored the idea of domains, studying the ways that different actors used territory, how those uses resulted in partitioning: in which places, at what times, and how the movement of time and space happened in a unified way. This union of space-time must necessarily be treated in terms of historical process, according to Ullman (1973), who argued that the use of the planet demanded an organization of space and time.

Albert Einstein, Hermann Minkowski, and many others have also commented on the inseparability of time and space and rejected the concept of absolute space, shifting toward of the idea of relative space. The fusion of relative space and relative time inspired J. M. Blaut (1961) and made it possible for Ullman (1973) and Parkes and Thrift (1980) to insist that when they are completely integrated, time and space reciprocally replace one another.

Amos Hawley's (1950) argument that we can only separate space and time in the abstract seems self-evident, but to affirm this proposition we must develop it further. For example, if we wanted to argue that there is a temporal pattern in every spatial pattern, we would need to first define both categories. To do this is to clarify the difference between the discourse and method of time in geography.

Ullman (1973) argues that space is "a more concrete dimension than time." And yet it can be a "measure" of time—but also be measured in terms of time. This is the entire problem. In other words, the problem is not to determine whether one of them is more concrete. This reciprocal measurement indicates that time and space are one thing, each transforming themselves into the other all of the time. If we want to move beyond discourse to make this idea a reality, we need to analytically equalize space and time by analyzing them with equivalent parameters.

Jacques Maritain argued that "true time . . . based in movement is, like space, inseparable from corporal material" (cited in Watkin 1950: 48n3). Given that space always has a material component where we can see its concrete and empirical nature, if we want to unify space and time, time must also be made empirical.

Time, space, and world are historical realities that must be mutually convertible if our epistemological concern is totalizing. In any given moment, the point of departure is a human society in process, that is, being realized. This realization takes place upon a material base: space and its use; time and its use; materiality in its different forms; actions and their diverse characteristics.

We thus make time empirical by making it material, and in doing so we also assimilate space, which has no existence without materiality. In this process, *technique* appears, historically and epistemologically, as the trace or vestige of that union. That is, on the one hand, technologies make empiricizing time possible, and on the other hand they provide the possibility for a precise description of the materiality over which human societies work. This empiricization can be the basis for systematizing the characteristics of each epoch.

People work through techniques to realize this union between space and time. Karl Horning (1992: 50) argues that all technique conceals, in some way, a theory of time. We have already also seen that technique can be founded in a theory of space.

Techniques are dated and include time both qualitatively and quantitatively. They are a measure of time: the time of directing the work process, the time of circulation, the time of territorial division of work, and the time of cooperation.

Space is made up of technical objects. The space of work contains techniques that authorize the types of things that can be done, how they can be done, according to which rhythms, and in which orders—all of which is time. Distant space is also modulated by techniques that command a typology and a functionality of displacements. Work posits a place, and distance posits an extension. The direct productive process is related to place, and circulation to extension. These two expressions of geographic space come together through these two expressions of the use of time.

Techniques contribute to the perception of space and time through their physical existence, which marks sensations relative to speed, and through and their imaginary, which also has a strong empirical base. Space imposes itself by creating the conditions for production, circulation, residency, communication, for the exercise of politics, for the exercise of beliefs, for leisure, and as a condition for "living well." Operationally it lends itself to objective evaluation, and perceptually it is subordinated to subjective evaluation. The same space, however, can appear as a terrain of individual and collective actions, or as a perceived reality, although in fact the operational and the perceived are intertwined. Both originate in technique, and to evaluate them we must synthesize the objective and the subjective.

Technique is, then, a constitutive element of operationalized time and perceived space (Broeck and Webb 1968; Fischer 1980). We therefore seek a common referent, a unitary element, in order to ensure the *equivalence* of time-space.

Space becomes concrete time through the process of production. As a result, the idea of work and instruments of work are key to geographic explanation and to the study of modes of production. The work carried out in each historical epoch is based a particular historically determined set of techniques. Following an oft-quoted statement by Marx, "It is not the articles made, but how they are made, and by what instruments, that enables us to distinguish different economic epochs" (Marx 1906, 200). Each concrete geographic place corresponds, in each moment, to a set of technologies and instruments that result from a specific combination that is historically determined.

THE AGE OF A PLACE

Can we say that place has an "age"? The assertion that a given city was born with colonization is often understood to mean that the city was actually founded in a given year. For example, the city Salvador da Bahia "was founded" in 1549 by Tomé de Sousa, by order of the King of Portugal. This date is its legal birthday and, from that moment on, its civic anniversary date.

Could we determine the age of a place according to different criteria? Is there a properly "geographic" criterion that we should use? Geomorphologists, for example, do this all of the time. They date entire areas according to the observed sequence of layers marking different phases of natural history. They dig ditches and make observations about the nature and thickness of the different layers and their order of superposition. Could we create a similar method of observation that would produce the same results for human landscapes? Is there a geographic technique that might parallel the ditch-digging done by geologists and geomorphologists?

We could, perhaps, date artificial materiality through techniques—techniques of production, transport, communication, money, control, politics, and also of sociability and subjectivity. Because they are historical phenomena, we can identify their moment of origin. This dating is equally possible at the scale of a place and at the world scale, or the national scale—if we consider a national territory to be a group of places.

Since the beginning of historical time, technique has tended toward universalism (Leroi-Gourhan 1945). Capitalism accelerated the process that internationalizes technique until it culminated, at the end of this century, in its globalization: today the universality of technique is not a tendency but fact.

The universalizing tendency of early human society allowed for the creation of particular technical solutions in different places, but those techniques did not appear simultaneously, nor did their appearance in one place necessarily have implications for other places. The process that began with capitalism and that today we call globalization allows us to speak of a universal age of techniques, which can be calculated from the moment that they appeared.

Techniques' scientific age—the date they are first known in a laboratory—is only important to the history of science. They also have a historical age, meaning the point at which they were incorporated into societal life. At this point a technique stops being science and starts being properly technical. If society does not utilize it, we may have an object or a machine but not an actual technique. The other key historical moment for a technique is that point at which it becomes universal. The autonomous existence of a technical object should not be confused with the relativity of its historic existence.

Each technique can thus have its own particular history from a global, national, or local perspective beginning at the moment it is established in a particular location. But universal history would be an absolute technical history and is therefore located much more in the domain of chronology than in history. Seen in this way, techniques appear absolute and abstract, despite their empirical reality.

Place provides techniques with their principle historical reality by relativizing their use, integrating them into the whole of life, taking them out of their empirical abstraction and making them effective historically. Because there are no isolated techniques in any given place, the effects of the age of any given technique always depend on the other techniques operating simultaneously in that place (which may include technologies of agriculture, industry, transportation, commerce, etc.). Social groups manage "industrial techniques" and are the bearers of diverse sociocultural techniques acting on a technologically diverse territory. These techniques, including the techniques of life, create the structure of a place.

A purely "historical" interpretation of techniques would imply that they had an absolute character, as if each technology could be defined in and of itself. But taken in isolation, a technique is a pure virtuality, waiting to be historicized.

Places, as we have argued, redefine techniques. In them each object or action that occurs there is placed into a preexisting fabric such that its real value can only be found within the concrete functioning of the whole. Their presence also changes other preexisting values, as is demonstrated in the ways that the respective times of industrial and social techniques intersect, intrude upon, and accommodate one another. All objects and actions change their absolute (or tendential) meaning and take on a relative meaning that is provisionally true, different from that of the previous moment, and impossible in another place. This is how something like the time of place is constituted—this spatial time that is the *other* of space (Santos 1971).

Consider a working tool, a factory: its technical characteristics engender the conditions for a particular outcomes, depending on the type of working capital, a specific quantity and quality of labor, and a specific quantity of energy. The age of the work instruments thus have implications for the rest of the economy (by virtue of the concrete possibilities of relations) and for jobs (by virtue of the concrete possibility of jobs). Because these relations preside over the hierarchy among productive places, possibilities for expansion or contractions differ from place to place. This relative difference is a product not only of local production, but of what is produced in all of the places within a given space, including those close by and far away, thanks to the expansion of contexts made possible with progress in transport and communications and with the standardization of production. Ultimately, we can measure the age of the variables present in each place with reference to internal and external factors, especially in underdeveloped countries where the history of production is intimately linked to the creation, in the countries of the center, of new forms of production.

2

Space
Systems of Objects, Systems of Action

INTRODUCTION

At the beginning of the last century, in his now classic book *La géographie humaine,* Jean Brunhes (1947) developed a definition of geography through a series of successive approximations. After he found his first attempt unsatisfactory, he made a second attempt and then a third one. The book's *démarche* is original in that the reader actually accompanies the author's thought process through his successive attempts to perfect his intellectual construct and arrive at his final definition of geography. Here we attempt a similar exercise, not in relation to geography but rather to geographic space.

In my first working hypothesis, I proposed that geography could be constructed based in a conception of space as a set of fixtures and flows (Santos 1996c). Elements fixed in a given place allow for actions that modify that place—new or renewed flows re-create environmental and social conditions and redefine each place. The flows themselves are the direct or indirect result of actions, and they intersect or settle in the fixtures, modifying their meaning and value and simultaneously modifying themselves (Santos 1991b: 53; Santos 1996a: 75–85).

Fixtures and flows interacting together express geographic reality and in doing so appear together as a possible object for geography. Although these processes have always been ongoing, today fixtures are increasingly artificial and more fixed in place and flows are increasingly diverse, larger, more numerous, and faster.

We might approach space instead through a different set of categories: territorial configuration and social relations (Santos 1996a). A territorial configuration is made up of the complex of existing natural systems in a given area and the things that people superimpose on them. Territorial configuration alone is not space, because its reality is based only in its materiality; but space brings together materiality with the life that animates it. Territorial configuration or geographic configuration has a material existence and a social existence—its real existence that comes from social relations.

For example, at the beginning of human history the territorial configuration was a simple ensemble of natural complexes. As history progressed, human production increasingly defined territorial configuration: roads, farms, houses, warehouses, ports, factories, cities, and so on. In other words, territorial configuration increasingly results from historical production and tends toward a negation of natural nature, replacing it with an entirely humanized nature.

Currently, I propose that we understand geography as a discipline that studies the indivisible group of systems of objects and systems of actions that form space. It does not analyze these systems separately, nor does it endeavor to revive Berry and Marble's (1968) idea, based in the systems theory then in fashion, that "all space consists of a set of objects, the characteristics of these objects, and their inter-relations" (cited in Beaujeu-Garnier 1971: 93).

To restate: space is formed by an indivisible, interdependent, and contradictory group of systems of objects and systems of actions, not considered separately but understood as forming a unique framework within which history takes place. Historically, wild nature existed first and was made up of natural objects that over the course of history were replaced by fabricated, technical, and mechanized objects, and later by cybernetic ones which have created an artificial nature that tends to function as a machine. Contemporary space thus has a highly technical content marked by the presence of an increasing number of technical objects: dams, factories, modern farms, ports, highways, cities.

Today space is a system of increasingly artificial objects, populated by systems of actions that also have an artificial character and that increasingly serve purposes that are external to a given place and its inhabitants.

Objects have no philosophical reality—we cannot know them separately from systems of actions, and vice versa.

Systems of objects and systems of actions interact with one another. On the one hand, systems of objects condition the way that actions take place, and on the other, systems of actions lead to the creation of new objects or act on preexisting ones. This is how space finds its dynamics and is transformed.

If we were to explain this in a simplified way using Marx's terms, we might say that we have a group of objects synonymous with a set of productive forces, and a system of actions that would produce a group of social relations of production. We would need to note, however, that the simplistic interpretation of the dialectic relationship between productive forces and relations of production long ago ceased to have real relevance. It is insufficient to say that we have productive forces on the one hand and relations of production on the other, and it has become irrelevant today to argue that the development of the forces of production leads to the development of the relations of production.

Today what we call productive forces are also relations of production and vice versa. In other words, the interdependence among productive forces and relations of production is intensifying, their influences are increasingly reciprocal, and one increasingly defines the other.

A study of space based only in this famous dialectic cannot provide methodological clarity, given that today these two classic categories appear confused and, as a result, lack analytic value. We must therefore find different starting points for an analysis. Considering space as an indivisible set of systems of objects and systems of actions, as we are proposing here, allows us to simultaneously work with the whole that results from this interaction, as both process and outcome, and also to base our work in categories that allow for an analytic treatment that can account for the multiplicity and diversity of situations and processes.

SYSTEMS OF OBJECTS

Some people differentiate objects from things, arguing that things are the product of a natural development and objects of a social one, or in other words that things are gifts from nature and objects are created through work. For example, in his famous book, *Vie des formes*, Henri Focillon argues that things (natural forms) are works of God while objects (artificial forms) are works of humans (1981: 4). Jacques Monod has a more reserved take on this differentiation, arguing that "the difference between natural and artificial objects seems immediately and unambiguously apparent to all of us. A rock, a mountain, a river, or a cloud—these are natural objects; a knife, a handkerchief, a car—so many artificial objects, artifacts" (1974: 15). As nature is objective and not projective, things can have neither purpose nor project. He goes on to ask the reader to analyze this proposition in order to arrive at the conclusion that such assessments are neither given, nor exactly objective. In his first chapter, "About Strange Objects," he reminds us that our conclusions are drawn "through reference to our own activity— intentional and purposive." Were our criteria strictly objective, we would be able to, say, develop a computer program that could "distinguish an artifact from a natural object" (1974: 16).

Let us return, then, to a more intuitive differentiation between objects and things and remember that today objects increasingly take the place of things. In the beginning, everything was things, although today everything tends to be an object, and even things themselves, created by nature, when they are used by humans according to a set of social intentions, become objects. As such, nature is transformed into a true system of objects rather than things, and, ironically, it is the environmental movement itself that completes the process of denaturalizing nature, by designating it as the thing with the highest value.

According to A. Moles, an object is "an element of the external world, created by man who can assume it or manipulate it" (1971a: 14). For him, neither a mountain nor a house would be objects, because "an object is some-thing independent and mobile" (1971b: 222). Following this logic, a flint scraper is an object, but flint itself is not. This definition complicates the concept's use in geography, which frequently studies fixed objects: a bridge, a house, a port, a train station, a dam, a city, the country, and a farm. For the geographer, these are all geographic objects. A. Woeikof (1901: 98) was the first among many to make the distinction between movable and immovable objects: for him, "objects over which men have control are movable things."

Henri Van Lier argues that "we must apply a universal definition to ob-jects" (1971: 129). Jean Baudrillard (1973: 62) departs from Moles's line of thinking, arguing that a house brings together a totality of objects, but a car is also an object. Objects are what people use in their daily lives and are not confined to the domestic realm, and, while they may appear to be tools, they are also symbols, signs. The car is, for Baudrillard, one of the most important signs of our times, and its role in the production of the contemporary imagi-nary has profound repercussions for the whole of people's lives, redefining society and space. Cities would not be what they are today if the car did not exist. People think of the car as indispensable, and this psychological fact becomes a lived reality. Although it may be an illusion, the car provides its owner with the idea of freedom of movement, making them feel like they have the ability to gain time, to not lose a single minute, within this century of speed and haste. A person with their own car can imagine themselves to be more fully realized, more able to respond to the demands of status and of narcissism, the characteristics of postmodern life. The car is part of the contemporary wardrobe, practically like clothing. When it is used in the streets, it seems to extend the body of a person, like a prosthesis or other tools, and even when people are in their houses, it is always at arm's reach.

Vilhena (1979: 197) draws on the philosopher Messer's (1929) argument that an object is anything that we can direct our consciousness toward. He argues that the object has an essence and an existence. It has an essence because it possesses a certain and determined nature by which it can be distinguished from other objects, which makes it possible to speak of a given thing and know that it is different from another. It has existence because it behaves in relation to consciousness in a way that can be observed, or, consciousness can observe it because it exists (1979: 196).

For Vilhena, an object is separate from the subject that knows it. It has its own existence, which is the product of its own history—even if that history is not independent of the history of society. The individual comes face to face with this external objectivity, a reality that does not depend on him but that, as I mentioned, concerns him. Thus, the assertion that the object precedes our thought (and is independent from the subject that knows it) is only relatively true: if the object truly preceded our thought, we would not be able name it. The simple fact of recognizing and naming an object supposes a learning, explicit or implicit. Language has a fundamental role in the life of people, in that it is how we identify and recognize the objectivity around us, through its already-existing names. For some authors, to name something is the fundamental act, and it is through naming that we produce thought and not vice versa.

In his research on cultural and geographical differences among various "primitive" peoples, Leroi-Gourhan (1945) made a similar observation about their fundamental tools, which led him to formulate a hypothesis about the universality of technique. Created objects, he argued, are not restricted to the location of their creation. While they may originally be conceptualized in a particular place, objects tend to be reproduced and dispersed, generating other similar objects (Hewitt and Hare 1973: 13). History is full of such examples, such as the diffusion of castle and cottage architecture. In São Paulo, for example, at the end of the nineteenth century, the first duplexes made their appearance. Then, later, others appeared with the same design, and today they are a hallmark of the Paulista landscape. Similarly, today in the era of the elevator and reinforced cement, successive generations of builders have constructed buildings that were initially up to twelve stories tall, then twenty or twenty-four stories and, today, forty (Souza 1994). This diffusion of objects, which today easily occurs on a global scale, obeys Gabriel Tarde's law of imitation. Today diffusion is much faster and more generalized, at least for those objects that correspond to new modes of contemporary production.

All object creation and reproduction respond to the social and technical conditions present in a given historical moment. Some people adopt novelty quickly, while others may not have the conditions to do so or prefer not to, continuing to use their older models. Although each epoch creates new versions of things, their use is not necessarily generalized. The key fact is that replicas are reproduced that are more or less true to the original object. George Kubler (1973), Focillon (1981), and André Malraux (1951) refer to this as an "illusion" of a reproductive power that appears to reside in things.

According to F. Rossi-Landi (1968), without including objects formed by unworked natural elements, there are currently more than ten successive levels of complexity within objects (cited in Krampen 1979: 14–15). Level one would be objects that are "premeaning," such as raw extracted materials, comparable to phonemes in the secondary articulation of language; while level ten, our contemporary level, brings together objects in "global production." This is the highest level of evolution of mechanical objects, which have been present since level six, with its simple machines, followed by aggregated machines (level seven), automation (level eight), and nonrepetitive goods or unique prototypes (level nine).

Another approach argues that there are two levels of object complexity—functional and structural (Moles 1971b). An object's functional complexity is related to the repertoire of functions that come together in its use. To say that a typewriter is made for writing implies its job, based in its elementary functions, directed toward realizing a particular number of products. For Moles, "functional complexity is the statistic dimension of uses": what we can do with an object, what it can offer us, how we can use it (1971b: 78). From this point of view, objects may have a greater or lesser level of complexity.

The structural complexity of an object has a direct relation to the variety of its fundamental elements, which indicates that there is no difference between structural and informational complexity. In other words, the structural complexity of an object *is* its information, because it is how that object communicates with other objects, or serves a person or institution—be it one that works directly with that object or one that, even remotely, has control over an object's local social and economic operations. The more structurally complex an object is, the more quickly and efficiently it offers an adequate response. In the geographic milieu it is similar.

There are many different kinds of object classifications that vary, depending on who developed them and on which aspects they want to place emphasis. For example, Max Bense (1971), drawing on C. S. Peirce (1960), identifies four categories of objects, differentiated according to their degrees of functional determination: natural objects, technical objects, art objects, and "design" objects. "Design" objects, "like all other man-made objects, are planned, but their functions are not completely determined" (cited in Krampen 1979: 10). According to Ferrara (1989), industrial design is meant to produce a "stimulus for the sagacity of the user," that does not necessarily represent a "function inserted into a form."

Bense argues that art objects are less functionally determined than other objects because they are valued based on factors external to them, located in the observer, or subject. This argument echoes Eduardo Subirats (1989: 102), for whom art is "the place that modern culture reserved for this transcendent dimension of the object."

Abraham Moles (1971a: 22) proposes that the task of recognizing a true ecology of objects is interdisciplinary, one based in developing a description of the *population* of objects. Contrary to what is usually understood as ecology, in which species are fixed, new species in this conceptualization are constantly emerging. From the moment they are chosen and located, in a house or a landscape, the new objects—with their age, characteristics, and functional behavior—change their local system of relations, redefining their environment. Moles defines this "park" according to its respective function within a whole, which he sees as a "life situation" (Moles 1971a: 23).

To understand this life situation, we should supplement the already rich idea of *population* with the idea of *system*, because as Baudrillard had argued (1970), few objects today occur alone or function in isolation. As an example, we might analyze the relationships among the elements of a cold chain, today so essential to the everyday life of much of humanity. There is a necessary relation between the domestic refrigerator and freezer, the refrigerated truck, the refrigerated storage units in businesses, and the massive refrigerators in factories. It is a whole whose individual elements are only viable as a whole. Or in another example, we might be able to look at the screen of the home television without even thinking about the system within which it is located, but we would not be able to enjoy its benefits without the simultaneous production of the program, the station that emits the signals, and the towers that distribute and redistribute them, or the electric systems and electronics housed in specially designed buildings. In 1925, Carl Sauer wrote that the objects of the landscape exist in correlation. Although his correlation might not have been as clear and indispensable then as it is today, thinking of objects related in a system was fundamental for geographic work even then.

In his book *Système des objets (The System of Objects),* Baudrillard (1968) insists on this systemic life of objects. In a similar line of thinking, Roland Barthes (1967), in *Système de la mode (The Fashion System)* (1967), proposes a system of objects defined as a "set of unions of functions and of force." The idea of a fashion system itself is very instructive, because in fashion objects are born with a planned expiration date (for their appreciation and value). The speed with which objects lose value and are replaced is also a feature of many contemporary technical objects.

By recognizing objects in the landscape and in space, we are alerted to the relationships that exist among places, which respond to productive processes in the broad sense, from the production of commodities to symbolic production. This is what Thure von Uexhüll referred to as "pragmatic systems" of objects—objects that facilitate pragmatic relations (cited in Krampen 1979: 9).

A GEOGRAPHIC OBJECT?

First, we must ask whether a geographic object actually exists. Like other disciplines that study a social or an anthropological object, it seems that a discipline like geography that is so eager for autonomy—and epistemological legitimacy—would also want to claim its own object. But what would this geographic object be?

Geographers are interested in both movable and immovable objects. Cities, dams, streets, roads, ports, forests, farms, lakes, and mountains are all geographic objects. Physical and human geographies meet in the history of these objects—studying the way they were produced and changed.

Everything that exists on the surface of the earth is an object for geographers. Objects in this sense are objective things created outside of people that become their material instruments for living. Whether they are created by nature or by humans, objects remain an exteriority.

The objects that constitute geographic space are necessarily continuous, and the population of objects that geographers must study are not selected by the researcher, no matter how wise and methodological they may be. In other words, space, for geographers, must include all objects existing within a given continuous extension, without exception, or it would not be possible to make sense of any given object. Ortiz's (1994) concept of "serial space" privileges a part, a subsystem, within the world of existing objects in a place, studying a part as if it were the whole. The idea of deterritorialization as it appears in the work of Ianni (1993), among others, also expresses this same conception of object, common among sociologists and anthropologists, that is often called the space of objects, and can be made up by either natural or artificial cultural objects (Augé 1994a). The geographic lens, on the other hand, examines the existence of objects as entire systems and not simply as selected collections: their current, past, or future utility comes, precisely, from their combined use by the human groups that created them or inherited them from previous generations. Their role can be purely symbolic but tends to be functional as well.

The conception of the object in archaeology better approximates that in geography. In both fields, the object is first a piece of data, and the analysis of that data allows us to intellectually construct its reality. The archaeologist tries to identify a culture and a time based on the specimens that they find. The geographer is interested in the set of conditions characteristic of the different periods, but they begin in the present and move, frequently, to the past. The archaeologist's "objects, their method of fabrication and their function" are also stable terrain for the geographer, but their respective démarche are different (Demoule 1994: 19).

Buchsenschutz (1987: 18) argues that, for the archaeologist, an object is any solid element that was used by people to protect themselves, to work, or to transport things. The geographic object would be all of this and much more; its analysis would reveal its previous use and also add the current use.

If for the archeologist the object is only the vestige of past action (Thévenot 1994: 75), for the geographer the object is a contemporary testament of action, and thus different models are dynamic and movable. In the geographic démarche, we see how present actions can act on objects that come from the past.

Sociologists conceive of their object in at least two ways. One approach treats the object as something objective, and the other refers to objective phenomena that are not necessarily materialized. At the end of the last century, Durkheim (1962) proposed that social facts are things. He was pointing to the reality of the social fact, stressing its effects in order to justify the assertion that the discipline of sociology that he had helped found was in fact a science. His proposal that there were reified social facts—objects—and social facts that existed in the domain of the real but that were not reified was subject to intense criticism.

German sociologist Georg Simmel's (1980) notion of the crystallization of social action raises similar points. For him, any explication of the world necessarily passes through forms and life. He explains that that which comes from the past and crystalizes as a form, along with that which exists in the present or in ongoing life, together explain the world around us and are therefore the starting point for any geography. For Simmel, the same shape or form can be realized by very different contents, and forms can comprise an infinite number of logically possible contents.

In his famous definition of social facts imposed upon society and individuals regardless of their actions or beliefs, Durkheim (1962: 12–13) distinguished among modes of action and modes of existence. He defines "modes of fixed action," which are different from "modes of existence," which are themselves modes of crystallized action. According to Durkheim, this crystallization of the modes of action is the equivalent of Marx's "dead labor" and would be better represented today by the set of cultural objects that—alongside or in the place of "natural" objects, whose meaning changes—form what we could call a spatial configuration, a territorial configuration, or a geographic configuration (of which landscape is just one aspect). In current geographic terminology, the terms *geography* and *landscape* are often mistakenly substituted for the word *space*. In this sense, the spatial configuration is a technical given, while geographic space is a social given. We will return to this theme later.

Other crystallized modes of action would be the law, which comes from the past and imposes itself on the present, and things like customs, music, and art. In other words there is an entire gamut of relations that prevail in the present, despite the fact that they were created in the past.

Building on Durkheim, we would argue that nongeographic social forms eventually become geographic social forms. Things like the law, custom, and the family become a type of geographic organization. Property is a good example, because it is simultaneously a juridical and a spatial form. Social evolution creates spatial forms on the one hand and nonspatial forms on the other, but then, in another moment, nonspatial forms are transformed into geographic ones. These geographic forms appear as a condition of action or mode of existence, and human action should, at some point, account for these modes of existence. This is what led Durkheim to propose a subdiscipline of sociology called social morphology, which geographers saw as a competitor to geography and fought (and fight) ferociously (Berdoulay 1978). This really was tragic, because for anyone who saw the milieu as composed of "things and people," Durkheim's idea could have approximated an epistemologically functional geographic definition of its object (1962: 113).

The question of what constitutes a geographic object remains unanswered. John Pickles (1985) puts his finger in the wound when he asks about "the mode of being characteristic of geographical objects" and emphasizes that we must understand this particular mode of being. Based in his phenomenological vision of geography, Pickles (1985: 95–139) draws attention to the fact that with all things being things in the world, we must avoid the risk of taking their appearance as reality, confusing being with the object.

But what, substantively, are geographic objects? How do they exist? How are they born and how to they evolve? What is their entitative reality? Can we really speak of a geographic object? (Bailly and Bégion 1982: 31–33).

There are other ways to formulate these questions as well. Must we stop searching for the materialities that we, exclusively, define as geographic objects in order to fully circumscribe an object for geography? To have legitimacy, would it be necessary to distinguish among geographic objects, ethnographic objects, and anthropological objects, among sociological objects and economic objects, as well as artistic objects, aesthetic objects, and religious objects?

Or could we begin from a different starting point? What we are seeking here is not a mythological structure to objects, but an epistemological construction of an object of thought, beginning from the province of experience. If we understand Schutz correctly, this constitutes reality (1987c: 128).

Pierre Boudon (1971) argues that there is a difference between the classification of objects and their epistemological construction. We should not confuse the two. The same object may have different epistemological constructs, but we must bear in mind, following Joseph Schumpeter (1969: 3), that the social process as a whole is indivisible.

Different disciplines can enter into dialogue with the same object. For example, the sociologist Raymond Ledrut (1984) dedicated an entire book to the question of the social form, and geography may seek to understand the world through geographic forms, but from an epistemological point of view, the very same things are social objects on the one hand and geographic objects on the other. Authors such as Gilles Ritchot (1991: 117), however, have also pointed to the reductionist danger of superimposing levels of organization, projecting the geographic object onto the semiotic, anthropological, or economic object.

The question at hand is above all a question of method, a question of constructing an intellectual system that allows us to approach reality analytically from a particular angle of vision. This approach is not a given in and of itself, not *a priori*; it is constructed. In this sense, social reality is constructed intellectually. Writing in the 1940s, Maurice Le Lannou (1949) caused a scandal when he argued that geography was a "point of view," an assertion which was, incidentally, more precise than Henri Baulig's (1948) idea of geography as a "state of spirit." Bernard Stiegler (1994: 44) wrote, referring to linguistics, "here is the point of view that creates the object."

We therefore do not believe that it is necessary to continue seeking to define an object with a separate existence—a strictly geographic existence, a geographic object in and of itself. Based in our understanding of geography's object, we would argue that we can approach all objects *geographically*. This proposition, however, would be tautological if we did not develop the analytic categories that allow us to approach everything as reality and as process, as a situation and as movement. We are trying to formulate a system of concepts (never only one concept!) that accounts for the interaction of the whole and its parts, and we think that understanding geographic space as an indissoluble system of objects and system of actions can be useful in this endeavor.

These objects and actions come together in a logic that is simultaneously the logic of the past (its dating, its material reality, its original causation) and the logic of today (its function and present meanings). It seeks to recognize the social value of objects through a geographic lens. The geographic meaning and the geographic value of objects comes from the fact that they are contiguous, forming a continuous extension, and systemically interlinked, and that they have a role in social processes.

SYSTEMS OF ACTIONS

The geographers Philippe Pinchemel and Geneviève Pinchemel (1994: 40) remind us that "men are beings of action: they act on themselves, on others, and on things on Earth." But what does it mean to act? What is action? What is an act?

Drawing on Parsons and Shils (1952) and Rogers (1962), we can say that an act is made up of: 1) a directed behavior that 2) happens in situations, that 3) is regulated by norms, and that 4) involves an effort or motivation.

In other words, an act is not just any behavior, but one directed "toward achieving a given goal" (Rogers 1962: 236). Authors such as Hindess (1987:

138–39) and Schutz (1967: 61) also make the distinction between behavior and action. For Schutz, action is the execution of a calculated act, and the meaning of any action corresponds to that calculated act. Further, the act presumes a situation on which an action is projected. This, Moles (1974: 264) argues, marks a visible shift in being in space; it creates a change, a modification, in the milieu. One of the outcomes of action is, then, that it alters the situation in which it acts. But action is also a process endowed with a purpose, following Morgenstern (1960: 34), in which an agent changes things and, in doing so, changes themselves; the two movements are concomitant. This understanding of action was also foundational for Marx and Engels, who argued that through work a person acts on or modifies nature (the environment) and in doing so change their own intimate nature (1947).

Action is subject to norms, whether those norms are explicit, formal, or informal, and realizing an action always requires the expenditure of energy. The idea of acting is directly linked to that of praxis, and we can understand practices as regularized, routine, or nearly routine acts that contribute to the production of an order. Following Pagès et al. (1979: 50), "the entire field of action of each individual is coded by a system of rules, as is their field of relations." Even the choice to act and the necessary energy expended to implement an action has always depended in part on norms—from the early period when techniques tended to be those of the body to the current moment where techniques tend to be informational.

Anthony Giddens (1978: 80) distinguished among act, action, and agency. For him, an act is a particular part of an action, which itself is a set of acts or a process made up of subprocesses, consecutive acts. He understands action as "the stream of actual or contemplated causal interventions of corporal beings in the ongoing process of events-in-the-world" (1978: 81). According to Morgenstern (1960: 40), the structure of an action's time has three periods: an initial, incomplete one that belongs to the condition of action; an intermediate causal period that is neither complete nor incomplete; and a strictly understood present that occurs at the end of the process of action.

Giddens (1978: 82) also distinguishes between intention and purpose: intention is central to daily practice, while purpose presumes ambitions or long-term projects. He recognizes that people seldom act with a clear goal in mind and that frequently our actions are made without first having clarity in our spirit, which we would argue is even more true today than in past decades—as evidenced, for example, by today's impulsive consumption that is highly responsive to advertising.

Reflecting on the relation between action and what he calls the "project," Gaston Berger (1964) argued that the time of action is the time of the project. For him, a project requires that we first recognize what needs to be done; then, how to do it (e.g., the set of tasks and their steps). A project should not be confused with a dream or a wish, because in a dream one can simply express a desire, an image, without knowing exactly what to do or how to do it—it does not require a set of actions, with the urgency of the steps in the process, or an objective, a solidly defined time. For a project to "prepare a [given] execution" effectively, it requires methodical application and work based in a particular order.

Because actions are increasingly disconnected from people's own purposes and places, we must increasingly distinguish between the scale at which we realize our actions and the scale that they control or affect. Today this distinction is fundamental: many actions that are implemented in a given place respond to needs generated far away but whose fulfillment is located in a different, particular point on the surface of the Earth.

An effect of this contemporary distancing, and the schizophrenic nature of the process of event creation more generally, is that we experience what we might call regional or local alienation, similar to what Giddens (1991) called "phantasmagoric" place.

We should also distinguish actors who make decisions from other actors. A "decider" is that person who can choose what will be disseminated and, more importantly, that person capable of determining an action that will be realized. Jean Masini (1988: 112–13) identified governments, multinational corporations, international organizations, major news agencies, and religious leaders as the great deciders. Common people's capacity to choose their actions may be more limited. Frequently, actors are conduits of actions rather than motors of them; people always participate in actions through their corporality. This notion of "corporality" is gaining traction in the human sciences under globalization. Geographers such as Neil Smith (1984), for example, writing about the problem of scale, argue that scales begin with the human body and move progressively to the world taken as a whole. Human corporality may be an instrument of action, but we must account for the fact that people's capacity to govern their own body is limited today, and that there has been a limited evolution of norms to change this situation.

The limitation on peoples' ability to choose is two-sided (Giddens 1978: 69). On the one side there is a limitation of consciousness. Is it possible in this postmodern world to distinguish clearly between good and bad? How, for example, can we distinguish between the discourses of politicians and of businesspeople, given that they are both subordinate to the same rules of marketing? Limits on consciousness limit how we can act and what we can choose to do. Once we possess a certain consciousness, we recognize that the kinds of actions really available to us are few.

How, then, can we account for what sociologists call a rational action? In *Legitimation Crisis* (1971), Jürgen Habermas proposes that we first distinguish the subsystems of rational deliberated action from others and then later open the theme to a broader discussion. In the past, objects revealed each society's purpose and were tools to realize that purpose. Increasingly today, "rational action" is based in the rationality of others—that is to say, "rationality" is largely determined by the nature of the technical objects themselves, which were designed in order to implement someone's precise rational action through technical means (Humbert 1991: 55). Actions are more and more precise, but they are also more blind to the situation in which they are acting because they were designed serve a project alien to that very situation. In other words, with the proliferation of technical objects, action is increasingly rational, but that rationality is an increasingly technical one. Within a pragmatic order, a relationality that serves alien or external goals becomes a rationality of the technical means and not of the subject.

Human action, however, is not exclusively rational. Weber made this clear in *Economy and Society*, where he outlined four basic forms of social action: instrumental-rational, value-rational, traditional, and affective (1971: 3–60). Similarly, Habermas (1973: 22) speaks of an opposition between "instrumental activity" related to work and "communicational activity" related to symbolic interaction.

Building on Gilbert Hottois's work (1994: 79), Simondon, writing in the 1950s, also clearly distinguished between two types of actions—technical and symbolic—with the former transforming nature and the later enacted on human beings. Braun and Joerges (1992: 81–2) identify three types of action: technical, formal, and symbolic. Technical action includes interactions formally required by technique. Formal action presumes obedience to juridical, economic, and scientific formalism. Symbolic action is not regulated by such calculations but rather relates to affective, emotional, and ritual forms, determined by general models of signification and representation. In certain cases, there may be conditions for technical action but not formal action, or vice versa. In both of these schemas, the forms of "rational" action are similar, while symbolic action is confused with cultural forms of the appropriation and utilization of technology.

There are also three parallel orders that organize daily life: the technical order, the juridical order, and the symbolic order. While the technical and normative orders tend to appear as *givens*, the forces of transformation and change, surprise, and a rejection of the past come from symbolic action, where force is located in affectivity, in the models of meaning, and in representation. The importance of place in the formation of consciousness comes from the fact that these means of acting are inseparable, even if, in each situation, their relative importance may be different.

Action belongs to humans alone, because only humans have objectives, goals. Nature, on the other hand, has no capacity for action because it is blind, it has no future goals. Human actions are not, however, restricted to individuals; businesses and institutions, and so on, also act, even if their actions may be realized through individuals (Hindess 1987).

Actions result from natural or created needs. These needs—material, immaterial, economic, social, cultural, moral, and affective—move people to act and carry out particular functions.

In one way or another these functions will culminate in objects. Actions are realized through social forms and lead to the creation and use of objects, geographic forms. Paraphrasing Alfred North Whitehead (1938: 139–40), we can say that "outside of space, nothing is realized," given that space is produced "by a *particular conjunction* of material and meaning making processes" (Lagopoulos 1993: 275).

A GEOGRAPHY OF ACTION?

Benno Werlen (1993: 100) argued that, in mistakenly focusing on space, geography failed to give proper attention to what he called an "action-based theory of social geography, highlighting subjective agency." But later he argued that "if 'action' rather than 'space' becomes the central theoretical concept of social geography, the spatial arrangement of objects becomes significant as a necessary condition and consequence of human action rather than a cause" (143).

Werlen's insistence on the central role of action in social geography does not necessarily exclude thinking about the role of what we call the "spatial dimension," but for him, space is not the cause of actions or events (142–43). He repeatedly emphasizes this point to defend his premise that social geography is a science based in action, and thus action and the act must be the primary units of analysis, not space (139). He does recognize that the spatial dimension of reality is important, but he thinks it should be understood as a framework for actions rather than as their cause.

He is not even arguing that "action in space" should be the basis of research in his new social geography. He seems to be primarily drawing on the work of a number of Anglo-Saxon geographers, including Derek Gregory, among others, in arguing that, as all action takes place *in space,* such an approach (action in space) does not advance an explication, from a spatial point of view, of diverse social systems. The primary tasks of social geographic research based in a theory of action, for him, would therefore be the following: first, to understand and explain human actions; and second, to clarify the relation among human actions and the social and physical world (1993: 139–40). He also gives great importance to subjective action, that is, to the role of the individual. This methodological choice marks all of his work, despite the fact that at every point he also emphasizes the role of the physical-material conditions that frame human action (174).

In sum, Werlen's geographic theory can be articulated in the following propositions: 1) geography should be considered a science of action, not of space; 2) geographic research should emphasize subjective action; and 3) the spatial dimension should be considered, but it is not the cause of events or of actions.

Although the idea that space influences human actions appears in every chapter of his book, he continues to actively assert, in all of his chapters, the prominence of action and its central role in geography. He presents action and space as if we had to choose between one or the other, or as if selecting one necessarily negated the relevance of the other. Perhaps here we again encounter the old and stubborn inherited dualism that has marked the discipline for more than a century? Even those who disagree with this dualist approach often use a methodological approach that recreates this dualism, which can lead to ambiguous postulations and Manichean attitudes.

We are left with the impression that Werlen hesitates in making the definitive step that would allow him to arrive at another vision of geography. Because Werlen, like Karl Popper, allows for the possibility integrating a focus on the course of action and on the objective structure (1993: 203). His work constantly alludes to the central role of space, and even includes a discussion of the different meanings ascribed to the word by geographers and other social scientists. He repeatedly refers to other work that he has done and to that of other authors to demonstrate that he is actually accounting for the importance of material even prior to that of action. For example, to Simmel's work on the constraints of distance he adds the idea of "functional distance," essential data to the calculation of costs (1993: 186). He uses the idea of the relations of action with artifacts and the physical world from Weber (183) and the role of localization as a base of operations from Parsons (190). He continually insists on the importance of the physical material conditions of action (200–1), on the meaning of immovable material artifacts (165), on the influence of the material, physical positions of the body of the agent (125). He even cites Schutz and Niklas Luhman on the purpose of the material reach of the human body, its actual or potential reach, and it influence over social interaction.

Werlen comes closest to solving the theoretical problem of defining space in his use of Durkheim. Of all of the sociologists and philosophers that he cites, Durkheim provides the clearest idea of what, at the time, geographers considered space to be—an idea that he, Durkheim, sought to refine. Back then, geographers did not understand his work, and even today Durkheim is still waiting for his ideas on space to be taken up again and refined.

Werlen did not take up all of Durkheim's ideas. For example, Durkheim (1962: 70) argues that forms "are like molds in which we are forced to place our actions," and in doing so he opens a path toward the construction of a geographic theory. Werlen (1993: 172) cites this passage to argue that "material artifacts can drive actions," but then he pivots back to his previous argument, insisting not only on the relevance of action but on its supremacy, and he fails to give the importance deserved to the idea of "mode of action" that Durkheim introduced in his theory of social morphology.

Objects do not act, but, especially today, they may be born predestined for and indispensable to a particular type of action. In the final analysis, actions define objects and give them meaning. Today, however, objects "valorize" actions differently depending on their technical content, such that considering actions or object separately does not account for their historical reality. A social geographer should consider objects and actions "acting" together.

The two categories, object and action, materiality and event, should be treated unitarily, because events and actions do not geographize indiscriminately. At every moment, there is a relation between the value of an action and the value of the place where it is realized. If that were not the case, then all places would have the same use-value and the same exchange-value, and the movement of history would not affect those values. There is a difference between saying that space is not a cause and denying that it is a factor. Acknowledging the "existence" of space is not "geodeterminist" as Werlen (1993: 6) argues. The value of space is not independent of the actions made within it.

Geographic space should be considered something that participates equally in the condition of the social and the physical—a mix, a hybrid. In this sense, there are no meanings independent of objects. Simmel's argument, later taken up by Werlen (1993: 147), that the same meaning can be invested in different objects and the same object can symbolize different social meanings does not make sense when an object is examined from a geographic point of view.

Giddens (1987: 433–34), in an aggressive text, attacked geographers sarcastically, claiming that sociology would have a lot to gain from the theoretical contributions coming from geography: geographic concepts would help sociologists to incorporate the reality of space into their analysis. Giddens attributed what he saw as geographers' lack of curiosity to the fact that geographers were content to take and to use the theoretical production of sociologists, who were primarily responsible for theoretical advances in geography. But this is not actually the case. Concepts in one discipline frequently function as mere metaphors in another. Metaphors are isolated *flashes* [English in original]; they do occur systematically, and they do not allow for theorization.

We cannot find a consistent definition of geographic space in the metaphors that come from other disciplines. Nor can conceptions of space created by these disciplines pass automatically into geography. Just as Einstein's (1923) seminal ideas of relativity and of the equivalence between time and space need adequation to function in geography, geography must elaborate its own concepts before trying to borrow formulations from other fields.

3

Geographic Space, a Hybrid

We can use the notion of "intentionality" to make another critical reading of the relations between object and action. Drawing on Husserl's idea that intentionality can be understood as the presence of things and also as a presence in things," Jean Beaufret (1971: 182) argued that "*intentionality* is the fundamental characteristic of living in general."

According to Franz Brentano (1935: 29), "There is no act of thinking without an object that is thought, nor a desire without an object that is desired." Or for the Portuguese philosopher Magalhães Vilhena (1979: 203), who quotes him, "To have an idea is to have an idea about something: all affirmation is the affirmation of something; all desire is the desire for something." That is why intentionality raises, in the words of Bruno Latour (1991: 59), "what had been only a distinction, then a separation, then a contradiction, then an insurmountable tension" between the object and the subject "to the level of an incommensurability."

Undoubtedly there are objections to the idea that intentionality only has utility when reconstructing a theory of knowledge. Husserl had criticized the ambiguity of the Cartesian *cogito* and the duality between *cogito* and *percipio*. He saw these two categories as integrated and inseparable operations whose unity should serve to simultaneously refuse the simplicity of idealism and realism. Consciousness itself, he says, is intentional, and "when we carry out an act of knowledge . . . when we are living in this conscious act, we are dealing with an objective thing that this act thinks and exposes precisely through its mode of knowing" (Husserl 1959: 249); or, in the words of William Luijpen (1966: 31), "The intellect is an *intellectus agens*. . . . The intellect also is *intellectus patiens*.

The idea of intentionality also helps us to contemplate the process of production and the production of things, understanding both as resulting from a relation between people and the world.

Luijpen (1966: 88–89) proposed that this "mutual implication of subject and world," this "meeting of man and object," was a "primitive fact" of an existentialist philosophy. He suggested that "dialogue" might be a better word to describe this phenomenon, given that "neither of the two participants . . . can be thought separately from the other, because if we separate them, we destroy the dialogue between them" (89). For Luijpen, the expressions *meeting* and *dialogue* are, in the phenomenologist vocabulary, synonymous with Maurice Merleau-Ponty's idea of "presence" and Gabriel Marcel's (1965) "participation."

Human action defines itself. According to Wilhelm Szilasi (1973: 35), the word *act* "does not refer only to an action, activity, or process, but to the relation of intentionality itself." He develops his argument, claiming that "acts are the events of consciousness that have the character of intentionality." For him then, the product is already contained within the intentional act, and, in this way, the faculty of consciousness that makes these actions possible is always outside of itself. Thus, as the consequence of intentionality we find ourselves, from the beginning, implicated in the "web of things" (41–42).

Gabriel Marcel's work (1965) is also relevant here, because the simultaneous distinction and union between *being* and *having* is at the center of his work. Furthermore, having is related to taking, and thus, the things that we have/take are necessarily separate from us (1965: 144–45). Marcel proposes that the relationship between having and spatiality follows from this.

Human action has a retroactive effect on the things that it brings to life, which Marcel aptly equates to a sort of *boomerang effect* [English in original] (1965: 163). Intentionality, for Marcel, would be a sort of pathway between subject and object. Things are therefore not only external to a given agent; they reach that agent "clandestinely." Thus, Marcel argues, the act of having initiates a tendency toward self-destruction (164–65).

In other words, the loss of the subject occurs through that very thing that they first possessed and sought to control but that then absorbed them. Refining this argument, Marcel argues that, in reality, this process is not the destruction of *having* but rather its sublimation and transformation into *being* (165).

The Italian philosopher Carlo Diano (1994: 90) takes this argument perhaps even further, arguing that "in the theoretical act, subject and object constitute a union, but the subject appears as object." He argues that one can claim that subject and object are mutually constituted, that they are, respectively, each made real at the cost of the other in its "empiricity," where, through the form's action, they are revealed in the event. Abraham Moles (1974: 106) addresses something similar in his discussion of how action is determined by its surroundings rather than by its being, and how it is by nature more or less unpredictable.

The intentional action is the "conscious and voluntary movement" of the agent toward things (Petit 1990: 71–72), involving the projection of the agent (Quéré 1990: 87–88), and the agent's beliefs, desires, and intentions imply an object.

O. F. Bollnow (1969: 241) argues that because people are subjects who relate to their surroundings and not simply objects among other objects, we can understand people as defined by their intentionality. He goes so far as to suggest that understanding intention might be adequate to understand the essence of space (242). Perhaps he was thinking of K. Lewin's (1934) "hodological" space, a space opened by pathways, which is, in our point of view, a limited understanding. Geographic space is much more than the sum of available pathways, even if it is also this.

Psychology and psychoanalysis offer a different understanding of intentionality that we argue we can appropriate into geographic analysis, albeit with one key exception. For Elliot Jacques (1984: 144), "the idea of an intentional event is implicit in the idea of conduct, of action"; and within this general category, I would emphasize the concept of the episode, "implicit in the idea of intentionality and of direction of this conduct and action." The episode contains a "determined and analyzable" structure that allows us to distinguish it from intentional conduct in general. Following this conception, an activity develops and, based on a *meta-image,* results in a behavior directed toward acquiring a satisfactory *meta-object.* This is represented by available means, in "the form of things, people, and ideas that already objectively exist and that can be utilized . . . either as they are or by being adequately transformed" (1984: 145–6). Such an idea of the *episode* fits well with our assertion that actions and objects have a unitary life, and that events and geographic space are produced simultaneously.

In his version of the intentionality thesis, Hägerstrand (1989) refines ideas previously proposed by David Ley (1979), Neil Smith (1979), Seamon (1982), Pickles (1985) and others. Drawing on the Swiss philosopher Jakob Meløe (1973), he explains human action as a projection of matter. Landscape, according to Hägerstrand, provides an extreme example of the intentionality thesis. According to M. A. Díaz Muñoz (1991: 132–33), Hägerstrand's geography of time is not based in the actual activity of individuals, but in the conditions for their potential activity, which set the terms for how "actions are converted into spatial-temporal trajectories of material" (Hägerstrand 1989: 114). This is one way to reinterpret Heidegger's (1992: 90) proposition that "the *where* determines the *how* of Being, because to Be means presence." According to the Swiss geographer, action is action *in a landscape,* and landscape gives form to action, but where Hägerstrand uses the term *landscape,* we would use the term *space.* With this caveat, we must emphasize the inseparability between action and object in order to affirm, as we are doing here, that the central theme in geography is not separate objects or actions, but objects and actions taken together.

Action is much more effective when it has adequate objects. The intentionality of action joins with the intentionality of objects, and, today, both are dependent on the roles of science and technology present within territory.

We must also remember that the outcomes of human action do not depend solely on the rationality of decision and execution. There is always a certain unknown in the result of any action that is due, on the one hand, to human nature and, on the other, to the human character of the milieu.

Actors engage in actions that are not the consequence of decisions (Hindess 1987: 141), and intentional actions can also bring about unintended results, which is quite common in the process of social or spatial change (Hägerstrand 1991b: 113). In his book *Du texte a l'action: Essais d'hermeneutique,* Paul Ricoeur (1986: 193) offers a paradigmatic example of this, where action separates from its agent and produces its own consequences and unintended effects. Unlike in the production of knowledge, here it is impossible to separate the process from its cause in the domain of action, as René Guénon (1945: 61) reminds us: "results are always separated from that which produced them" due to the "essentially momentous character of action."

Ricoeur (1986: 193) calls the unpredictable nature of actions' outcomes the "autonomy of action." One reason that we cannot fully predict the outcome of action is because action always happens within a milieu, a complex and dynamic combination of elements that has the power to deform and impact action—as if the arrow of time becomes warped as it moves through space. According to Moles (1974: 106), the "event" itself would be an interpretation of this autonomy.

An event is the result of a bundle of vectors, driven by a process, and it gives a new function to a preexisting milieu. But we can only identify the event once we perceive it, that is, when it is whole and completed. And the event is only complete once it is integrated into the milieu. According to Georg Simmel (1903: 42) "rendez-vous" indicates both a meeting and the place where that meeting happens. If that bundle of vectors could be stopped in its path before it were manifested, then there would be no event. Action does not take place without an object, and, when it is implemented, it redefines itself as an action and redefines the object. That is why events are at the heart of the interpretation of social geographic phenomena.

THE INSEPARABILITY OF OBJECTS AND ACTIONS

In his critique of the epistemology of modernity, Latour (1991: 127) ironically comments that the "modern" way of seeing the world would lead us to believe that society is "only the symmetrical artifact of nature, what is left when all objects are removed." In truth, however, what we call society only becomes concrete when we understand it as both the context and content of objects. As Whitehead (1919: 196) puts it, our understanding of the particular life of an object must be based in an understanding of its relation to the event that it is situated in.

Moles (1972) argues that objects are double mediators in that they are placed between individuals and society and between individuals and their material situations. Similarly, for Baudrillard (1973: 16), it is insufficient to simply define objects in a system. We must also define the system of practices exercised on those objects. There is a continual interchange between the two—the evolution that affects the work process and social relations also creates real changes in geographic space, both in its morphology and functions and processes. We can identify different epochs by analyzing these changes.

Every historical period has a corresponding list of techniques and set of objects. Over time, the emergence of each new system of techniques also produces a new set of objects. And in each period, there is also a new arrangement of objects—new objects, new models, and also new forms of action. If we define "place" as a point where bundles of relations come together, then a new spatial model can occur in place even if the existing things in that place do not become new things or change location themselves; this is possible because a spatial model is both morphological and functional. In other words, when a place changes morphologically, and there are new objects created in order to meet new functions, old objects may remain even if their functions change. In fact, in 1802 Kant noted that objects change and create different geographies. We can understand this assertion in two different ways: it could mean that new objects emerge over time, such that in each moment the population of objects contains many different objects of different ages; or it could mean that the same object, over time, changes meaning. Even if its internal configuration remains the same, its external relations are constantly changing. As a result, its value might shift, even if its material structure does not, because its web of relations changes it, making it substantively other. A new geography is therefore constantly being created.

In each new moment, we must ask what defines the new system of objects and actions, especially given that new arrangements tend to be more productive and to constitute, in a given place, hegemonic systems. New systems tend to be either created specifically for the most powerful social forces or placed at their disposal. New actions can work on old objects, but their effectiveness might be limited.

The fundamental properties of any thing determine how it will relate to other things. For Hegel (2010: 463), "A thing has *properties*; these are, *first*, its determinate reference to *something other*; the property is there only as a way of reciprocal relating." Based in these relationships, systems of objects are constructed and take on meaning. And, as Ernesto Laclau (1990: 109) argues, reading objects is tantamount to reinserting them into the given relational conditions, which both include space and manifest through space. In this sense space functions as a kind of whole that redefines the objects that constitute it, which is why we would say that the geographic object is always changing its meaning—which is what Laclau called the "instability of objects."

The theoretical physicist Bohm's proposition (1957: 146) that a thing cannot exist outside of context also extends to geographic space. A geography that is only interested in a particular type of object, (for example, technopoles) or objects of a particular age (for example, contemporary technological objects), will not be able to account for reality, which is total but never homogeneous.

It would be an understatement to say, like Krampen (1979: 25), that space can be seen as "a stage where humans enter into relation with other humans and with objects." And it would be even less acceptable to say, as Henri Van Lier does (1971: 137), that space is a "firm system of reference . . . emerging from the fact that things maintain, internally and externally, precise and constant relations." It would be better to argue, along with Berry and Prakasa Rao (1968: 21) that "the network of space is a series of interdependent and superimposed networks in which changes in one affect the others." But we would need to specify that these networks are also human, formed by inseparable objects and actions.

We also cannot forget that the object hides itself, or, in G.-N. Fischer's words (1980: 90), that "we do not understand the interior of things" because "the technical meaning of things is no longer visible." By investigating the technical content of objects we begin to learn about them and take up the task of understanding them. Subirats (1989: 102) argues that objects are subjected to an order that is not at all mysterious, given that ultimately, objects have an, "analytic and conceptual defined transparency." Following Jacques Ellul (1964: 162) "technique demonstrates, in practice, that mystery does not exist." When we begin to investigate the type of work that an object might offer, we encounter the nature of the object. Or we might say, following Henri Van Lier (1971: 137), that the meaning of the object appears in pragmatic situations.

But would attributing meaning to objects not also be metaphorical? B. Ollman (1971: 145–46) argues that an object does not have a life of its own. Baudrillard proposes to resolve the problem that objects do not exist outside of the symbolic activities of society through a discussion of the symbols that objects embody (cited in Krampen 1979: 7). In symbolic work, needs are satisfied and in that process symbolic activity gives these needs existence. In response, Moles (1971a; 1973) prefers to argue that the meaning of an object is located in its function.

Form certainly provides us with a starting point for knowledge, but it is far from an endpoint—form alone cannot offer us a comprehensive explanation. Simmel argues that form is indispensable for knowing life, but that "the language of form is incomplete" (1980: 17). A great number of thinkers argue that form and life are the two poles of the production of knowledge. Among them, Cassirer, in *Symbolic Forms,* and later in *The Logic of the Humanities,* uses the concepts of form and cause to analyze the world (1974: 159). Because form and cause, form and life, do not exist autonomously from one another, they should be thought together. R. Ledrut (1984: 38) similarly emphasized the inseparability of context and content, arguing that separation destroys the unity of both.

The logic of an object logic emerges precisely from this unity. When we alter the functionality of one of its parts, we reduce its effectiveness and could even fatally adulterate it, turning it into something else.

Form and content exist separately only as "partial truths," as abstractions that only reencounter their value when taken together (Ledrut 1984: 32). The relation between the context and the content, between background and form, is not merely functional. As Simondon (1989: 64) argues, "The participational relationship connecting forms to their background is a relationship which straddles the present, brings the future to bear upon the present, that which brings the virtual to bear upon the actual. This is so because the base is a system of virtualities, of potentials, of moving forces, whereas forms are a system of the actual." We know that if forms constitute the current system, it is only because the actions within that system are constantly evolving. In sum we might say that understanding geographic space as the result of the concurrence of a systems of objects and systems of actions allows us to travel from the past to the future by considering the present.

GEOGRAPHIC SPACE, A HYBRID

If, as we propose, space is a product of the inseparability between systems of objects and systems of actions, we must be careful to avoid, following Bruno Latour (1991), modernity's epistemological mistake of seeking to work only with pure concepts. He argues that on one side of this problem we find Thomas Hobbes, founder of political science and the social sciences, and on the other, Robert Boyle, the great author of the natural and exact sciences. This separation between "a scientific power charged with representing things and the political power charged with representing subjects," is one of the points of departure of the modern paradox, with "a complete separation between the natural world (constructed, nevertheless, by man) and the social world (sustained nevertheless, by things)" (Latour 1991: 29–31). Latour insists that we do not need to tie our theorizations to two pure forms: on the one side, the object, and on the other, the subject-society, because "Nature and Society are no longer explanatory terms, but rather something that requires a conjoined explanation" (81).

Given that history does not separate the natural and the artificial, the natural and the political, we need another way of seeing reality that opposes this secular work of purification. Today it is often impossible for the common person to distinguish the works of nature and of humans, or to identify where the purely technical ends and the purely social begins. In fact, the technical objects that we encounter daily "are not meat or fish," but rather intermediary beings in which "men, products, utensils, machines, [and] money" connect to one another (Akrich 1987: 50).

Michel Serres asks (cited in Latour 1991) whether in our construction of an epistemology, would we not prefer to begin from hybrids rather than from pure concepts? Hägerstrand (1989; 1991b) proposes something similar in his efforts to simultaneously explore the material world and the world of human meaning.

When Simondon (1989) explores the role that background exercises over forms, it is quite possible that he is also discussing the inseparability of systems of objects and systems of actions that we have placed as central to a definition of geographic space.

Georges Balandier (1991: 9) further suggests that we explore the present unstable universe where these compositions or mixtures of men and techniques occur, and where "the definition of social and of modes of power would be as important as the control of techniques." This is why, as Maurice Godelier suggested in the 1960s, "all systems and structures should be approached as 'mixed realities'" (1966: 254–55). For him, the "mixed" are a set of objects and norms. Intermediary beings, such as robots, belong to neither art nor nature and are part of the world of accidental beings, which is different from the world of natural beings (Queau 1987: 8).

These objects do not have their own history or geography. Isolated from their corporal reality, they may appear to be carriers of diverse individual histories, beginning with the history of their intellectual production, as fruit of the scientific imagination of the laboratory or of the intuitive imagination of experience. However, their historic existence depends on their insertion in a series of events—a vertical order—and their geographic existence depends on the social relations that they are subject to and which determine their relations to other objects—a horizontal order. Their meaning is always relative.

These "quasi-objects" (Latour 1991) would be the same as Whitehead's (1919: 195–96) "living objects" or "objects expressing life," or even Stiegler's (1994: 30) "inorganic organized beings."

My concept of content-form (Santos 1996c) is the geographic corollary to this idea of mixtures and hybrids, and also to Diano's (1994) idea of "monumental" form, which itself may be a legacy of Aristotle. The form recreates itself in each event, so it cannot be understood only as form or as content. This means that when an event is realized, it takes on the available form most adequate to carry out its functions. However, beginning at the moment the event happens, that form—the object—takes on a new meaning that emerges from this encounter. In other words, meaning and reality cannot be understood separately, and in fact, one does not even exist without the other.

The idea of content-form brings together process and outcome, function and form, past and future, object and subject, natural and social, and it presupposes the analytic treatment of space as an indivisible set of systems of objects and systems of actions.

AN EPISTEMOLOGICAL NECESSITY: THE DISTINCTION BETWEEN LANDSCAPE AND SPACE

Landscape and space are not synonymous. Landscape is a set of forms that, in a given moment, express the legacies of the successive localized relations between humans and nature. Space is both these forms and the life that animates them.

The term *landscape* is much more commonly used than *territorial configuration*, which we would define as the set of natural and artificial elements that physically characterize a given area. Strictly speaking, landscape is the part of the territorial configuration that can be apprehended visually. In practice we usually use the term *landscape* to refer to the territorial configuration, and in many languages the two terms are used interchangeably.

Landscape occurs as a set of real, concrete objects; it is transtemporal, bringing together past and present objects in a transversal connection. Space is always present as a horizontal construction, a unique situation. Each landscape is characterized by a given distribution of object-forms with a specific technical content. Space is the result of society's incursion into these object-forms, which explains why in space these objects do not change their place as much as their function, their meaning, and their systemic value. So while landscape is a material system that is relatively immutable, space is a system of values in permanent transformation.

Space, one and multiple, in its diverse parts, and through their use, is a set of goods whose individual value is a function of the values that society attributes to each of them (e.g., each fraction of the landscape) in a given moment.

Space is society, and landscape is society. But space and landscape do not overlap completely, and the attempt to make them do so is ongoing and unending.

Landscape exists through forms created in different historic moments that coexist in the current moment. In space, the forms constituting a given landscape find *a present function in the present moment* that responds to society's needs. The particular forms in a landscape have been born in different successive moments to meet the needs of different societies, and only the most recent forms are determinations of the current society.

Following Carlos Reboratti (1993: 17), "Human landscape is a combination of various times present in a given place." In truth, landscape and space are always a type of palimpsest where the actions of different generations are superimposed upon one another through accumulations and substitutions. Space itself is a matrix where new actions are substituted for previous ones, making it present precisely because it is past and future.

François Ricci (1974: 132) calls landscape and space two sides of the same coin. When using these concepts, we risk either not distinguishing between the two sides or separating them in such a way that we end up only considering one side at a time. Our analysis of them can only be effective when "the side that may be ignored, but not eliminated, comes to impose itself as a face hidden behind the more recognizable face."

The author of an article entitled "La géographie aux champs" (Grataloup 1975: 26–28), in the very first issue of the journal *Space-Time*, implored us to distinguish between "the perceived landscape, whose only uniting element is the man who perceives it, and the significant space of a phenomenon." But their provocation seems to have gone unnoticed, as evidenced by the fact that today banal space is a neglected subject (we certainly speak more about the space of a given phenomenon than about the space of all phenomena) and that geography's epistemological legacy poses an obstacle to a nondualist treatment of the problem. Pierre George (1974: 7) argues that this idea of landscape, as it is currently used, is "one of the ambiguities of geography, a Janus-faced science, always tempted by sources of reality that they should be studying."[1]

Space cannot be studied as if the material objects that make up a landscape had lives of their own and could explain themselves. Of course, the forms are important. This materiality serves the modes of production that created them. But following Baudrillard (1973: 16), "the only thing that allows us to account for the real are not the structures of technology, but the incursion of practices onto technology, or better yet, the obstacles created by practice on technology."

Technical objects have no meaning outside of their landscape, but they do exist in the landscape, awaiting social content. Marx argued that "political economy is not technology" (Marx 1904: 270). If humans, through their work—as producers, residents, or occasional occupants—do not give life to a thing, the life that only they hold, the object will forever remain technology, and will not become economy. Franz Jakubowsky (1971: 60) argues that, just as the material forces of nature only become productive through human work, the same is true of social material forces, which are created by people through past or present processes of production. In the *Economic and Philosophical Manuscripts* Marx cited Pecquer, saying that "the material element, which is quite incapable of creating wealth without the other element, labor, acquires the *magical virtue* of being fertile for them [who own this material element]" (cited in Korsch 1967: 273).

During the Cold War, Pentagon laboratories talked of producing a neutron bomb capable of annihilating all human life in a given area without destroying any buildings. If President Kennedy had allowed this project to move forward (which he did not), then *space* would exist on the day prior to such an event, while on the day after there would only be *landscape*. This is a paradigmatic example of the difference between these two concepts.

In our point of view, the question at hand is about the nature of space formed, on the one hand, through the material accumulation of human actions over time, and on the other, by current actions that give it a dynamism and functionality. In other words, landscape and society are complementary elements whose synthesis is constantly remade in human space.

The movement of society gives geographic forms new functions, transforms the organization of space, creates new situations of equilibrium and new points of departure for new movement. In taking on life, always renewed by societal movement, forms—turned content-forms—can participate in a dialectic with society itself and as such make up part of the evolution of space.

Landscape's palimpsestic nature—it's living memory of a dead past—transforms it into a precious work instrument, because "this permanently frozen image" (Bloch 1974: 49–50) allows us to look back to the past in order to gain perspective on the whole. Historian Marc Bloch is one of the original creators of this retrospective geography, which was later produced definitively in Braudel's 1949 book *La mediterranée*.

Bloch warns against imposing this image "on every past moment." In this image we only encounter material fragments of a past—of successive pasts—whose simple reconstruction does not help us much. In fact, landscape only allows us to presume a past. If we want to interpret each step in social evolution, we need to examine the history represented by these fragments of different ages together with the history written by those societies that were writing it moment to moment. This is the only way to reconstitute the past history of the landscape; what's more, the function of contemporary landscapes can only be understood through their encounter with contemporary society.

No part of the landscape has the ability to generate change the whole. According to Isachenko (1975: 635), "even if all of the components of landscape are present, in one way or another, directly or indirectly, a true change in the given relation cannot 'automatically' and 'without delay,' affect, in the same proportion, all parts of the system." Changes are always whole and each aspect or part is only a piece, an element, in the movement of everything.

Landscape congeals historically, and participates in lived history. Its social function in space is realized through its forms, and so through those forms we can investigate how landscape functions (Monteiro 1991). If, as Whitehead argues (1938: 225), knowledge "is only that which analyzes the functioning of functions," then knowledge of landscape must understand its role in the global functioning of society. Landscape is a result of accumulated history, and in particular it stands as a testament to successive means of production. Human space is an always provisional and constantly remade synthesis of contradictions and the social dialectic. What interests us is what this understanding might offer to help resolve our epistemological problem.

Marx proposed that we analyze phenomena according to two qualitative aspects: their natural or specific qualities. V. Kusmin (1974: 72–73) drew on this proposal to argue that, in the former, the more general and abstract aspects take precedence, while in the latter, the phenomenon is seen as an element or component of a given system, that is, as a systemic phenomenon.

Despite its concrete, material nature, if we analyze landscape in isolation, it can only be an abstraction, because its reality is historic and based in its association with social space. To fully analyze landscape we must be attentive to the distinction that different authors have made, between "substantial existence" and "relational existence," two complementary and opposed forms of the objectivity of nature. This parallels the distinction made by Marx and taken up by Kusmin (1974: 67) between social qualities of the first order and social qualities of the second order.

Can we imagine a dialectic relationship between society and different spatial forms, say, between society and landscape? Or does the dialectical relation take place exclusively between society and space?

We would argue that society animates spatial forms, giving them content, life. Only life is capable of this infinite process that goes from the past to the future, and only life has the power to transform everything substantively. Everything whose meaning does not emerge from this interaction with society is incapable of moving on its own and cannot therefore participate in a contradictory movement, in any dialectic.

An empty house or an empty field, a lake, a forest, or a mountain do not participate in this dialectical process. Rather, when they are transformed in space they are attributed certain values. The simple fact that they exist as landscape is insufficient. The form used is not the same as its content—it becomes space because of its content-form.

There is no dialectic possible between forms as forms, nor, for that matter between landscape and society. Society geo-graphs itself through these forms, assigning them a function that changes through history. Space is the always provisional synthesis between social content and spatial forms. The primary contradiction is between space and society, between an invading and ubiquitous present that is never completely realized and a localized present that is objectified in the social and geographic forms it encounters.

When society acts on space, it is not acting on objects as a physical reality, but as a social one, as content-form. In other words, society seeks to endow already valorized social objects a new value. This action is projected onto objects that are already the bearers of previous, and still present, actions and as such, these objects of actions are endowed with a human presence.

The dialectic occurs between new actions and an "old" situation, an inconclusive present that seeks to realize itself on a perfect present. Landscape is only one part of the situation that, as a whole, is defined by contemporary society, so, as in society, as in space.

In each moment, in the final analysis, society is acting on itself, and never exclusively on materiality. The dialectic is therefore not between society and landscape, but between society and space, and vice versa.

THE
PRODUCTION
OF
CONTENT-
FORMS

4

Space and the Notion of Totality

Geography has been timid in its approach to totality. As a discipline, it has not exactly abandoned this theme, but it has also not approached it systematically.

There are two common approaches to thinking about totality in geography. The first, more common approach treats geographic fact as a "total social fact," in the tradition of Marcel Mauss. Its overarching goal is to bring together all of the elements that define a region or a country and to align them with all possible factors affecting a given local situation. However, this line of thinking gives rise to innumerable ambiguities. For example, place itself almost always appears to be self-contained, and the various factors considered are rarely examined as they actually occur, that is, as a system.

The second approach, which often inspires fastidious philosophical debate, is based in the idea of world-totality, using Fernand Braudel's concept of a *world system* (popularized by Immanuel Wallerstein) as an epistemological solution to the question of totality. The pitfall that geographers fall into here is imagining that this framework, which was constructed specifically for other approaches to understanding reality, could be readily applied to the investigation of geographic fact. In fact, the more we seek this central concept of the world system in other disciplines, the further we get from a concept that is analytically useful for geography. In our view, an emphasis on the idea of the world system creates two problems. First, in these discussions the world-totality tends to be reduced to only one of its many characteristics. And second, this focus generally leads to analyses based on ideas external to geographic fact, and, as a result, geographic fact is then explained only through allusions, comparisons, analogies, and metaphors that are never adequate to provide comprehensive analyses of geographic phenomena.

Roger Brunet (1962: 13) argues that "geography endeavors to achieve what had been the dream of philosophy: to apprehend the real in its totality," but this is not geography's ambition. A geographer could certainly develop a totalizing vision of the world, but that vision would have to be based in his or her own particular area of knowledge—located within one aspect of the global reality. The geographer's first task is therefore to construct a smaller philosophy, a metageography that offers a system of concepts capable of reproducing, intellectually, real situations as they are seen from the point of view of this area of knowledge. We cannot do this without first delineating our object of knowledge.

Today this problem is more acute and urgent than ever. The world is globalizing to such an extent that people are discussing the idea of a global space. Although we may have reservations about the legitimacy of this particular idea, it is undeniable that spaces of globalization are emerging. And further, progress in science, technique, and information makes it increasingly possible to explore the idea of totality more objectively. For the first time in the history of humanity, we are living with an *empirical universality* (Santos 1984), which makes it both urgent and possible to return to the question of totality.

Although recently geographers have tried to incorporate the idea of totality into geographic analysis, both implicitly and explicitly (Brunet and Dollfus 1990; Durand, Lévy, and Retaillé 1992; Johnston and Taylor 1986; Peet 1991), we have not yet fully explored totality's value as an analytical category for helping us to build a theory and epistemology of geographic space.

One approach might begin with an examination of concrete totality as it presents itself in this period of globalization—an empirical totality—to examine the effective relations between the *world totality* and *places*. This would be tantamount to revisiting the universal equivalent in order to understand the particular and vice versa, reexamining, from this angle of vision, the role of events and the division of labor as key mediations between the two elements.

In the following sections, we explore the concept of totality—identifying its processes and metamorphoses and analyzing its consequences for the existence of space.

The concept of totality is fundamental in order to know and analyze reality, and it is one of the richest legacies of classical philosophy. It proposes that everything present in the universe forms a whole. Each thing is no more than part of this whole, but totality itself is more than simply a sum of its parts. The parts cannot explain the totality; rather, it is totality that can explain the parts. Totality B, or, everything that results from the movement in the transformation of Totality A, again divides into parts. The parts that correspond to Totality B are no longer the same parts that corresponded to Totality A. They are different. The parts from A (a^1, a^2, a^3 ... a^n) no longer exist in Totality B, and only Totality B can provide an explanation for its own parts (b^1, b^2, b^3 ... b^n). It is not that the parts a^1, a^2, a^3 ... are transformed into b^1, b^2, b^3 ..., but that Totality A transforms into Totality B.

Thais is why they say that the whole is more than the sum of its parts. Let us examine the case of a given society, a *social formation*. That which characterizes it in Time 1 is not the same as in Time 2. Imagine, for example, that a growing global population, a growing urban population, and growing industrial production characterize said social formation. In Time 2, we encounter different situations. The total population, the urban population, and the industrial production are no longer the same. Given that in Time 2, which immediately follows Time 1, everything is different than it was before, does that make it a different entity? Or are we encountering a society in movement?

When society moves, all of its functions move in quantity and in quality. Such functions are realized concretely in the particular places most adequate to that realization. We can understand these geographic areas as having an exclusively functional role, while the changes that occur because of that realization are global and structural, extending to all of society—the world, or the socioeconomic formation.

The increase in total population, in the urban population, and in industrial production is not due to the influence of the localized places in different regions, but to the global movement arising from more general forces responsible for the geographic distribution of the different variables across the whole. This can also be expressed in different terms.

Totality is reality in its entirety. For Ludwig Wittgenstein (1961), in the *Tractatus,* reality is the totality of the states of existing things, the totality of situations. Totality is the ensemble of all things and all people, in their reality—in their relations and their movement. In his book *Origim da dialética,* Lucien Goldmann (1967: 94) similarly argues that totality is the "absolute set of parts in their mutual relationships," which is how totality simultaneously evolves to become something else and to continue being totality. This totality of the real, as Lucien Karpik (1972) calls it, is understood together with "the planet," that is, with nature and the human community.

Historical process is one of complexification, meaning that through history totality becomes denser, more complex. But the universe is not disordered, and thus we must seek to identify the order in the universe, to discover its laws and internal structures (Kosík 1967). We should not look for the order that organizes things according to our liking, but the order that things themselves actually have—what Karel Kosík calls concrete totality.

THE SCISSION OF TOTALITY

We seek to comprehend reality, but totality is a fleeting reality that is constantly unmaking itself in order to remake itself. The whole is something that is always seeking to renew itself, to become, again, another whole. How, then, can we comprehend it?

Merleau-Ponty warns against the tendency to work with a confused or empty understanding of totality. And Wittgenstein (1921: 4, 1961: 462) warns against conceptualizing a tautological totality, where representational relations cancel each other out, because they have no reference to reality.

Bearing such warnings in mind, we must first account for the fact that knowledge presupposes analysis and that analysis presupposes division. Then we must understand the processes through which totality is divided. Hobbes (1841: xiv), for example, in discussing the state, argues that "as in a watch, or some such small engine, the matter, figure, and motion of the wheels cannot well be known, except it be taken asunder and viewed in parts." Kosík (1967: 30) considers the decomposition of the whole to be "the feature most characteristic of knowledge."

Thus, knowledge of totality presupposes its division. The real is the process of separation, subdivision, and decomposition. This is the history of the world, of the country, of cities: to conceptualize the totality but ignore its division is to disregard its movement.

TOTALITY AND TOTALIZATION

One way to approach this problem is to use Sartre's distinction between totality and totalization, understanding the former as outcome and the latter as process. According to Urs Jaeggi (1969: 52), totalization would be constituted by the past, present, and future. In other words, the arrow of time only occurs through totalizations. Furthermore, Gurvitch (1971) explains that for Sartre there are no static totalities, only totalities in movement. As Benetti (1974) puts it, totality, the product of a real movement, appears in each moment "as an inert set and a movement of totalization that is unfolding."

Could we place this understanding alongside Merleau-Ponty's (1994: 281–82) idea of "spatial space and spatialized space?" Or, could we return to Benedictus de Spinoza's (1910) expressions of *natura naturans* and *natura naturata*, the complementary and contradictory pair that reveal the march of history and the relationships of society with the environment? Nature-becoming-nature and nature-made-nature, however, are no longer natural nature but historicized nature. And there is no precedent for choosing between *natura naturans* and *natura naturata*. Each in its way provides the basis for and explains the other.

Structured totality is simultaneously a perfect, finished totality, an outcome, and a totality *in fieri*—in movement, a process. In other words, we should distinguish a produced totality from a totality in production, but the two coexist, side by side, in the same places. For geographic analysis, this convergence and distinction are fundamental for encountering a method.

If, following Sartre, totality is always in movement, in an incessant process of totalization, then all totality is incomplete because it is always seeking to totalize. Is this not precisely what we see in the city, country, or any other geographic unit? This permanent movement is geographic analysis's central interest: the perfected totalization, represented by the landscape and territorial configuration and totalization that is making itself, represented by what we call space.

If, again following Sartre, being is existence in potential, and existence is being in act, society would be being and space would be existence. Space is the key element that ultimately allows global society to realize itself as a phenomenon.

As such, space is first and foremost a specificity of the social whole, a particular aspect of global society. Production in general, society in general, is nothing more than a real abstraction, the concrete-real—an action, specific relation, or production—whose historicity, or concrete realization, can only happen in space. Thus Eric Dardel (1952: 59) argues, "Terrestrial space appears as the condition for the realization of all historical reality, as that which gives it body and assigns a place to everything that exists. You could say that it is the Earth that *stabilizes* existence."

THE PRECEDENCE OF PROCESS

Historical process is a process of separation into particular, specific things. Every new totalization creates new individuals and gives old things new content. The process of totalization moves from the old to the new totality and constitutes the knowledge base for both of them.

The whole can only be known by knowing its parts and the parts can only be known by knowing the whole. These two truths are therefore partial. To access the true totality, we must recognize the combined movement of the whole and its parts through the process of totalization.

The process of the whole becoming another whole is a process of undoing, of fragmentation and recomposition, of simultaneous analysis and synthesis. In this movement the one becomes multiple and vice versa. As Regis Debray (1991: 83) puts it: "The multiple is the future of the one." The multiple whole becomes one again and then as a new whole, it is again ready to be undone.

The metamorphosis of abstract-real into concrete-real, of essence into existence, of potential into act is, consequently, the metamorphosis of unity into multiplicity (Spinoza 1910: 61).

In *Search for a Method,* Sartre (1968: x) argues that totality "is perpetually in process as History and historical Truth." According to Barnes (1968: x) Sartre's existentialism contains two legacies from Hegel: truth is something that is always emergent; and truth tends to become a totalization. As Alain Badiou (1975: 61) explains, the being of the transitory state is the process—a state of division—through which the whole is seen as a scission. "Movement is not a succession of wholes but a series of divisions."

The problem of time remains unresolved in this framework because what Riu (1968: 21) calls the "dynamic interpretation of phenomena" occurs through the recognition that definitive reality is actually located in the process itself. That is to say that a finished thing might provide us with a crystallization of movement, but that is not the same thing as life itself. We can only really arrive at meaning when we understand what Whitehead

(1971: 56) calls "the specious Present," the immanent, unfinished present, the not-yet-finished reality. For Whitehead, the essence of existence resides in the transition between what is already given and a new alternative, but the present is always seeking a not-yet-realized future. Georg Lukács (1972) also draws attention to this passing moment, this present whose perception demands that everything be surprised in its movement. The best way to surprise this movement is to observe the scission of totality.

THE UNIVERSAL AND THE PARTICULAR: THE PRESENT

The present should be seen as the realization of the objective interest of the whole, through particular ends. The meaning of the present, according to Whitehead (1938: 128), comes from the value that things have for themselves, for others, and for the whole. The particular originates in the universal and is dependent on it. J. J. Goblot (1967: 16) argued that Stalin's mistake was transporting the universal to the particular and then expelling that particular from the universal—a "double and contradictory" approach.

From Cassirer (1965: 1:105) we take the idea that the movement of totality allows it to be understood, in a first moment as a whole and in a second moment as a differential. As a whole, totality is seen as one thing and often *in the abstract*. As a differential, it is understood through the particular manifestations of its form, function, value, and relation, that is, *in the concrete*.

Totality is simultaneously the abstract-real and the concrete-real. It only becomes existent, is only completely realized, through social forms, including geographic ones. Totality undergoes a new transformation in each moment of its evolution. In other words, in each moment of its evolution it again becomes the abstract-real.

The movement that creates multiplicity also individualizes totality through its forms. The *fragments* of totality become *objects* that continue to integrate the totality. In other words, fragments become the essence and activity of objects, but always as a function of the totality, which remains intact. Each individual is only a *mode* of the totality, a way of being: it reproduces the whole and only really exists in relation to the whole.

TOTALITY AS POSSIBILITY

In *Phenomenology of the Spirit* Hegel describes the metamorphosis, through experience, of the Idea into Object and Object into Idea. Following Hegel, "Spirit becomes object because it is just this movement of becoming an other to itself, i.e. becoming an object to itself, and of suspending this otherness" (1966: 3:21). The Hegelian Idea is what we are calling totality, and phenomenology the transmutation of the abstract-real into the concrete-real (and vice versa). This metamorphosis is ongoing because totality is in perpetual movement.

In his *Metaphysics*, Aristotle (1979) argues that while all acts contain potential, potential does not always become an act. As abstract-real, totality is *potential*: and through its relations to its forms it becomes an *act*, or concrete-real. For Aristotle, the essence is that which a being has to do. The movement of totality is also a movement in search of objectivity.

We can therefore understand totality as simultaneously a whole of essences and of existences. The whole of essences, yet unrealized, is made up of *perfect objects*. The word *object* is used here in the same way that sociologists tend to use it, as all that exists in the world of the concrete and the world of representation and imagination (Godelier 1972). The word *perfect* can be applied to these entities, these *objects*, to indicate the fullness of their being—or in other words their maximum potentiality, an absolute. They are possibilities, like a perfect technology, a perfect technical object, a perfect action, a perfect norm. They are possibilities that have not yet been realized by actors and that are therefore latent.

Serafin Meliujin (1963: 226) distinguishes between possibility and reality. For him "*possibility* represents a real tendency, hidden in objects and phenomena, that characterizes the diverse directions in the development of a system. *Reality* is all that exists objectively as realized possibility." He adds, "For possibility to transform into reality, two factors must be present in nature: first, the action of objective laws, and second, the creation of propitious conditions" (227).

Thus, the world's existence is latent, a set of possibilities that are drifting until called to realization, when they transform themselves in *extension*—in qualities and quantities. Those essences would be, then, the possible-real, real possibilities and not ideas. This real is a viable configuration of nature and of spirit in a given moment: a new technique, a new action that has only just occurred.

Totality as latency is defined by its real possibilities that have not yet been historically or geographically realized. They remain latent until they are realized (historicized, geographized) through action. It is action that brings together the universal and the particular—by bringing the universal to *place*. In other words, action creates a particularity that continues to be particular in relation to the movement of the whole, until it is ultimately overtaken by new movements. The overtaken particularity precedes the current universality and succeeds the defunct universality. In other words, there is an interactive moment in which particularity and universality mutually foster one another.

Existences are particular manifestations of being, which itself precedes existence and is its conditions of possibility. Existences are functioning technologies, operationalized objects, historicized and geographicized actions, norms created by of the interplay of possible forces in a given moment and place. Through historical process, the whole of existence manifests as relativity. For example, a technology may be nominally full or absolute, but it is rarely utilized in its fullest extent. Each actor takes it up in a different way. So, it may be theoretically full, but in practice it is not. Through facticity, we pass from the unrealized "absolute" to the realized "relative," which in each case is a certain combination of quantities and qualities. These combinations will, in turn, condition new possible qualities and quantities.

The resulting particularity combines some of the possibilities currently offered by the whole, along with some of what remains of the outdated particularity. From this formulation, we can understand space's resistance to the impact of new events, the *dynamic inertia* of content-forms (Santos 1975; 1984).

INDIVIDUATION, OBJECTIFICATION, SPATIALIZATION: CONTENT-FORMS

Totality (of which there is only one) is selectively realized according to differential impacts, such that only some of its possibilities actually become realities. People, collectives, classes, businesses, and institutions are characterized according to the effects of their different forms of knowledge. Similarly, places are often defined according to the effects of what happens within them. This selectivity happens on the level of both form and content. The movement of totality toward objective existence is driven by its spatialization, which is also a form of particularization.

The transformation of the whole (which is integral) into its parts (which are its *differentials*) also occurs according to an ordered distribution in space of the whole's effects through its different variables. Actions are not located blindly, nor are people, institutions, or infrastructures. This principle of differentiation among places produces specific combinations where the variables of the whole take a particular form.

As such, places reproduce the country and the world according to a particular order (Silveira 1993: 204–5). Because the determinations of the whole occur in a qualitatively and quantitatively different way differently for each place, this unitary order actually creates diversity. This evolution is diachronic, establishing nonhomologous changes in the relative value of each variable. Uneven and combined development is, therefore, an order that can only be understood through the process of totalization, that is, the process of one totality transforming into another one.

However, we must also investigate the "conditions," the "circumstances," of this historic—and also geographic—milieu because "they cannot be reduced to the universal logic." Goblot (1967: 10) argued, for example, that within the same object we can find unity with difference, indicating that when we analyze which processes constitute an event, it would be insufficient to only consider the universal.

We cannot, therefore, understand a dialectic that creates a hierarchical structure (essence, naked totality), process, function, and form in a linear movement or in a univocal manner because, on the one hand, the structure needs form to become existence and, on the other hand, the content-form has an active role in the movement of the social whole.

In making content-form through action, form becomes capable of influencing the development of the totality and thus participating fully in the social dialectic. According to Sartre (1960: 139), "The whole is entirely present in the part as its present meaning and as its destiny."

This fresh vision of the concrete dialectic breaks new ground for understanding space, given that through this vision we will give new status to geographic objects, landscapes, geographic configurations, and materiality. This approach is clearer, because space is not merely a receptacle for history, but a condition for its realization. Today this concrete dialectic also includes ideology and symbols.

THE ROLE OF SYMBOL AND IDEOLOGY
IN THE MOVEMENT OF TOTALITY

For a long time, philosophers thought it necessary to counterpose essence and appearance. We would argue that this approach is no longer productive, despite the fact that ideology is also essence, appears as reality, and is lived as such. Perhaps it would be better to counterpose essence and existence, which would force us to remake the path from between them wherever we encounter things in movement.

Following James Anderson (1985: 2), ideology cannot be seen in purely subjective terms, as if "everything is only in the heads" of people. It should also be based in concrete, factual reality. Ideology produces symbols that constitute part of real life, and frequently takes the form of objects. At the end of the twentieth century, we can say that ideology is simultaneously a fact of both essence and existence; it is located in the structure of the world and in things; and it is a constitutive factor in the history of the present.

Reality includes ideology, and ideology is also real. It was once considered false and thus not real, but today it is not far from reality, nor is it mere appearance.

When, in a place, essence transforms itself into existence, the whole is transformed in parts, and thus totality takes a specific form—real history arrives in place with its symbols. Objects are born as an ideology and as reality at the same time, and they can therefore exist as individuals and participate in the social reality. In other words, the social totality is formed by a mixture of "reality" and "ideology." That is how history is made.

It would not, then, make sense to think that an object would consist of a "real" part and a "false" (i.e., ideological) part, or that separate "real" and "false" parts would form totality, structure, or essence. And we must recognize that these so-called real and false parts of the structure have a constitutive and structuring role.

Ideology is a level of the social totality that is not only objective, real, and constitutive of the real but is an abstract-real that increasingly manifests as a concrete-real, which complicates social life.

Ideology occupies the position of referent in representation, but not in real movement (the movement of the real and of ideology together), precisely because the symbol, by its very nature, has autonomy. With a society in movement—making history—the movement of the whole is simultaneously the movement of the elements of "truth" and the movement of ideological elements.

As Cassirer (1965: 282) wrote, "The question of truth appears to apply only to particular parts and not to the whole of reality. Within this whole, different layers of validity are demarcated, and reality seems to separate sharply from appearance." How then are we to take up the task of analysis? The notions of real and symbolic, real and ideological, essence and appearance, all have analytic, epistemological value. For R. M. Eaton (1964: 205), "Any symbol is equivalent, for symbolic purposes, to itself; it can replace itself in any context without altering the meaning, since every symbol can have one and only one meaning."

When society, in each movement, is split, the symbol is released from that general movement and continues on in the same vein as it had before. The present unifies things, but in the next moment separates them, or allows for them to be distinguished from one another. Each symbol holds the same identity, regardless of the context, both in a situation of movement and change. In other words, the movement of society, the movement of totality (and of space) changes the meaning of all of the constituent variables, and also of the symbol, precisely because it does not follow that movement.

Therefore, in every new division of labor, every social transformation, there is a demand for the renewal of ideologies and symbolic universes, at the same time that it becomes possible for others to understand the process and search for meaning.

5

From the Diversification of Nature to the Territorial Division of Labor

INTRODUCTION

The division of labor can be explored most broadly in geographic studies, which systematically bring together the notions of totality and time, linking the question of the distribution of resources to the idea of the event. The division of labor is a motor of both social life and spatial differentiation.

FROM THE DIVERSIFICATION OF NATURE TO THE DIVISION OF LABOR

Through the exchanges of energy among its elements, the natural world is in a perpetual movement in which its identity is constantly renewed, and, in that process, some of its aspects change. Whitehead (1919) defines the *diversification of nature* as the process through which natural elements are constituted. Natural elements derive their particular characteristics from each movement within a given mode of diversification. Then each mode of diversification is succeeded by another mode (as changes in characteristics accumulate). That is how nature makes itself other: as its aspect changes, so does nature as a whole.

Kant (1999) noted this in *Critica de Razão Pura* and affirmed that history progresses infinitely when he remarked, "Creation is never at an end, is never complete. At one time it had a beginning, but it will never end. It is always busy, producing new objects, new scenarios, new Worlds. The work that it presides over corresponds to the time that it extends over."

For Whitehead (1919: 62–63), "an object's changes come from its different relationships with different events," and "without objects, comparing one event to another would be impossible." Whitehead's argument thus presumes the indissociable relationship of objects and events. Their process of interaction within the same movement creates and re-creates space and time. For him "objects are only in space and in time because of their relationships with events," whereas, if an object were to exist alone, it would have no time or space (63).

Whitehead's theory draws on R. G. Collingwood's work (1946: 166), seeing "nature as consisting of movable patterns, whose movement is essential to its existence." These patterns are analyzed through what Whitehead calls "events or occasions," which coincide with S. Alexander's (1963) "point-instants," or pure events. Both Whitehead and Alexander, in Collingwood's opinion, concede that, in complex things, essence and structure (or pattern, as Alexander prefers) are identical. Different moments of the diversification of nature create specific patterns that define them.

We can compare the diversification of nature in the natural world to the division of labor in the historical world. This division, moved by production, provides a new content and function to places with each new movement. As a result, the human world changes and diversifies, which is to say that it reencounters its identity and unity as its various aspects change. In this geographic version of Whitehead's theory, "entities" and "natural elements" should instead be read as "places."

When nature was still completely natural, the diversification of nature played out in a pure state. The movement of its parts, cause and consequence of its metamorphosis, emerged from a process that could be attributed entirely to the unleashing of natural energy.

The first appearance by humans was a new factor in the diversification of nature, because they attributed value to things, adding a social fact to the process of change. In the first moment, when they were yet to be fitted with the prostheses that would augment their transformative power and their mobility, humans were creators, albeit subordinate ones. Later, technical innovations increased humans' power of intervention and their relative autonomy, and thus the socially constructed "diversification of nature" increased.

The world economies theorized by Braudel mark an important step in this process, in that the changes that affect places increasingly originate externally to them. Within the march of capitalism there is a tendency for global diversification by social forces to dominate the diversification of nature by natural forces. At first, the "social" was located in the interstices of nature; today the "natural" is housed or takes refuge in the interstices of the social.

With industry, this tendency became even more accentuated, thanks to the human technologies that now interfere in all phases of the production process, through the new forms of energy that people command. Today, the motor for the division of labor has become international; it is information.

The diversification of nature is both process and outcome. The international division of labor is a process whose outcome is the territorial division of labor. The two processes undoubtedly appear similar, in that the energy that moves them changes. On the other hand, nature is a repetitive process, while the division of labor is a progressive one.

THE DIVISION OF LABOR AND THE DISTRIBUTION OF RESOURCES

The division of labor can also be seen as a process by which available resources are socially and geographically distributed.

The world's resources constitute a totality. I understand resources to mean all possibility, whether material or not, of human action (whether of individuals, businesses, or institutions). Resources are things, natural or artificial, compulsory or spontaneous relationships, ideas, feelings, or values. People change themselves and their environment based on the distribution of resources. Thanks to this transformative action that is always present in each moment, resources are others—that is, they renew themselves, creating another constellation of data, another totality.

The resources of any given country also constitute a totality. Each discipline seeks to enumerate them according to their own more or less specific, detailed, and often misleading classifications. In reality, no resource, whether an inventory of products, a population, a job, innovation, or even an amount of money, has an absolute value. The real value of each thing is not contingent upon its separate, individual existence but upon its geography, on the collective meaning that each and every thing has because it is part of a place. As concrete as things such as products, innovations, populations, and money may appear to be, if they are not located in place, then they are merely abstractions. The collective and individual definition of each thing depends on a given localization, which is precisely why it is the sociospatial formation, rather than the mode of production, that is most adequate for understanding the past and present of any country. Each activity is a manifestation of the total social phenomenon. And its effective value is provided by the place where it manifests, along with other activities.

That distribution of activities, that is, that distribution of the totality of resources, emerges from the division of labor, which is the value that allows the totality of resources (nationally or globally) to functionalize and objectivize itself. These processes happen in places. Space as a whole combines with all of the local forms of functionalization and objectification of the totality.

In each moment, each place receives particular vectors and not others. The movement of space is the result of this movement of places. Seen through the optic of space as a whole, this movement of places is discrete, heterogeneous, and together "uneven and combined." This movement is not unidirectional; rather, such constituted places then become the conditions for the division of labor itself, which is also simultaneously a condition and outcome of that process. But the division of labor has a causal precedence, in that it is a bearer of the forces of transformation, conducted by new or renewed actions, and located within new or old objects that make that transformation possible.

Take money as an example. We know that finance is a great common denominator in a world where banks—which have become global—incorporate and amalgamate added value in its different manifestations, independent of their particular location or scale. All types of profit and loss are processed by the financial system. Banks can clarify, qualify, and classify everything that pertains to finance according to their own interpretation of the law of value and, in the end, through reinvestments, relocalizing products according to their whims. Because of the way that their actions affect the division of labor, banks are today an important geographic factor.

But financial instruments, which have become quite numerous, are different in different places. We call all of these instruments "money" in order to simplify our discourse. In reality money appears in different modalities and different types in different places. National currency is the simplest and most banal and generalized form. It is also the most ubiquitous form. In today's world, it is rare for money to circulate in a form other than national currency. Money can, however, also circulate in other forms—as foreign currency, checks, local national and international credit cards, promissory notes, bonuses, actions, obligations, applications, funds, certificates, and many other products. In fact, one of the highest forms of financial intelligence today is the capacity to invent new products.

This multiplicity of financial forms, however, is only selectively distributed geographically. Places can be distinguished according to the type of money available or located in them. We do not encounter all kinds of money everywhere. Rather, each place is marked by a particular combination of that money, more or less abundant and rich, that forms the basis for a financial hierarchy among places. Simple statistics allow us to map the dense and rarified areas of financial circulation across any territory.

Therefore, the types of money that "run" in these places actually "run" every night to the metropoles where they are transformed. This drain toward the center happens according to a hierarchical model which corresponds to the particular strength of the center and which is served by computer networks localized hierarchically within the system, one which is simultaneously a chain of capture and distribution. This information is instantly collected in the banks of the intelligence centers and allows them, easily, to make financial decisions and even to selectively relocate money.

Each situation, for nearly all social actors, constitutes a limit on their capacity to act financially, simply because the physical access to any given financial instrument depends largely on the place where it is located. In most countries, there is a limited number of locations where all possible financial forms can be utilized. Moreover, countries distinguish themselves by the types of financial instruments available there. This reasoning also extends to other parts of economic and social life because they are all subject to the territorial division of labor. This territorial division of labor creates a hierarchy among places and, according to its spatial distribution, redefines the capacity for people, firms, and institutions to act.

The division of labor presupposes the existence of conflicts, which we must consider in our analysis of it, although some of these conflicts are more relevant for our purposes than others. The first is the conflict between state and market, although we cannot discuss these two entities as if they were simply given. Within the market, different businesses, according to their differential powers and respective productive processes, provoke a division of labor that corresponds to their own interest. And different scales of public power also compete for a territorial organization that is adapted according to their particular prerogatives. The modalities for the exercise of public power and the politics of businesses are based in the territorial division of labor and seek to modify it in their image.

THE TIMES OF THE DIVISION OF LABOR

Can we say that the division of labor has times?

We could approach a study of the division of labor and the question of time in at least two different ways. The first would be to analyze successive divisions of labor, meaning the chain of transformations over the course of history, their causes and consequences, the established periods and their duration, and the places where they occur. The second would be to study divisions of labor superimposed on one another in a single historical moment. This latter approach is more specifically geographic and demands a more objective understanding of the often vague concepts of time and space.

Each place, each subspace, bears witness, as observer and actor, to the simultaneous unfolding of different divisions of labor. Let us comment on two situations, remembering that each new historical moment changes the division of labor. It is a general law. In each place, in each subspace, new divisions of labor arrive and establish themselves, but they do not do so separately from the previous divisions of labor. The particular combination of diverse temporalities in any given place distinguishes it from other places. For the purposes of analysis, we should also recognize the fact that that within a given situation, each agent promotes their own division of labor. The labor of a given place is the summation and synthesis of the individual labors that can be identified as a singular mode in each historical moment.

It is in this latter sense that we can say that the division of labor *creates a time*, its own time, which is different from the previous time. This is also very general because this "time" ends up being abstract, becoming concrete only in its interpretation, in active life, through the action of diverse social agents. That is how, beginning with each agent, with each class or social group, *temporalities* are made (interpretations, that is, the particular forms of the utilization of that general time), "practical temporalizations," in the words of Sartre, which are the matrices of lived spatialities in each place.

The generic time of the division of labor would be the time of what we commonly call the mode of production. The defining elements of the mode of production would be the general measure of time, and that general measure could even be extended to the relative times of more "backward" existent elements, legacies of previous modes of production, in order to account for them. Seen in its particularity(that is, objectified) and therefore with its geographic aspect, time (or better, temporalities) leads to the idea of the sociospatial formation (Santos 1977). In this formation, different competing times work together and all recover their complete meaning through this functioning and this shared existence.

The more that the temporal and spatial manifestations of these successive divisions of labor are separated by time, the more effective and visible they are. Or, from an analytical point of view, the more the interested observer can historically divide time into periods and subperiods. Today, as history passes through a formidable acceleration and, with the computer, the measure and division of time becomes even more possible (Siegfried 1955: 160) and the consequences more scientifically tangible. We have a greater capacity to accurately periodize phenomena, to make better divisions of time in order to better recognize the stages and the meaning of historic and geographic events. And as defining phenomena becomes easier, our analysis can be finer and more complex and thus richer.

Although the computer and other technical gains are key to this outcome, periods are not the result of the homogenous time of machines but rather of the lived time of (global, national, and local) societies, which are created by the different divisions of labor.

It is true that the latter can be the object of a more detailed and precise analysis, based in the assessment of its contents of the abstract times of clock, today more detailed and precise. If, however, these divisions created by technology create the conditions for many different particular activities to be carried out, this does not affect the totality of these activities, much less of life. In the interpretation of the division of labor, especially at the level of a country—or, moreover, of a place—we must also take the nontechnical and the non-technical-economic into account, whose role is increasingly important in the production of behaviors.

The time of the world is the time of multinational corporations and supranational institutions. The time of nation-states is the time of national states and big national firms: they are the only ones who can take full advantage of national territory through their actions and trajectories. Between these two there is a regional time—of regional supranational organizations—along with common regional markets and continental or subcontinental cultures. The next scale below that of the nation-state is that of national subspaces, regions, and places, whose time is that of medium and small-sized businesses and of provincial and local governments. But what scale is smaller than that of places? What place deserves to be called the smallest place?

Let us dedicate a few paragraphs to the earlier question of both superposition and of different divisions of labor. This would mean discussing the presence, in a given subspace, of different scales of simultaneous time.

All places exist in relation to a world time, the time of the dominant mode of production, even if not all places are necessarily affected by it. To the contrary, places differentiate themselves, either by their historic period, or due to the fact that they are differentially affected, either quantitatively or qualitatively, by these times of the world. The time of the world would be the most external time, related to all spaces, independent of scale. There would be, in this hierarchy and this order, the times of the nation-state and the times of places.

Here there are two problems. Could we, for example, also speak of supranational times that are not global, like continental times? Is there a "European time," as well as "African time" or "South American time"? This discussion must be had, but we quickly find that only some of the existing nonglobal trajectories have supranational implications. The second problem comes from the fact that the word *place* is, like other parts of the geographic vocabulary, full of ambiguities—a region could also be a place, and the word *region* itself can be used to designate different kinds of areas. We know a priori that the most external geographic dimension of time is that of the world, but we don't know what extension of time is the most internal. Only a laboriously established method could allow us, *a posteriori*, to recognize this most internal or smallest time, whose observation cannot be absolute.

Regardless, what is fundamental here is not the management of the instruments of measure, but rather the recognition that each place is a theater of multiple "external" times. Based in world time—the absolute extension of time—other times appear as internal times. The time of the nation-state is internal in relation to world time and external in relation to regional times and the time of places. And compared to the minimum internal time—that of the place or the point—all the rest are external.

ROUGHNESS OF SPACE AND
THE SOCIAL DIVISION OF LABOR

The social division of labor is often understood as the distribution (either in the world or in place) of living labor. This distribution, seen through the localization of its different elements, is called the territorial division of labor. These two forms of approaching the division of labor are complementary and interdependent; however, this approach is insufficient unless we account for the fact that, beyond the division of living labor, there is also a territorial division of dead labor. Dead labor, in the form of the built environment, plays a key role in the distribution of living labor. Furthermore, territory's natural features, whose influence was determinate at the beginning of history, still influences how the division of labor happens. Natural and artificial forms are virtualities, which may or may not be utilized, but whose presence in the labor process remains important (conditioned by its own internal structure). Marx (1956: 165–66) has already called attention to the economy of nations, but he fails to explore its relevance for geographic explanation.

Geographers have long explored the role of nature and the different proposed explanations for its influence on geography have contributed to a vigorous debate in human geography in this century. The question of the constructed environment, which has recently come into fashion, is still far from exhausted, and we have much to learn from an exploration of these forms.

Simmel, like Durkheim, began raising these issues at the end of the nineteenth century. Sartre's concept of the *practico-inert* is equally key to this conversation. The social process is constantly leaving behind a legacy that creates the conditions for new phases. Things like a plantation, a port, or a road—but also the density or distribution of a population—are part of this category of *practico-inert,* practice deposited in things, that becomes the condition for new practices. In every moment the social process is redistributing its factors. And this redistribution is not indifferent to the preexisting conditions—the natural and built forms inherited from previous moments.

Representations of the past in the contemporary landscape are not always visible as time, nor are they reducible to meanings, only to knowledge. What we call roughness (*rugosidade*) is that which remains from the past as form, as built space, landscape, what is left over from the process of suppression, accumulation, and superposition, that with which things replace themselves and accumulate in all places. Sites of roughness present themselves as isolated forms or as arrangements and are part of a space-factor. Even without being immediately translatable, roughness brings us the sediments of previous divisions of labor (all scales of the division of labor), the remnants of the types of capital utilized, and their technical and social combinations with work.

In each place, then, current time encounters the past crystallized in forms. For contemporary time, the remnants of the past constitute that type of "slavery to previous circumstances" that John Stuart Mill discussed. This is what we mean when we speak of the *dynamic inertia* of space (Santos 1992).

The previous divisions of labor allow us to return to previous forms according to a logic that reestablishes them in the very moment of their production. Either seen individually or in their patterns, roughness reveals the combinations that were possible in a given time and place.

The built environment constitutes a patrimony that we cannot fail to account for, especially given that it plays a key role in the localization of contemporary events. In this way, the built environment stands in contrast to the purely social elements of the division of labor. These groups of forms are there waiting, ready to eventually exercise their functions, even if they are limited by their own structure. The work that has been done in the past imposes itself over the work yet to be done. The current territorial division of labor rests upon the previous territorial divisions of labor. And the social division of labor cannot be explained without an explanation of the territorial division of labor, which depends, itself, on inherited geographic forms.

6

Time (Events)
and Space

In current parlance, the word *event* has different meanings and
is used to refer to different things. In philosophical dictionaries,
what we are here conceptualizing as an "event" also has different
names.

Every author develops their vocabulary internal to their own
system of ideas. Henri Lefebvre uses the word *moment* for what
Gaston Bachelard calls an *instant* and Alfred North Whitehead an
occasion. For Bertrand Russell (1966: 289), an event is the outcome
of a series of instants. While these different words may not exactly
be synonyms, for the purposes of building a geographic theory of
the event we can use them almost interchangeably. That said, a
geographic theory must be internally coherent and must therefore
give these terms their own particular meanings.

Lefebvre (1958: 348) defines the moment as an attempt to fully
realize a possibility. This possibility "happens," it "discovers itself"
and can be lived as a totality, which is to say that it is realized and
extinguished.

If we consider the world as a set of possibilities, then the event
is a vehicle for one or more of these possibilities to actually exist in
the world. But the event can also be the vector of existing possibilities within a social formation, that is, in a country, region, or place,
if that country, region, or place is understood as a circumscribed
set more limited than the world.

Place is the final holding place for the event. While Eddington argues that an event is "an instant of time and a point in space," we might more precisely describe it as an instant of time that happens at a point is space. For Arthur Eddington (1968: 186), the event-point is the most elementary concept in a theory of nature that accounts for relativity. An event, for Eddington, is precisely "a point in this space-time," "a given instant in a given place." The principle of differentiation then derives from the combination of a temporal order and a spatial order.

All events happen in the present. They happen in a given instant—a fraction of time determines them. They are a matrix of time and of space. In *A Philosophy of the Future*, Ernst Bloch (1970: 124) writes, "Time *is* only because something happens, and where something happens there time is" [English in original]. He emphasizes the word *is*, but as geographers we would also emphasize the word *where*.

As bearers of action in the present, events create time (Schaltenbrand 1973: 39). Or, as Henri Focillon argues (1981: 99), the idea of the event completes that of the moment. If we speak of a past event, we are discussing its previous presence at a given point in the arc of time. In other words, we are speaking of a "past present." When we speak of a future event, we are talking about a possibility that will be realized in a future present. As Whitehead put it (1919: 61), "Events are, essentially, elements of actuality"; and when they occur they extinguish their possibility, or, in Whitehead's words, "they pass." Events do not repeat themselves, according to Bertrand Russell (1945), given that, as Bosi (1992: 222) argued, their "principal character" is a fact that "can be situated precisely in the coordinates of space and time." Sir Lewis Namier argued (cited in Freeman 1961: 77) that this is because the circumstances for a given event are never the same twice. Each act is therefore different from the both the previous and the following ones (Kubler 1973: 105), which is what defines its singularity (Morin 1972: 6–20).

Each event is therefore entirely new. When events emerge, they create an inescapable, new history. This is what Lefebvre (1958: 346–47), referring to the "moment," and Bachelard (1932: 30–31) to the "instant," mean when they argue that these concepts are absolute and thus efficient and irreversible. Sartre (1938: 85) argues that it is precisely this irreversibility that gives people their "sense of adventure" in encountering events. In other words, in realizing that no moment repeats or returns, we decide to act within these tight nets [*malhas estreitas*].

This absolute presence is the basis for the impact of any given event. Where the event takes root, there is change, because, as Focillon (1981: 99) argues, the event itself is an effective brutality. In a similar line of thinking, Nora (1974: 191) argues that there is no natural difference between an event and a crisis, which he defines as a complex of events. Following from this, we can say that within each new event preexisting things change their content and their meaning. Samuel Alexander (1963: 16) argued that, "We don't need to explain the idea of novelty so much as that of repetition, regularity, uniformity." Repetition would be the exception, the deviation, and the abnormality. Novelty, on the other hand, is the essence of history.

Events change things, transform objects, giving them new characteristics even while they remain situated in the same exact place. In *Human Geography*, Jean Brunhes explained this problem in his discussion of the complications arising from the existence of different successive phenomena in the course of time and in space. The geographic, Brunhes argued, "remained the same, but the people who live within it have greater needs, changing and growing complexes" (1947). Although we could argue that his statement confuses the "geographic" with what is actually the "material," the fundamental idea is still interesting. Like human geography more broadly, however, the statement still fails explicitly to reference the event as a category of analysis.

Events dissolve things (Diano 1994: 91); they dissolve particular identities and propose others—indicating that identities are not fixed and thus, following Deleuze (Boundas 1993: 41), challenging us to a "test of knowledge." In other words, in the face of a new history and new geography our knowledge [*saber*] also dissolves, and we are forced to reconstitute it through our perception of the movement of things and events.

There is no event without an actor. Or, following Diano (1994: 66), there is no event without a subject. Following this line of thinking, we could argue that every theory of action is also an event, and vice versa. A geographic theory must integrate the ideas of the event and action.

A good explanation of events must also be able to differentiate among them. As Kubler (1973: 105) argued, "We cannot apprehend the universe without classifying it according to types or categories, ordering the infinite flux of non-identical events in an finite system of similitudes."

The first level of differentiation would be the separation of natural events (a strike of lightning, the beginning of the rain, an earthquake) from social or historical ones (the arrival of a train, a rally, an automobile accident). The movement of nature, the diverse expression of natural energy, produces natural events, and nature changes according to its own dynamic. Human action and its effects on natural things produces social events. Here, the movement of society produces change through the diversified use of labor and information.

The history of humanity emerges from a world of things in conflict into a world of actions in conflict. While initially actions established themselves in the interstices of natural forces, today it is nature that occupies the interstices. In other words, in the past, society established itself on and in natural places that were only partially modified by humans, while today natural events occur in increasingly artificial places, changing the value and the meaning of natural events.

Historical events presuppose human action. In fact, event and action are synonymous terms, which means that in classifying events we are also classifying actions. Events are not merely facts, they are ideas. An innovation is a particular type of event, characterized by its relation to a given point in time and space, from which it changes its mode of doing, of organizing, or of understanding reality.

We can also differentiate between finite and infinite events. The former results from the distribution of finite possibilities or resources: the limits on time (if I choose to go to one place I cannot go to another at the same time); the money available; the population of a country. Infinite events, on the other hand, result from the distribution of possibilities and resources that aren't exhausted through use, such that their distribution can be cumulative rather than competitive. Freedom, democracy, and information are examples of infinite events.

We can also differentiate between unplanned events and planned ones. And the will to shape the future takes shape along different temporal horizons, from the very short to the longest term.

DURATION, EXTENSION, SCALES, SUPERIMPOSITIONS

The event is always present, but that present is not necessarily instantaneous, raising the question of whether duration, or the lapse of time during which a given event—determined by its constituent characteristics—has an effective present. This distinction is key for distinguishing between consecutive and simultaneous events.

An event can have an organizational duration in addition to its natural duration. The natural duration derives from the original nature of the event—its individual qualities or intimate structure. A principle of order can also make the event last beyond its internally determined time. In other words, rather than allowing a given event to play out on its own terms, we can change its natural process, using organizational forms or structures to, for example, reduce or limit an event's existence or period of action. By this we mean that things like laws, governmental decisions, decrees by central banks, or the rules of a private bank or company are organizational forms that can adjust or even determine the duration of events.

Events do not occur in isolation, but in systemic groups—true "situations"—that are increasingly organized in their establishment, functioning, control, and regulation. Such organization simultaneously depends on the duration and the amplitude of the event. The level of organization itself depends on the scale of the event itself.

For example, the national determination of the school calendar is an organizational mandate that delimits and categorizes social time. In doing so, it determines from above and from afar the duration and the level of economic activity in a large number of vacation destinations. In another example, bank hours regulate the rhythms of activity in other parts of economic life.

The omnipresent role of formal organization within all life processes is one of the key markers of our time. Lucien Goldmann was perhaps the first to recognize contemporary capitalism as the capitalism of organization. Whether a given resource is used completely or incompletely, absolutely or relatively, effectively or ineffectively, profitably or not, as well as the forms in which their determinations should fit, depend largely on the mode of organization. Even the most basic geographic relationship—that of humans to the earth—is itself increasingly determined by the characteristics of the given area involved and by the processes of production, which are themselves increasingly outcomes of a result of the organization of production taken as a whole.

If we understand time not only as a duration or intensity but as an extension—or a spatiality, others might say—we come close to understanding, from a geographical point of view, the concept of the extension of an event put forward by Whitehead (1919) and others.

This is more easily recognized within the domain of natural events. For example, what terrain does a flood affect, in a given moment? Within a given period, which areas register a particular temperature?

In the domain of action—events of a social nature—the same phenomena occur, although identifying them may be more difficult. It is clear that without much difficulty we can trace the areas where a given element—an agricultural product, an industrial product, or a service—might be present.

To explain this presence, one would need to distinguish between organizational factors and technical ones, which tend to be easily confused.

Technical factors can be used alongside natural factors to analyze events in the physical world. A particular vegetative species—for example, a variety of corn or grain—has natural behavioral rules. But its ultimate yield will depend on the organization of production. The hard part is remembering that "natural" or technical characteristics induce particular organizational forms and vice versa.

If, following Marcelo Escolar (1992: 42), we hold that the event is not the same as localization, then the content of different areas must be related to the events that occur within them. In an economic example, each product is directed toward certain goals related to its technical and organizational characteristics. Technical characteristics, which are different for different products, include the productive process (quality of inputs, problems of conservation and runoff, physical relationship to markets, etc.), which can also be translated in terms of time. These conditions are not fixed or absolute but rather are also modulated according to "organizational" vectors: credit, fiscal and tax policies, price minimums, transport, accessibility and quality of information and technical assistance, international prices, speculative forms, external value of currency, and so on.

Locations of different occurrences might have similar content, but they are never identical. For example, in small-scale agriculture where there may be similar plots of corn or flour, but the actual content of different areas is never the same. Each place is a quantitative and qualitative specificity of different vectors (seeds, fertilizer, time spent working, irrigation, transport, etc.).

It would clearly be insufficient to refer generically to an area of flour or corn production. Rather, we absolutely must refer to a specific area, where, together with the production of a particular corn or flour, other events come together to form a single coherent formation and to occupy a determined extension. The concept of "situation," used by a philosopher of sociality, can, in geography, be assimilated to the idea of area of occurrence. This combination of means and ends, of intermediate and final goals, changes over the long term. That is why the surface of occurrence, the area of occurrence, the situation, and the situation's extension also change. Seen in this way, scale is both a limit and a content, which is always changing according to the different dynamics that make decisions over local and regional occurrences.

Which forces can produce events over extended areas?

The first of these is the state, through its "legitimate use of force," whether or not it is made explicit in law. Law is general by its very nature and therefore a public norm acts on a totality of people, businesses, institutions, and territory. This is the superiority of state action over other macroorganizations. Neither supranational institutions nor multinational ones have this power—while they may indirectly have global effects, their direct effects are pointed or linear.

The "intermediary" authorities (states, regions, metropolitan areas) exercise their role as "official" producers of events over surfaces smaller than national territory.

The idea of scale has two meanings when applied to events. The first is the "original" scale of the variables involved in the production of an event. The second is its scale of impact, of realization. Historical events generally do not take place in isolation. This nonisolation can be translated into two types of what we can call "solidarity": the first is based on the cause or origin of an event, which simultaneously occurs in different places that may be far apart or close together. Here we are talking about events that are in solidarity but that are not superimposed on one another—their link comes from the movement of a totality over the place that they occur. The second type of solidarity is based on the place where the event is objectified, its own geographicization. In this case, different but concomitant events are in solidarity because they are superimposed in a common area.

In the former, the relevant scale is that of the forces at work, and in the latter it is the area of occurrence, the scale of the phenomenon itself. In fact, the word *scale* should be reserved for this latter meaning. In other words, scale is actually a temporal fact and not a spatial one; or, even more specifically, scale varies with time, since the area of occurrence is given by the extension of the events.

In considering the scale of the forces at work, we must also account for the geographic, political, or economic place where the relevant variables occur. For example, a world event may originate in a multinational organization, a transnational bank, or a supranational institution—the World Bank and the International Monetary Fund create world events. And in the respective territorial dimensions, there are national, regional, and local events.

The scale of origin of an event is also related to the power of its creator. Rarely does the governor of a state or the mayor of a municipality have the ability to create something beyond a regional or local event. Simultaneously, vectors of action from larger scales are also operating within the geographic context of a region or a place. These vectors from different hierarchical levels combine to jointly constitute a common area of occurrence—the scale of realization.

Would it really be adequate to distinguish events according to the scales at which they originate and are realized? At their point of realization, we might think of events as flows and would need to ask whether a world event-flow can exist. At their point of realization, the possibility of a world event is also subject to question. Through imperial power, a country could either make or fail to make decisions that affect what happens within its frontiers. The same could be said for any other entity that exercises power over a totality: of people, businesses, institutions, relations, or places. A multinational corporation, however, does not have direct power over the world totality of corporations. And supranational organs have relative influence over the world taken as a whole.

But there are actions that can affect the entire world, in the sense that, in a given instant, its impact can be felt beyond the local, regional, or national level, extending to numerous points situated in different countries and on different continents. It is only in this sense that we could speak of global, national, regional, and local events. Could we also say that there can be a superposition of events?

What Alexander calls a place-moment, Eddington calls a place-event. Bachelard argues that we must understand the moment as a point in space-time, which is to say that it is not merely a point in time and a point in space. Rather, Bachelard situates the moment precisely at the intersection of a place and the present—the *hic et nunc*. The moment is not here and tomorrow, nor is it there and today; it is here and now.

Diano (1994: 67–69) argues that "it is not the *here* and the *now* that locate or temporalize the event, but rather the event that temporalizes the now and locates the here." He insists that "there is no event if not in the precise place where I am and at the precise instant in which I recognize it."

Chronologically aligned events succeed one another, which is to say that there is a temporal order to events. According to Eddington (1968: 36), this order is quadruple, because we can arrange events according to four modalities: from the right and the left, from the front and the back, from above and below, and before and after. If, at first, someone could consider these four orders independently, later they will attempt to combine some of them—which is how, Eddington argues, one can begin to distinguish between time and space.

Events do not occur in isolation. When we analyze multiple events (whose order and duration are not the same) occurring at the same time, we can verify that they are in fact superimposed on one another. This group of events is itself an event, in which the various singular events are elements of the broader event. This is an example of both superimposition and combination, because the outcome is greater than the sum of its constituent parts. The order of combination is one thing, the point in which they occur is another, and the result is another. When Russell (1966: 287) defines the event as a series of instants, he could be referring to this geographically interesting fact.

This is also how Focillon must have understood things when he described the event as a node, a place of encounter. It is as if the event tied together the different manifestations of the present, unifying these different contemporary instants through an actual chemical process in which they lose their original qualities in order to participate in the production of a new entity, which appears with its own particular qualities.

For Whitehead (1971: 34), "The passage of events and the extension of events over each other are, in my opinion, the qualities from which time and space originate as abstractions," and "theory requires that we are aware of two fundamental relations, the time-ordering relation between instants, and the time-occupation relation between instants of time and states of nature which happen at those instants."

For Whitehead, this happens in relation such that place is a fusion of actual occasions that are interrelated in a particular manner and in a given extension (cited in Paul 1961: 126). The concept of event scale could also be based in a concept of geographic scale. We could argue that each combination of events simultaneously creates unitary phenomena, that is, unitarily endowed with an extension and imposed over an area, which necessarily act in conjunction with one another. Therefore, the idea of the event can occupy a central role in the contribution of geography to the formulation of a social theory. In other words, through the event we can understand the current constitution of each place and the joint evolution of different places, an outcome of the parallel change of society and space.

Events are current, absolute, individualized, finite, and successive. But to the extent that they extend over one another, interacting with one another, they create the continuity of a world that is alive and in movement (Paul 1961: 126), or, in other words, they create temporal continuity and spatial coherence. That is how geographic situations are created and recreated.

TIME AS AN INTERPRETATION OF
THE REALITY OF OBJECTS

From the point of view of the event, we must also discern between an object's existence and its value. An object has a reality *per se* that comes from its material constitution. An object taken in isolation has a value as a thing, but its value as a social fact comes from its relational existence (Laclau 1990: 119).

Forms secure the continuity of time through successive events, which change their meaning. An object's corporality may give it an autonomous existence, but it cannot have an autonomous meaning, as we will see. "Changes in an object come from the different relationships that it maintains with different events," according to Whitehead (1919: 63). In this sense, space is a testament to the realization of history, because it is simultaneously past, present, and future. Or, as Relph (1976: 125) writes: "Places are themselves the present expression of past experiences and events and the hope for the future."

We should then distinguish between being an object and having value as an object (Vilhena 1979: 195). The valorization of an object is linked to the way that its society makes use of it. Kubler distinguishes between absolute value and systematic value. The former emerges from the object itself, and the latter emerges in considering this object within a system of objects (Kubler 1973: 140). That is to say that the absolute value of an object has to do with its intrinsic characteristics, its attributes, or what it might contain, what type of force it evokes, what type of work it can do. On the other hand, the systemic value of the object presupposes an analytic side and a synthetic side: if we begin from the existent, an analytic; if we want to propose a different form of use for the object, a synthetic.

Kubler suggests that we work with three coordinates: place, age, and sequence. Place, because each object occupies a place, which becomes clearer as an object becomes more fixed. The place of a dam is much more particular to that dam then the place of, say, a refrigerator. But objects also have an age, or a temporal content. How can we determine an object's content when it is marked by several different factors? The object's age is determined in part by the technique that produces it—that means that a cybernetic object is young, but a chipped stone or a ground stone is very old. But this absolute age is age taken out of context.

We still need to consider the fact that an object exists geographically in a place, and at the moment that it becomes located there it takes on another element of age. Being located into a particular environment is not the same thing as existing in an absolute form as a possible geographicization that is as yet unrealized. For example, a forty-story building has one age, which is the age of the first object with forty stories that was built in the world or in a country. But the building would also have an age in a given place that comes from the moment that it was built in that place. That means that each and every object has diverse ages: the moment of its means of production, when the possibility appeared in the world to create a given object; the moment of the social formation when this object first appeared in a country; and a third moment, when the object became localized in a particular place.

A geographic interpretation of Kluber's idea of sequence would force us to ask how sequence relates to the production of space. The real history of life in places shows that objects are inserted into a given milieu in a given order, a sequence, which determines the meaning of that milieu. It is different if, on a given path, we build a building before we pave the road, or if first we pave the road and later we build underground infrastructure, if we first build a school or a hospital, a hospital or a bank. The outcome of the different combinations is not the same, depending on the order in which things are done.

We cannot separate the idea of time from that of objects and their value. But it is complicated because we cannot know, a priori, the moral and physical duration that things, instruments for working, have. We cannot fully know physical duration in advance, because although we might be able to imagine the behavior of objects in any given milieu according to the known resistance of their materials, it is really only after an object is located and utilized that we can we know how long that initial structure will endure. It is even more difficult to discuss the social age of an object. Its moral aging depends on many factors that are not known *ex ante*, only *ex post,* which is why Laclau (1990: 118–19) explains that objects have a historical contingency.

The existing connection among objects emerges from events, which is to say, from the time that they are made manifest and can therefore encounter other objects. All events are children of the world, its attentive interpreters, its particular manifestations. The world in movement presumes a permanent redistribution of events, whether they are material or not, with a differential valorization of places. Geography is founded on the idea that the world is always being redistributed, re-geographized. In every moment, the world's unity produces a diversity of places.

The *instant* valorizes objects differently. The value of the whole changes (its quantity, quality, functionality) in every moment. The processes that ensure that an event will happen change, which changes the function of things, which is to say, their particular value. The whole value of things also changes in every moment, and the value of each individual thing changes along with it. The distribution of values is not random. It reveals the determinations through which the whole of reality changes in order to fit within forms that are either preexisting or created. The model of systems of objects and systems of actions can only be understood as a spatial-temporal mode.

DIACHRONY AND SYNCHRONY: THE AXES OF
SUCCESSIONS AND OF COEXISTENCES

In each location different periods are differentiated by the successive systems of social events, which makes it possible for us to distinguish yesterday and today. We call this the axis of succession. In each place, different actions and actors have different times and they utilize social time differently. But in the common life of each moment events are concomitant rather than successive—we call this the axis of coexistence.

Flows have different speeds. The speed of a letter differs from that of a telegram or a fax. People run the same distance at different speeds. In geographic space, however, despite the fact that temporalities may be different for different social agents, they still happen simultaneously. We have an asynchrony in the temporal sequence of different vectors and a synchrony of their common existence in a given moment. To understand places as they are now and as they evolve we must understand both the axis of succession and the axis of coexistence.

Each action happens on its own time; different actions occur together. Particular individual objectives, functionally perceptible, are merged into a common goal, which is difficult to discern. Social life, in its differences and hierarchies, happens within different times that join, intersect, and become linked in what is called life in common. This life in common happens in space, regardless of the scale—in a village, a big city, a country, the entire world. The spatial order is the general order that coordinates and regulates the exclusive order of each particular time. According to Leibniz (1994) space is the order of possible coexistences.

Time as succession, historic time, was long considered the foundation of geographic study. It is an open question whether that continues to be true or whether, to the contrary, geographic study is actually different way of seeing time as simultaneity: since there is no space where the use of time is identical for all people, businesses, and institutions. We think that the simultaneity of different temporalities over a piece of earth constitutes the domain of geography. We might also emphasize that time as succession is abstract and time as simultaneity is concrete, because it is the time of life. Space brings everything together, with all of its multiple possibilities, which are the different possibilities of the use of space (of territory) related to the different possibilities for the use of time.

UNIVERSALITY AND LOCALITY: TOTALITY IN MOVEMENT AS A TAPESTRY

While the event exhausts its own possibilities, it cannot exhaust or even utilize all of the possibilities in the world. The event inscribes the characteristics of a particular moment into the totality, but it does so as a part of the whole, as Lefebvre argues when he says that the possibility lived by each event is "limited and partial" (1958: 348). It is not, however, a question of seeking a measure of its completeness or incompleteness, or of its effectiveness in light of the full range of possibilities. Its destiny is to realize the totality in the particularity, to live this particularity fully and actively, and thus to contribute to the permanence of the whole, allowing it to be reborn with new characteristics.

It is only in this sense that we could say that one event causes another. In fact, only the totality in movement creates new events. But the totality in movement also includes actions made possible in particular places, from which they influence other places. And actions are not indifferent to the reality of space, rather the very localization of events is conditioned by the structure of the place. Perhaps this was what Whitehead meant in *Modes of Thought* when he said that "the whole antecedent world conspires to produce a new occasion" (1938: 164). Thus, as actions do not have an existence independent from the object to which they give life, neither do events have a reality external to this association with objects.

At the beginning of history, only physical events were universal. The climate is one such example. What we call continental, local, or regional climates have a global behavior. Human facts first occurred locally. The expansion of their relevance happened slowly. It took millions of years for them to register broader geographic effects with the crises of the world economy, as defined by Braudel, comprising the set of economies that are geographically distinct but that survive through exchange. And the process known as globalization has only existed for decades. Only today can we actually speak of historically global events.

As Simmel (1980: 154) argues, our thinking remains incomplete when we seek to understand the process through which the content of an event is inscribed into the cosmic totality. Today, thanks to technical progress and the globalization of the economy, the still incomplete existence of a universal human community (as proposed by Goldmann 1967: 41) allows us to recognize, in each event, a spark of the world.

In our current moment, through the globalization of the international division of labor, human facts also become universal. This happens at the same time that humans become capable of creating natural events and producing physical facts, or ones that change, through their action, the meaning, the reach, and the consequences of natural phenomena, including within the current of universalized human history.

Now we can again and even more strongly take Wittgenstein's position that the world is constituted by the totality of events rather than of things (Wittgenstein 1961: 5). Or, as Russell (1974: 209) argued: "The world offered to our imagination by the theory of Relativity is not so much a world of 'things' in 'movement,' but rather a world of events." When they are carried out simultaneously, in a given stage in the arc of time, events constitute, according to Whitehead (1938: 225–26), "a community of actualities in the world." For Eddington (1968: 168), "The aggregate of all event-points has one name: the world."

What gives events universality is not simply the fact that they happen, but that they are imbricated with one another. Their interwovenness is universal, according to Victor Li Carrillo (1968: 7). In Sartre's *Critique of Dialectical Reason*, he reminds us that "facts do not appear in isolation, they are produced together in a unity that is greater than a whole. They are united through internal bonds and the presence of each one changes the others in their profound nature" (1970: 1:11). It is not only that one event follows the other but that "one event causes the other," according to Whitehead (1938: 225), and "that each event is a factor in the nature of every single other event."

The event is marked by the preeminence of its two levels of existence: the global and the local. Again, following Whitehead (1938: 225), we learn that "no event can be wholly and solely the cause of another event."

In other words, one event may cause another, but it does so by way of the universe, with the intermediation of the totality and in accordance with the totality. This is as true for the major factors of world change as it is for lower-level and banal episodes. A change in one neighborhood affects others, and not only the ones nearby. Improving transportation in one area impacts other areas positively or negatively if the streets or other infrastructure are not altered. Creating a light signal at a street crossing can have effects for miles.

Alexander argued that it is insufficient to analyze events in isolation if we do not take apart their structure or pattern. If events happen in patterns,

Collingwood (1946: 166) argues, we must also remember that these patterns, whether natural or societal, are moveable—which is to say that they are always changing in order to produce a new tapestry and a new truth.

The world can be seen as a kaleidoscope of situations, which makes it possible, through this prism, to see the current definition of subspaces and the historical processes that affect their existence and evolution.

Leslie Paul (1961: 125) argued that the event is "a drop of existence" that "reflects the macrocosm of the universe in the microcosm." From that follows Simmel's (1980: 131) lesson that the totality of events makes it possible to understand an individual event. Events are individual but not isolated. They are interrelated and interdependent, and it is within these conditions that they participate in situations. In reality, there are only situations because events follow one another at the same time that they are superimposed and interdependent.

The interdependency of events happens at various levels, two of which are most relevant from the geographic point of view: the levels of the world and of the place. We argue that events are the consequence of human existence on Earth, acting to create the world. One could also read "humans" as states, businesses, institutions of all kinds, entities that are, together with individuals, capable of action—remembering that action and event are imbricated movements.

In the era of globalization more than ever before, events have global solidarity, by their first origin, their ultimate motor. People do not step out of the world in order to act; rather, they find possibility in it, which can then be realized in particular places. In this way, simple events are amalgamated into situations. In other words, events exist in solidarity locally as a result of their concrete realization. Different situations can result from a solidarity event, and the result can be that the integration between the universal and the individual takes on a new historical content in our current world.

These are, in the final analysis, the two essential forms of the interdependence and simultaneity of events. According to Einstein (1905: 893), "We have to take into account that all of our judgments in which time plays a part are always judgments of *simultaneous events*." But be careful. Eddington (1968: 51) calls our attention to the fact that "the simultaneity of events in different places has no absolute meaning." Whitehead (1938: 229–30) reminds us that "each occasion, although involved in its own immediate realization, concerns the universe."

The global and local levels of events are both essential for understanding the concepts of world and place. But a local event, in the last instance, refers to the global event. From its birth, the event is included in a system to which it attracts the object that it had previously inhabited. The event is the crystallization of the movement of a totality in the process of totalization. This is to say that other events, brought into the same movement, are inserted into other objects in the same moment. Together, these events reproduce the totality; that is why they are complementary and are explained within themselves. Each event is simultaneously the result of a world and a place.

SPATIAL PROCESS: THE SOLIDARITY EVENT

We began by recognizing that the planet, as a material and human entity, is a totality, and that in each moment, history is also a totality. Therefore, the planet and history are realities that are in a permanent state of transformation in order to once again become planet and history. Or, paraphrasing Sartre, they are totalities in a permanent process of totalization. The international division of labor could be considered the energy driving this movement. With the acceleration that we are witnessing—itself a product of the simultaneous evolution of science, technology and information— "moments" of the division of labor become much more numerous. It is as if, in each moment, totality is splitting in order to be reconstituted in the next moment, when a new scission renews the movement again. We would not distinguish between unity and diversity if we did not understand that the unity we are referring to is that of the planet and of history and the diversity that we are referring to is that of places. Events operate this link between places and a history in movement. Region and place, moreover, define themselves as the functionalization of the world and through them that the world is empirically understood.

Region and place do not have an autonomous existence. If we understand them apart from the totality, then they are merely an abstraction. All of the resources of the world, or even of a country, be they capital, population, the labor force, and so on, are divided through the movement of the totality, through the division of labor, and in the form of events. In each historic moment, such resources are distributed in different ways and locally combined, and this brings about a differentiation within the total space and gives each region or place its particular specificity and differentiation. Its meaning comes from the totality of resources and changes according to historical movement.

Both region and place are subspaces subordinated to the same general laws of evolution, where empiricized time is the condition of possibility and the preexisting geographical entity is a condition of opportunity. Each practical temporalization corresponds to a practical spatialization, which disregards the previous solidarities and limits and creates new ones. The distinction between place and region becomes less relevant than before, when it worked with a hierarchical and geographic conception in which place occupied a geographical extension of space that smaller than that of a region. In reality, a region could be considered a place, according to the rule of unity and confirmed by the continuity of historic events. And places— take the example of big cities—could also be considered regions.

Both cases have to do with a solidarity event that defines a subspace, region, or place. This understanding of solidarity comes from Durkheim and has no moral connotation; rather, it calls attention to the compulsory realization of common tasks, even if they are not part of a common project.

In an agricultural region, this solidarity event is homologous. But within a single city, dominated by industrial production, it is possible to identify this homologous event. In the relations between the city and the country, and also in interurban areas, it is complementary. There is also a hierarchical event that is the outcome of commands and information that comes from one place and is realized in another, such as work. It is another face of the urban system. That is not to say that one place commands another; it is more of a metaphor. But the limits on the choice of behaviors in a given place can be due to interests that are located in a different place.

Such a homologous event is that of agricultural production areas or urban areas, which are modernized by specialized information, generating functional contiguities that give contours to the defined area. A complementary event is one of the relations between the city and the country, or of relations between cities, and is a consequence of both the modern needs of production and of nearby geographical exchange. Finally, a hierarchical event is one of the results of the tendency toward a rationalization of activities that are done under leadership, under an organization, which tend to be concentrated.

In every case, information plays a role similar to what in the past had been reserved for energy. Previously, energy in its crude state deriving from natural processes brought together different parts of a territory. Throughout history, information has taken on this function, and today it is the primary instrument that links different parts of a territory.

In the case of homologous and complementary events, that is, in the areas of homologous production in the country or homologous production in the city, territory is defined by an everyday shared through rules that are locally formulated or reformulated. Information used tends to be horizontally generalized. A hierarchical event, on the other hand, is marked by an everyday commanded by privileged information that is secret and power-ful. A homologous and complementary event is the domain of locally cen-tripetal forces, while a hierarchical event is the domain of centrifugal forces. In the latter case, there is also, undoubtedly, centripetal force present, but it is the centripetal force of something else.

In the first hypothesis (homologous or complementary), forces with technical relevance have primacy. In the case of a hierarchical event, norms have primacy and the political is more relevant than the technical.

Both homologous and complementary events assume a continuous ex-tension, in the city and the country, because contiguity is the foundation of solidarity. In the case of hierarchical events, the relations can be discon-nected. Here, solidarity can be independent from contiguity. It is the differ-ence between spatial proximity and organizational proximity (Gille 1987).

In the first case, copresence is a cause or an effect of action. In the sec-ond it is telegraphic (Moles 1974)—the presence of absent bodies, to use an image by poet Paul Valéry. In the former case *horizontalities* are created, and in the latter case *verticalities* are created.

As we saw earlier, the territoriality of a historical event is always chang-ing, leading to the creation and the re-creation of that which Hägerstrand (1973, 1985), in some of his work on the Geography of Time, calls "do-mains." In each moment, there is always a mosaic of subspaces that com-pletely covers the surface of the earth and whose design is supplied over the course of history: scale moves from being a geometric concept to one conditioned by time.

FOR A GEOGRAPHY OF THE PRESENT

7

The Current Technical System

INTRODUCTION

At any given moment in their evolution, the characteristics of society and geographic space exist in relation to a particular state of techniques. In order to make sense of the different historical structure, function, and articulation of territories, we must therefore understand the successive technical systems to which they are related. Each period has a meaning, shared by society and space, that embodies the way that history realizes the promises of technique.

TECHNICAL PERIODS

Drawing on J. Rose's (1974) three major time periods—the Neolithic revolution, the industrial revolution, and the cybernetic revolution—Jacques Attali (1982) argues that techniques evolved from techniques of the body to techniques of the machine and then to techniques of signs. In a different register, José Ortega y Gasset (1947) also identifies three moments in technical evolution: the technique of chance, the technique of the artisan, and the technique of the technician or the engineer. Carl Mitcham (1989: 62–63) elaborates this periodization, explaining that in the first phase there is no particular method for encountering or sharing a given technique. In the second phase, we see the development of techniques that are consciously understood and passed from generation to generation by a particular class of people known as artisans. Here, however, there is only "craftsmanship, not science." It is only in the third phase that we see the development of "conscious study" and "technology" along with "the development of an analytic mode of thinking that is linked to modern science." Heidegger simplifies the question of technical evolution by proposing that there is technique of ancients and one of the moderns, collapsing Ortega y Gasset's threefold division into two.

Lewis Mumford (1963) organizes the evolutionary history of techniques into three moments: the first consisted of intuitive techniques that utilized water and wind and lasted until about 1750; the second consisted of empirical techniques using iron and charcoal and lasted from 1750 to 1900; and the third was defined by the scientific techniques associated with electricity and metal alloys and began around 1900.

We might simplify the history of artificial instruments into three words: tools, machines, and automation. Their respective definitions illuminate the decisive moments in the evolution of relations between humans, the living world, raw materials, and forms of energy. A tool is moved by human force, entirely under human control; people also exert force over machines, but in this case human force combines with tools utilizing nonhuman energy as well; and automation responds to received information and so can escape human control.

The industrial revolution is considered a defining moment in the history of techniques because it marks the point where machines take on a major role in the production of world history. Because it also marks a major acceleration in the speed of key technical transformations, it is often seen as the starting point for the history of techniques; however, making this argument would be to confuse the history of techniques with the history of machinery.

Scholars commonly divide post–Industrial Revolution history into three eras. Following Ronald Anderton (1971: 117), they are marked by: "in the first place, the establishment of the methods for manufacturing plants, in the second place, the introduction of mass production, and in the third place, the development of computer-based systems of control and communication, in sum, automation." For Hannah Arendt (1981: 160–62), the stages of technological development since the beginning of the modern age can be understood as: first, the time of the invention of the steam engine, which imitated natural processes, in which coal mines were the great discovery; the second stage is characterized by the use of electricity; and finally, automation. Ernest Mandel also has a tripartite vision (1980: 9), and his

TABLE 7.1 Fu-Chen Lo's Periodization (1991)

TECHNO-ECONOMIC PARADIGM	First Mechanization, 1770–1840	Steam Engine and Railroad, 1830–1890	Electricity and Heavy Engineering, 1880–1940	Fordist Mass Production, 1930–1990	Information and Communication, 1980–
GROWTH SECTORS	Machine textiles Chemistry Foundries	Steam engines Railroads Machines Instruments	Electrical engineering Mechanical engineering Cables and wires Steelworks	Automobiles Aircrafts Synthetic materials Petrochemicals	Computers Electronic goods from capital Telecommunications Robotics Biotechnology
NEW INNOVATIONS	Steam engine	Steel Gas Electricity Artificial dyes	Automobile Airplane Radio Aluminum Petroleum Plastics	Computers Television Radar Machine-instruments Drugs	

first stage happens in the eighteenth century, the second dates to the end of the nineteenth century, and the third is the current century.[1] Mandel layers different machine systems on top of these stages, each organized around a particular technology and a particular form of organization of labor. He classifies a system of steam engines, of manufacture and craftsmanship, and a system of steam-powered industrial plants, before then considering the assembly line system, which links different machines equipped with electric motors, and, finally, continuous flows created by semiautomatic machines that are dependent on electronics. In their different expressions, they represent radically different types of techniques and machines (1980: 43).

Fu-chen Lo (1991) argues instead for five periods, characterized by early mechanization (1770–1840); steam power and railway (1830–1890); electrical and heavy engineering (1880–1940); Fordist mass production (1930–1990); and the period of information and communication, which began in 1980.

James Anderson (1985) also predicted that this fourth industrial revolution would be marked by multi-use systems of information linked to offices and residences, nuclear fusion, new advances in biotechnology, and control over time (Gross 1971: 272–73).

TABLE 7.2 Technological Changes and Strategic Advances

Period	Information	Energy	Mass
PRE-AGRICULTURAL	Language	Fire Animals	Primitive tools
AGRICULTURAL	Writing Printing press	Gunpowder	Plow Iron
INDUSTRIAL	Telegraph Telephone Phonograph Radio Cinema	Steam engine Electricity	Steel Advanced machinery Railroads
CURRENT	Television and satellite transmission Satellites Computer calculation, storage, and retrieval Control Systems	Fission atomic energy Electrical energy grids Lasers	Interplanetary super-sonic transport New synthetic materials Prosthetics
IMMINENT (BEFORE THE YEAR 2000)	Multipurpose informa-tion systems linked to homes and offices Office automation Multimedia	Fusion atomic energy	Biotechnology Time monitoring

As with any other decisive moments of historical transition, we must interrogate whether what we are witnessing actually constitutes a change from the previous period. There is ongoing debate as to whether the formidable recent advances in technique mark a new stage, or whether contemporary changes are merely a continuation of other conquests and processes that characterize this century.

Although the current moment holds a lot of technological potential, much of it remains unrealized. In his list of technoeconomic paradigms that followed the industrial revolution, Fu-chen Lo (1991) left space open for new innovations in the domains of information and communication, which is exactly where the changing elements of our current world appear to be situated.

From our vantage point, substantive developments based in contemporary techniques seem certain, but history tells us that it is difficult to predict how the contours of that development will actually emerge.

TECHNICAL SYSTEMS

Although the history presented above is brief and schematic, it clearly demonstrates that techniques never emerge alone or function in isolation. Bertrand Gille (1978) goes so far as to insist that even the term *technique* itself should always be plural (Perrin 1988: 24). Jacques Ellul (1977: 88), for whom the notions of system and technique are inseparable, always emphasized that technique should never be treated as merely additive or as an afterthought. In other words, it is simply impossible to understand a technique outside of its context (Ellul 1977; Hughes 1980; Salomon 1982; Tsuru 1961).

The techniques that constitute a system are functionally integrated. For example, "there is a default solidarity," as Debray (1991: 239) explained, "between an electronic telegraph and a railroad, the telephone and the automobile, the radio and the plane, the television and the spaceship, a chronological and a cultural relationship." Techniques' lives and evolution are systemic. Groups of techniques appear in a given moment and constitute the material basis for the life of a society until they are displaced by another system of techniques.

The first industrial system lasted for nearly a century, but the duration of the system that followed it was much shorter. In such systems stability is always relative and precarious, in that each step of technological progress also implies the parallel production of new rigidities, creating new dysfunctionalities alongside the emergence of new inventions.

One of many interpreters of the time of techniques, George Kubler (1973: 126), emphasized that techniques themselves are not isolated events, but rather are complex, structured realities whose constituent relations we can uncover through examination: "The idea of succession also presupposes that in the sequence of inventions there is a structural order, independent of other conditions."

It might be said that the internal evolution of technical systems is characterized by a search for coherence among its parts—its material and social elements. Each period contains a certain type of cohesion in which we can identify a set of self-regulating techniques (Miquel and Ménard 1988: 224). The complementarity among techniques is structural; Perrin (1988: 28)

argued that "techniques establish relations of dependence among themselves," and their historical development "multiplies the number of inter-
relations." This development, indeed, is due in a large part to the fact that
every modification of a given element affects other elements (Ellul 1977:
23), which also speaks to its systemic existence. This "technical environment"
(Simondon 1989), is also responsible for the fact that each invention's productivity depends on the availability of complementary technologies and a
new technical system simply does not function before the *mise au point* and
the establishment of technical tributaries.

THE CURRENT TECHNICAL SYSTEM

We can differentiate time periods from one another by analyzing their
forms of doing (in other words, their techniques). Technical systems include ways of producing energy, goods, and services, ways of relating among
people, and forms of information, discourse, and interlocution.

The marriage of technique and science that began in the eighteenth
century reinforces the relationship ongoing since that time between science and production. In their contemporary iteration as technoscience, the
material and ideological basis for these relations is located in the discourse
and practice of globalization.

While Whitehead (1997: 96) argues that the "invention of the method
of invention" is the greatest invention of the nineteenth century, Donald
Schon (1973) prefers to emphasize the invention of the organization of
invention, referring explicitly to the inventive work of Thomas Edison as
a symbol of what he calls "technical passion" (Hériard 1994). Today the
creative process for new objects, new machinery, new material, and new
appropriations of nature's virtuality is significantly larger, in part due to
the increasingly intimate association between science and technique. The
advent of technoscience made it possible to make predictions based on research, most commonly based on some attempt to establish a causal chain.

In his highly didactic work, Lojkine (1992: 73) designed a synoptic chart
of the differences between previous sociotechnical systems and the current one, which he characterizes as a "flexible, self-regulating [system] of
poly-functional machines," using "material and immaterial (informational)
means of circulation that are decentralized and interactive."

The present technical system includes so-called macro-systemic techniques, which are those technical systems without which other technical
systems would not be able to function (Braun and Joerges 1992; Gras 1992;

Gras 1993; Hughes and Maynz 1988; Joerges 1988). The macrosystemic techniques are the basis for the massive infrastructure projects (dams, highways, telecommunications, and so on) that Pierre George (1968: 192) described in *L'action humaine* and that are also the basis for power networks. But they also create technical microsystems, as Siegfried (1955: 71) predicted and as Jean Chesneaux (1983: 24) described as part of a miniaturization of society.

Victor Scardigli (1983: 24–25) places the products and services that result from the present scientific-technical revolution into five categories: 1) innovations related to radio and television media; 2) new services related to the telephone network; 3) microcomputers and home computers utilized for gaming, to manage activities, for domestic budgeting, for learning, or as an address book; 4) new products emerging from some combination of the above categories; 5) products that invisibly incorporate electronic components (home appliances, cameras, and so on).

One of the defining characteristics of the contemporary system is how fast it has been disseminated. Technical innovations introduced in the twenty years following World War II spread twice as quickly as those introduced following World War I and three times as fast as those introduced between 1880 and 1919. The speed with which these new technologies have been adopted can also be measured in terms of the length of their period of development, understood as the sum of two moments—the period of incubation (when it is found and used for industry) and the period of commercial development (when use becomes generalized). At the start of the twentieth century, the development of a new technology took approximately 37 years, a number that was reduced to 24 years in the period between the two world wars, and then to 14 years after the Second Great War. The speed of adoption in this last period is twice as fast as the one that preceded it and three times as fast as the first period.

Today, innovation happens at a gallop (Kende 1971: 118). The geographical diffusion of these innovations seems even faster when we compare it with previous phases—while in the past it was a process of gradual diffusion, today the process is brutal. As they spread, new technologies involve many more people and colonize many more areas. Witold Rybczynski (1983: 40) explains this when he says that "mechanization stopped on the railroad platform," while the radio and television penetrate into the heart of countries and are present in many more places, even entering into our own homes.

Although contemporary technical systems may be invasive, there are limits to that invasion. These limits are products of both the division of labor and the conditions of population density. The stronger the division of labor in a given area, the greater the tendency for hegemonic systems to become entrenched, and, as a result, the motors of the globalized economy are more efficient, which is to say that supranational institutions, businesses, and banks have greater influence. Density—as Marx and Durkheim have noted—is a factor in the division of labor itself because greater density facilitates greater cooperation.

Whenever new technical systems become entrenched, they create an integrated but not necessarily flexible system. In fact, as Humbert (1991) has noted, integrated systems that are not flexible, as well as autonomous systems that are flexible, abound. Integrated systems embody the hegemonic economic systems seeking to establish themselves everywhere, either displacing autonomous systems or incorporating them into their logic with varying degrees of dependence. The reality is that contemporary technical systems are imposed with ever-increasing strength, but, as in previous periods, their generalized presence does not signify a generalized homogenization of systems. Multiple levels of integration and flexibility persist.

Thierry Gaudin (1978: 186–97) approaches this question of flexibility differently, proposing to divide contemporary techniques into what he calls "mild techniques" [*techniques douces*] and "hard techniques" [*techniques dures*], the latter of which characterize inflexible integrated systems. We might add that this inflexibility, this hardness, is due both to the techniques contained within instruments or tools as well as the to method through which they are used. This is one of the major contradictions within contemporary discourse: there is endless discussion of flexibility and flexibilization as one of the primary characteristics of the present model of accumulation, at the same time that there is a real organizational hardening that results from the seemingly indispensable norms of action, which become increasingly rigid the higher the level of productivity and sacrosanct competitiveness.

Gaudin divides the technical extremes between elitist techniques and popular ones. The former responds to the demands of the prince, to mobilize substantial resources, and depends on specialists, while the latter is the product of the combination of the savoir faire and imagination of the masses, who invent the objects of everyday life. We do not generally encounter either of these extremes in their "pure" state. Rather, different modes of the technical exist simultaneously and alternatively coincide and conflict with one another using their respective weapons: institutionalized appropriation on the one hand and curiosity and necessity on the other.

Contemporary techniques are also characterized by their indifference to their context. Stiegler (1994: 80) argues that this abandonment of the "anthropological hypothesis" was imposed by what he calls the "technical industrial revolution." Today, to become part of local history, a technique does not need, a priori, to be part of the cultural inheritance of the given locale, nor must it be wedded to the virtualities of the given geographic milieu. Rather, for or the first time in history (Herrera 1977: 159) technology appears as an exogenous element for much of humanity. In its current iteration, technology functions in the service of production at a planetary scale, where limits are not set by states or by resources, and where human rights do not even enter into consideration. In fact almost nothing is taken into account beyond the frantic search for income and the elements that facilitate its growth.

It has become a truism to say that technique is generally irreversible, which is to say that once a technique is established, it becomes impossible to live without it. Or, following Daniel J. Boorstin in his book, *The Republic of Technology*, "We cannot go back and forth between the kerosene lamp and the electric light" (Cited in Witold Rybczynski 1983: 101).

Contemporary technology presents itself as practically inevitable. This "inevitability" is due to the fact that technological diffusion is propelled by capital operating on a global scale, directly or indirectly in every place, and also to the formidable force of the corresponding imaginary of that capital-driven inevitability, which facilitates its establishment everywhere.

Because they are practically inevitable, contemporary technologies become irreversible. Their irreversibility actually arises from their feasibility. In other words, even if it were possible to abandon some technologies as modes of doing things, the remaining technologies would be those that are entrenched as a mode of being—incorporated into nature and territory—as artificial landscape. They are thus irreversible in that, first, they are products of history and then they become producers of history.

There are, based on these new products, nearly countless characteristics that we can use to identify contemporary technical systems. All of these different aspects, however, can be categorized within Ellul's (1964: 64–79, 78–79) two dimensions of contemporary technical phenomena: rationality and artificiality.

The artificiality of a technical object guarantees its effectiveness for achieving the tasks it was developed in order to do. It becomes concrete, as Simondon (1989) puts it, as a bearer of precise virtualities that distinguish and distance it from the uncertainties of nature by specialization that is increasingly functionally restricted. That is, due to the extreme intentionality of the contemporary technical object.

An object's rationality is created from within this artificiality. Technique helps to produce standardization, supports the production of prototypes and norms, assigning only its logical dimension to the method, each technical intervention being a reduction (of facts, tools, forces, and contexts) served by a discourse. The resulting rationality is established at the expense of spontaneity and creativity, because the service of profit is universal. This is how a technique becomes self-propelling, indivisible, auto-expanding and relatively autonomous, carrying within it a particular rationality that it imparts to all places and social groups.

Technical systems increasingly demand coordinated control. From a multiplicity of locations and a plurality of sites of command, we move toward a single one, or at the very least, and unified one. This tendency is not exclusive to one technical system such as, say, that of electricity but rather applies to the totality of technical systems. As these technical systems function in unison with a system of actions, this could help us to understand the current importance of processing information.

INFORMATION TECHNIQUES

In today's "information age," information is the raw material for technological revolution (Dias 1990: 293). We are currently witnessing a massive change that would have been impossible without what Hall and Preston (1988: 30) call the "convergent technologies" that resulted from the second wave of technological innovations in the 1990s (Robin 1993: 72), which is to say from the combination of a second generation of information technologies (based in mechanics, electromechanics, and an early phase of electronics) and a third and current generation of information technologies with microelectronics. Philippe Breton (1991: 15) dates the beginning of this current phase, which he calls the "third informatics," to the 1980s. Information technologies are the lifeblood of many other technologies and the condition for their operationality (McBride 1986: vi), but this particular "technological convergence" between telecommunications, computation, and bureaucracy, Kevin Morgan argues (1992: 318), would not have been possible without deregulation, with which it possible for the "telematics coalition" to win out over the postindustrial coalition. This victory was the foundation for the "telecommunications era," based on the combination of digital technologies, neoliberal policies, and global markets (Morgan 1992: 314).

Many argue that we now live the mere continuation of a process. The "information society," however, would not have been possible without the "control revolution" (Beniger 1986: vi). This "revolution" began in the United States in the nineteenth century, but did not really take off until the arrival of microprocessing technologies, or what Wiener called "cybernetic science," which began in 1940s and focused on studying "communication and control of animal and machine" (Wiener 1948).

Because it is central to the physical circulation of commodities and the regulation of productive circuits for supplies (Paché 1990: 89–90), we might say that informatics is the new dominant mode of the organization of work (Pastré 1983: 9). While past economic analyses of Western societies (Perroux 1962: 177–78) often mistakenly failed to understand the central role of the "regular transmission of usable information" by those internal to the productive process, today that role is undeniable, given the way that unequal and concentrated information forms the basis for power to a much greater extent than it did three decades ago (Traber 1986: 3).

The informatics and control revolution made generalized mobility (of people, energy, uses, and products in time and space) possible. This mobility, which Pierre Naville predicted (1963: 254), is a measured and controlled one, capable of ensuring a real power over other points in space for the centers of decision making.

The computer, based in telematics and tele-information, is emblematic of this historical period. The computer brings together productive processes and makes possible an extremely accurate division of time that can be utilized rigorously. In other words, Taylor's clock becomes even more precise. Through the computer, the concept of "real time," one of the fundamental drivers of our era, becomes historically operationalized. Through this technical and social production of real time we live a perceived instantaneousness, a simultaneity of instants, a convergence of moments. The computer, itself the product of a real time created in a laboratory, produces the real time of institutions and of multinational corporations. First developed in university laboratories working in the service of the military, the discovery of *ivhirewird* was then taken up by the economy to become one of the bases of operation for multinational corporations engaged in production and above all, for multinational finance.

The computer was the vehicle for showcasing Informatics to the general public (Breton 1991: 11), and today, at the end of the twentieth century, it still captures our imagination. During the last century and long afterward, the only machine that had conceptual status in the social sciences was the machine-tool, but today that place has been ceded to the computer (Joerges 1988: 31), largely due to its role in decision making and in processes of coordination and concentration, which allows for coherent action and the possibility of forecasting the future. As a manipulator of information, the computer enhances the powers of communication, previously the domain of the car, the radio, television, and the press (Anderton 1971: 122–23), and makes possible the rapid or even immediate transmission of messages and commands (Ellul 1977: 106–7).

New techniques do not merely create a new perception of time. Rather they obligate a new use of time, an increasingly strict obedience to the clock, a behavioral rigor adapted to a new rhythm. Take, for example, the railroad. Prior to its introduction in France, each locality had its own time. In order for the rail lines to be coordinated, the railroad obliged them to use a common time. In this sense we can understand the history of techniques as the history of the convergence of moments, which began to advance much more rapidly with the introduction of the railroad.

In the realm of human behavior, techniques affect our ways of thinking, suggesting an economy of thought adapted to the logic of the instrument. Louis Pauwels (1977) called thought that is constantly preoccupied with being useful "calculated thought." The mathematization of humans, which began in the eighteenth century, is essentially a corollary of this tendency, which enables the numeric thinking of which Daniel Halévy was so critical (1948: 64).

The appearance of the computer was a fundamental moment in this evolution because rather than actually simplifying the complex, it allowed for its simplified presentation, which could only be done through a brutal process of reduction. Ellul explained this process, arguing that the computer detests difference and hates the particular. It functions based on the delimitation of knowledge, and the cost of its efficiency is the reduction of difference. As Chesneaux (1983: 121) explains, the rationality created by its calculations is based in a reductive logic that eliminates data not considered useful (because in order to function, it requires large homogenous series).

This means that its efficiency depends on eliminating accidents, and it submits intellectual elaboration to a practice in which systematization and standardization impose their own logic—the domination of the logic of math over the logic of history. In other words, it is as if math took on a life of its own (Queau 1987: 6), or as if mathematical space manifested materially.

Taken together, so-called smart machines and calculative thought testify to the transcendence of the technique that facilitates a true metaphysical concretization by producing artificial realities and synthetic images. This adds to the prevalence of what Rieu (1987: 51) calls "associated thought," the mechanical product of our subjugation to smart machines, and it works against what we should mobilize as critical thought. So, what does it mean to think in these circumstances? Rieu believed that informatics would bring back the time of philosophy, which is the only way to refuse what Carneiro Leão (1987) called radical blindness, a way of seeing that is completely subordinated to models and automatic processing.

This mathematical rigor will also be established within territory. The most flagrant example is that of contemporary urban life, where people are constantly trying to catch up with time. The modern city moves us as if we were machines, and an omnipresent clock commands even our tiniest gestures. Our minutes are someone else's minutes, and the interlinking of movements and gestures is a banal given of collective life. The more artificial the milieu, the more it demands this instrumental rationality that itself demands even more artificiality and rationality. But the modern realm increasingly invades these imperatives of urban life, where globalization imposes a strict rhythm of practices. The rationality that we are living in the current world is not only social and economic, but also resides within territory.

Unicities
The Production
of Planetary
Intelligence

INTRODUCTION

As we have just discussed, to understand the structure and functioning of the world we must understand the role played by contemporary technical phenomena in the production of a planetary
intelligence. Here, we want to highlight the emergence of what we
call three unicities: technical unicity, temporal unicity (the convergence of moments), and unicity of the motors of economic and
social life. These three unicities form the basis for the phenomenon of globalization and the contemporary transformations of
geographic space.

TECHNICAL UNICITY

At the beginning of planetary social history, there were as many
technical systems as there were places or human groups. These
groups only had access to techniques of the body, had limited mobility, and were dependent on restricted geographic areas, where
their intelligence and the available natural resources allowed them
to develop ways of doing that were dependent on the immediate
environment. Each point inhabited by a given group on Earth
therefore constituted a coherent set formed on a given fraction

of the planet by a local population, by local techniques, a local political system, and a local economic regime.

This unitary movement occurred with almost no mediation beyond that of the simultaneously horizontal and vertical relationship between a group and its environment. Place defined the conditions of life and the conditions (and processes) of its evolution. Technical systems were local.

Through history, exchanges and, above all, inequalities among groups resulted in certain groups imposing their techniques upon others. Regardless of whether those techniques were accepted passively or were resisted, or whether the imposition was brutal or subtle, the choice was nonetheless inevitable. As a result, entire sets of techniques or parts of them were incorporated into others, changing existing equilibriums and increasing the number of external elements present within previously autonomous histories. We might refer to this process as a "deterritorialization" of techniques. Once such new techniques take root in their new environment and mix with the preexisting techniques to form a new system, we have what we might call a "reterritorialization." As a result, the local movement of techniques stops being merely horizontal or anthropological and becomes subject to a vertical influence that incorporates the place into a more extensive social and technical history.

Such invasions, mixtures, and compositions ultimately reduced the number of technical systems. And with each new movement, as fusions, suppressions, and integrations became entrenched, the stock of existing technical systems was reduced, because the exchanges among groups intensified and expanded geographically, involving a greater number of societies and territories.

The creation of Fernand Braudel's "world economies" is a key moment in this evolution. Beginning in the sixteenth century with the expansion of capitalism, intercontinental and transoceanic exchanges of plants, animals, and people—along with their different ways of doing and being—became possible. Their technical particulars tended to mutually contaminate one another.

At the beginning of capitalism there were still multiple technical equations, various forms for the utilization and creation of resources. As capitalism developed there were fewer technical models and the choices became more restricted.

The last quarter of the nineteenth century is marked by the affirmation of revolutionary material techniques, which also entailed a fundamental transformation in the other techniques of social life. But the diffusion of

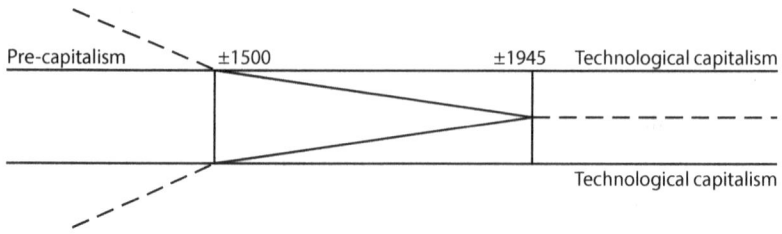

FIGURE 8.1 The Narrowing of the Choice

these techniques was, to some extent, attenuated for political reasons. The creation of the great imperial colonies reinforced the strength of the European powers. Their dominion over massive portions of the rest of the world grew because of their command over commerce, which had a political base. At that time, markets were still national (which should be interpreted in the broad sense, considering that the frontiers of the colonial states spanned distant dominated territories) and differences in technological power could be offset by the commercial advantages that each of them could freely take advantage of. The competition among the central countries was not based in technology but rather in trade policy.

The death of the empires precipitated by the Second World War coincided with the emergence of a universalizable technique. In fact, even before it was widely established, this new technical system had already won this enormous victory, having transcended the only frontiers that could impede its diffusion. The emergence of numerous national states, the creation of supranational organizations, and the arrival of information and consumption as the common universal denominator all facilitated a triumph of information-based techniques that would revolutionize economics and politics from then on, even before culture was included into the global process of change.

Beginning in the second half of the twentieth century, the choice of this form and the speed with which other options were eliminated made it such that soon there was only one technical model. In other words, there was no longer a choice (see figure 8.1).

The movement toward unification inherent in the nature of capitalism has continued to accelerate, and today it is reaching its apex, with the predominance, everywhere, of single technical system that is the material base of globalization. With the emergence of the technical-scientific period immediately following the Second World War, the technical system became common to all civilizations, all cultures, all political systems, all continents and places. In comparing the capitalist and socialist systems, Edgar Morin (1965: 72) questioned whether a more decisive analytic for understanding their relation would be an analysis of the antinomy of their forms, or the unity of their industrial technique. From this we can conclude that that under these conditions, the socialist system would represent a subsystem of the capitalist system.

But each period sees the birth of a new technical generation that comes to characterize it. This new subsystem becomes more effective than others and then becomes hegemonic. In the past, the different hegemonic systems were not truly global, because they were absent in certain countries or regions. Today the hegemonic technical subsystem has become globally ubiquitous, as Ellul (1964: 116–33) argued in his discussion of "technical universalism." That is to say that today the dominant form of technique works across the entire globe, such that technique itself becomes a "universal and uniform environment" (Miquel and Ménard 1988: 281).

This is extremely important, first, because it means that all of humanity has a single form of domination—it is implied that all civilizations should strive toward this mold. This situation is entirely new in the history of the world. Second, because it allows for a general understanding of hypotheses about the future.

Technical unicity does not mean that there is only one unique existing technique. There has not been any moment in history, except perhaps in its initial phase, that human groups have used only one generation of material or immaterial techniques. Each new family of techniques does not completely supplant the ones that preceded them. Rather, they exist together within an order established by each society in its relations with other societies.

This means that the past is not completely swept away. Some material inheritance continues to exist in proportions that vary according to different civilizations, countries, and regions. A new set of techniques characteristic of the contemporary period is imposed on the remains of successive previous elaborations.

The layers of the past are not all the same, because different civilizations were not all subject to the same influences and experiences during the different phases of technical evolution. Some areas were untouched by the technical changes in a given period. But contemporary techniques have been universally disseminated, albeit with different levels of intensity, and their effects may be felt directly or indirectly over the totality of spaces. This, incidentally, is one of the distinguishing characteristics of contemporary technique.

The anthropologist André Leroi-Gourhan, who argues that since the beginning of history similar objects were created in different times and places by different ethnic groups, introduced the expression "the universality of techniques" (1945). Marc Humbert (1991: 55) built on this notion, explaining that "the chipped stone tool was the same over the entire planet, at a time when transcontinental relations were at best rare and extremely slow." He proposed this generality of technical forms as a tendency, and that tendency is its universality. Today universality takes a different form. First, it is not a tendency but a reality. Second, this reality makes up part of different places in practically the same moment, without noticeable temporal delay. Third, this general phenomenon gives place to the actions that themselves also have a universal content. As a result, we see things like, for example, similar political programs proposed for all or nearly all countries, such as the famous "structural adjustment" plans of the World Bank and the IMF, with the support of the great industrial and financial powers. Fourth and finally, these similar contemporary technical objects are universalized but occur in isolation. Today an entire system of objects is universal.

One could speak of technical unicity due to the fact that technical hegemonic systems are increasingly integrated, forming sets of instruments that operate in an interconnected manner. This "interdependency of pieces" (Simondon 1989) owes a lot to the intentionality of technical objects. This is the way that "each important part is so closely associated with the others by reciprocal exchanges of energy that it cannot undergo any essential variation whatsoever" (Simondon cited in Baudrillard 1973: 11).

The systemic character of technique—essential to its definition— reaffirms itself now even more forcefully. Rotenstreich (1985: 63) warns that technology, in its contemporary form, "is more than the sum of all of the separate instruments and disconnected products." It is the "universalization of techniques and products" that marks the emergence of a "global industrial system" (Humbert 1991: 53).

Different thinkers christen this new reality differently—as a "universal mechanism" (Moles 1971b: 82) or an "essential motor of power" (Janicaud 1985: 117). This "planetarization of technique" (Tavares d'Amaral 1987: 35) is responsible for the planetary banalization that Chesneaux (1983: 258) addresses in his discussion of the fourth law of Partant.[1]

The contemporary hegemonic technical subsystem is, by its nature, an invasive system. This explains the rapidity with which its expansion becomes generalized in comparison to previous hegemonic subsystems. It ultimately imposes itself, directly or indirectly, through its unifying role in global systems.

This invasive force, combined with its systemic character, is responsible for two economic tendencies that appear antagonistic but which are actually complementary. On one side, economic process fragments at the global level because pieces of this unitary and dispersed technical apparatus are present in different points across the globe. The systemic character of technique assures that the technical process is complementary and coordinated, that there is a succession of steps, and it guarantees particular results. Otherwise, multinational corporations could not exist. Beginning in one designated point, singular control is exercised over technical, economic, and political processes whose bases of operation are found in various locations across the surface of the earth. Ingmar Granstedt (1980: 89) refers to these points, which "transmit products as they are being elaborated," as true "technical scales," considering, in this case, that it would be inappropriate to speak of the market.

So it is widely possible for different moments of production to be extremely dispersed, even while the control of them becomes even more condensed—a process of *concentration* (de Britto 1986).

J. Ladriere (1968: 216) calls this "technicist project" a global one, which he argues has been emergent in humanity since the nineteenth century. But he sees this global project as an implicit one, rejecting "the capacity to conceive a total project that approaches in a single gigantic plan . . . all future development." He argues that only partial projects are made explicit, but that they are induced by a larger implicit project. Citing Stanislas Breton, he argues that technique "is manifest as a concrete universal and no longer as a category of thought in its full expansion" (Ladriere 1968: 11).

According to Breton himself (1968: 115), "relational universality" can be obtained by "communicating all the techniques that unfold over one another, in an appeal to complementarity that is both the conditions for its existence and its effectiveness."

Here we should return to the difference between the universality of technique as a real tendency that is realized, in the definition of Leroi-Gourhan, and the universality of technique as it exists today, based in a technical conjuncture that is homogenized, systemic, completed, and commanded by globalized [*mundializadas*] relations that are systematically unified. Today, the global project becomes explicit.

What we call the *unicity of moments*, or a *convergence of moments,* is another amazing element of our times.

While some might argue that time is becoming unified, we would instead argue that today it is becoming possible to know distant events instantaneously, and therefore to perceive their simultaneity. The event is a physical manifestation of historic time, as if the so-called arrow of time pointed at and hit a particular point on the surface of the earth, populating it with a new event. When, in the same moment, another point has also been reached and we can know the event that happened there, then we are witnessing a convergence of moments and their unicity is established through contemporary communication techniques.

Although they happen at the same time according to the clock, these moments are not the same. They are unitary moments, united by a common logic.

This phenomenon is entirely new; it is a privilege of our generation. Today's ephemera remind us of previous generations' very different sensibilities regarding events. For example, on the bicentennial anniversary of the French Revolution we saw a series of mementos that included Louis XVI's diary. In it, on July 14, 1789, the night that the Bastille fell, the French sovereign described what had happened that day in a single word: *nothing*. Paris was the same distance from Versailles, where the court was located, that it is today, but at that time it was impossible for even the king to know what was happening in the capital. In other words, events were simultaneous, but there was no way to perceive it.

In *O nome da rosa*, Umberto Eco (1983: 22) explains, "In 1314 five German princes in Frankfurt elected Louis the Bavarian supreme leader of the empire. But that same day, on the opposite shore of the Main River, the Count Palatine of the Rhine and the Archbishop of Cologne elected Frederick of Austria to the same high rank. Two emperors for a single throne and a single pope for two: a situation that, truly, fomented great disorder." When the *Times* of London published its first paper, on January 1, 1788, "the news from Rotterdam and from Paris [were] dated December 25, 1787, the news from Frankfurt December 14, and the news from Warsaw December 5" (Mattelart 1992: 303). The news was simultaneous, but the events were not. The discrepancy can be attributed to the various distances and means for crossing them. In another example, Allan Pred (1966) has also noted that the death of George Washington in Alexandria, Virginia, was not announced in New York until seven days later (Giddens 1984b: 111).

We might say, from a geographic point of view, that the world had two key moments. The first occurred with the first great navigations, and the other happened more recently with satellites (with or without people in them). Our contemporary understanding of outer space and even of our own planet is based in the domain of the electromagnetic spectrum, one of the great accomplishments of our time. Today satellites photograph the earth, in real time, following established or fixed orbits, and emitting images taken in rapid succession, allowing us to witness whole processes such that we can actually see the evolution of phenomenon. Movements of bodies on the earth and in the air, deforestation, and population expansion are different phenomena whose dynamism we can now recognize and quantify, allowing for an extensive and profound knowledge of each place.

There is an unequivocal relationship between the new possibility for knowing the planet, this universal intelligence, and the generalization of possibility for using all resources, this "universal labor" previously discussed by Marx (see Markus 1973: 63). Paradoxically, labor becomes universal when the different pieces of the same processes are less and less geographically concentrated (see also Hiernaux-Nicolas 1994: 92).

In his *Economic and Philosophical Manuscripts*, Marx (1974) describes nature as man's inorganic body, the site of reciprocal exchange from which society extracts the means for its reproduction. Today, all of nature has become the inorganic body of all people to an even greater extent through the frequent and perverse intermediation of supranational institutions, beginning with multinational corporations. People have been transformed into that "universal natural being," but this change does not benefit everyone (Markus 1973: 19).

On the other hand, information can now flow instantaneously, communication can happen everywhere, without gaps. Without this ability, there would be no universally integrated technical system, nor transnational productive and financial systems, nor generally globalized [*mundializada*] information, and contemporary globalization would be impossible.

The process of the convergence of moments runs parallel to technical development, especially the development of techniques for speed and for measuring time. The conquest of speed allows for faster movement of both things and messages. "The global and the fragment, the part and the whole, the product and the process, the general and the particular all synchronize and in that exchange they create a single field, where both knowledge and action expand" (Ferrara 1993: 165). The techniques of accuracy in telling time, from the astronomic command of time to the development of ultra-precise clocks, allows us to be more conscious of the passage of time and to recognize its divisions.

Since the 1860s, electrical equipment has allowed for a greater approximation among events. Baudelaire (cited in Halévy 1948: 111), an enthusiast of this progress, wrote:

> *Dieu, que le monde est grand à la clarté des lampes*
> *Aux yeux du voyageur que le monde est petit!*

> *[Ah! How great the world is in the light of the lamps!*
> *In the eyes of memory, how small and slight!]*

It is true that the media began to play a role in the process of globalization at the end of the nineteenth century. Giddens (1991: 81) retells a story told by Max Nordau (1968) in his book *Dégéneration*, where he points to the fact that the reader of a newspaper in a small city in 1872 had a better understanding of current events than did a prime minster of a century earlier.

Today, the perceived simultaneity is even greater than it was at the beginning of the century, when the telegraph, the submarine cable, or the telephone transported signals and voices without the gaps previously created by working hours or distribution delays. Today these messages and information arrive in offices and homes directly, practically without intermediaries, and that is not even to mention the immediate transmission of images through the television. Today photographers and cinematographers are actors who actively interpret events by selecting how they will transmit them. But the existence of such intermediaries does not negate that what we are describing is happening—that is, the possibility of communicating events across distance, without losing information. In the end, following Barney Warf (1989: 259), "For a satellite, each place is the same distance from others." And time is also unified by the generalization of the fundamental needs that people have in their lives, made common at the world scale (Ianni 1992).

Through the "planetary communication system" (Rosnay 1975: 176), we live a situation of "generalized communication" (Vattimo 1992: 24), when distance no longer necessarily causes isolation (Mlinar 1990: 57).

As a result, the concept of *real time* becomes a reality, bringing possibilities into political and social life, especially for business. The adequate and precise use of time and space multiplies the effectiveness and the power of the firms that are able to take advantage of these new possibilities.

Financial activity benefits the most from this rigorous framing of time. Money, in its many forms, can now flow globally, twenty-four hours a day, utilizing real relays, connected to a "vast interactive web of communication" that is never exhausted (Barber 1992: 7). Points strategically located across the surface of the earth are interlinked through "computers, televisions, submarine cables, satellites, lasers, fiber optic cables and microchip technology" (Barber 1992: 7).

This shift makes it possible for financial operators to operate at all times and in all places, "with no respect for even the most minor juridical law and without being subjected to any kind of preventative control, mobilizing capital that is not theirs and of which they only actually control a small fraction" (Brie 1993: 28). It is the basis for the massive expansion of the information economy, whose increasingly concentrated and internationalized activities have been deregulated since the 1970s with the collapse of the Bretton-Woods Agreement (Warf 1989: 258), which made possible a deadly competitive game in which giant corporations seek to grow even further.

The role of finance in producing a new architecture of space has not escaped geographers, although they have been accused of paying insufficient attention to this phenomenon. For example, Peter Dicken and Peter E. Lloyd (1981: 62) contrasted geographers' interests in industrial and commercial activities with their disinterest in the financial sector. Some criticism has been quite personal, such as when Roger Lee (1991) attacked Iain Wallace (cited in Lee 1991) for his description of the global economy that completely neglected to include international finance, or "place-less money," as a key element alongside the state and large corporations. Finance without a place? This point inspired Richard O'Brien (1992) to argue that, thanks to financial globalization, geography no longer has any reason to exist.

Common places are established based on this new perception of time. The two most commonly discussed are the idea of a "global village" and the idea that in this new context, time annihilates space. Critiquing the first concept, Brzezinski (1976: 19) argued that "global city" would be a more suitable metaphor than "global village." Targowski (1990) described the architecture of this global village as composed of cities that are interlinked electronically, an instantaneous network in which economic, social, and cultural information flows such that they are both global and local. This depiction evokes the earlier "one world" imaginary that was celebrated at the end of the Second World War by the famous book by the Englishman

Harold Laski (1948). It makes it seem that virtual simultaneity is possible with the technical progress that has become a reality for everyone.

In reality, these global computers primarily circulate pragmatic information that is manipulated by a small number of actors for their own benefit. The information market is controlled by a handful of giant firms located in just a few countries. Europe realized only 36 percent of the informational sales in its own market, while the United States controls almost the entire global market. With 400,000 employees, present in 117 countries, IBM has a business volume that was worth $55 billion in 1990 (Weissberg 1990: 105), and it is understood as a "moderator" in the market, which essentially consists of competing through every means possible with homologous businesses.

The market of information—not only specialized financial information but all information—is concentrated and controlled. We must increasingly distinguish between facts and "the news," which is already an interpretation of those facts. If it were even possible to separate out the "global village," what reality would it be based in? The common suggestion—that the new ways to access information and inform ourselves indicate that we are again becoming more attentive to actual facts, as in primitive societies—is misleading (Morin 1972; Nora 1974). Rather, following Slater (1995: 367), we must understand that these "global perspectives" are laden with ideology.

The idea that time annihilates space comes from a delusional belief that the current progress in the way that people, things, and information utilize speed actually shortens distance. The truth is that "information does not reach every place. . . . There are innumerable intermediary filters . . . that interfere in the nature of information . . . that [allow] for the mischaracterization of the product" (Silva 1993: 75). In reality, a minimal number of people in the richest countries benefit from the new means of circulation. For these privileged individuals, space is not being suppressed; rather, what they have is a new command over distance. Space is not defined exclusively by this dimension (i.e., by their new power).

Today the number of and frequency of events is increasing everywhere. Space is becoming fuller, denser, more complex. This new accumulation of presences, however, this opulence of actions, does not happen blindly on any random point on Earth. The information that forms the basis for actions are selective, seeking out places where they can be most effective. This is an implacable law in a world thirsting for productivity because it produces profit.

In this situation, the preexisting conditions in each place, its stock of material or immaterial resources and of organization—this roughness [*rugosidades*]—constitutes the coordinates that guide new actions. If we consider space as it exists within a given movement, as an objective reality, and time as actions that insert themselves into that reality, then it is time that depends on space and not the other way around.

For millennia, the history of people has been constructed in different moments, as a sum of dispersed, disparate, and disconnected events. The history of our generation is one in which moments converge; the event of each place can be immediately communicated to any other, due to this domination of time and space on a planetary scale. The instantaneousness of globalized information brings places together, making it possible to be instantly aware of simultaneous events and therefore creating a unitary relation between events and places on a world scale. Today, at every moment we can understand, in every place, events are interdependent within a global system of relations.

The technical progress that allows satellites to photograph the entire planet also gives us an empirical view of the totality of objects existing on the face of the earth. Because the photographs are taken at regular intervals, we get a portrait of the evolution of the human occupation of the earth. The simultaneity depicted is truly new and revolutionary for our understanding of the real, and also for the corresponding focus on the sciences of humans, changing their paradigms.

Empirical knowledge of the simultaneity of events and the understanding of their interdependent meaning—the base for the empiricalization of universality (Santos 1984)—is a determining historical factor. The hegemonic actors of economic, social, and political life can select the best places in which to operate, and, as a result, the localization of everyone else is condemned to be residual.

THE SINGULAR MOTOR

Alongside the unicity of techniques and the unicity of moments, we should also investigate whether there is a unicity to the motor of economic and social life across the planet, emblematically represented by the emergence of a global surplus value and directly or indirectly guaranteed by the systemic existence of large organizations—the primary actors in contemporary international life (Carreras 1993: 132–33).

Along with the unicity of techniques and moments, global surplus value amplifies and intensifies the process of internationalization, bringing it to a new plateau. Today, everything globalizes [*mundializa*]: production, products, money, credit, debt, consumption, politics, and culture. This set of globalizations [*mundalizações*], each supporting, dragging, and helping to impose the others, truly merits the name globalization.

The productive sector is made up of a network of interdependencies (Boismenu 1993: 4) exemplified by the creation of political-economic communities and common markets. The liberalization that we are seeing of regional markets reinforces multilateral liberalization and strengthens the global market (Lloyd 1993: 38).

Universal surplus value's field of action is often referred to as the local market, "founded in global exchange and the universal law of value" (dos Santos 1993: 3).

GLOBAL BUSINESS

Thus, "the new space of businesses is the world" (Savy and Veltz 1993: 5). The largest companies are not simply multinational; they are global. Their organization is in fact quite different from transnational corporations that operate in a restricted region (Dulong 1993: 167).

One of the key differences between a multinational firm and a global one is a change in the concept of operational autonomy, which in a global firm is subordinated to an overall strategy adapted to new conditions of competition. As Dicken demonstrates (1994: 107), decisions, responsibilities, and strategically decentralized resources are subject to a strict management that integrates the conception, fabrication, and distribution of products at a world level (Veltz 1993: 52).

Alliances between large firms organize the markets and the circuits of production (Michalet 1994: 19) to benefit economies of scale, to select the best methods of implementation, and to take advantage of the productive specializations of the different associated firms in order to reduce their production costs (Berthelot 1994: 12).

As a result of this combination of the imperative for integration and globalization, the creation of networked firms becomes both a tendency and a necessity (Cooke 1992: 212). Global businesses function in networks, resulting in all kinds of global ramifications and interdependencies (McConnell 1982: 1634; Ramonet 1993: 6), also rendering these businesses more flexible and movable (Defarges 1993: 50).

Early on, B. Poche (1975: 19) articulated some of the primary characteristics of the new situation, namely of new possibilities for controlling global processes of production: control of innovation (the productive forces of science and the technical); control of circulation (the productive forces of commercialization and distribution); and control of the management of capital in its money form (the productive forces of financial management). Since then, these mechanisms have been further refined thanks to new information techniques that allow for even greater concentration of control.

As a result, we have seen a shift from a regime of competitive regulation to a regime of monopolist regulation (Attali 1981: 99), driving a system of power controlled by a few groups (Nze-Nguema 1989: 42).

But the phenomenon of the networks surpasses the limits even of the dominant firms and colonizes, directly or indirectly, permanently or occasionally, the entire productive fabric. The concept of the "transnationalized industrial complex" emerges from the interaction of all of these processes characteristic of globalization. From there we get what J.-B. Zimmerman (1988: 122) calls "systemic duality," or the combination of national productive systems and transnational industrial structures, "two categories whose structure, rationality, and nature are different."

These networks are tributaries of information whose importance within production has grown so significantly that today we can speak of a dematerialized economy. Just as the "globality" of a firm is related to the role of services in its activity, the businesses that are linked to information are the ones that globalize most forcefully.

THE GLOBALIZATION OF FINANCE

Georges Corm (1993: 119) noted that the electronic revolution would better guarantee the continuation of the major "technical-industrial feudalisms," allowing for "instant contact among all financial markets and stimulating the development of new techniques and new financial instruments," in addition to making operations of buying and selling more secure.

Bruno Lanvin (1988: 16–17) uses the term *pure information* to describe the prime material for the activities of the financial system and banks, whose products are highly "dematerialized" and where "the markets tend not only to globalize, but to become confused."

The current wave of deregulation had its decisive founding moments in the 1970s. In the United States in 1984, the importance of this deregulation became apparent with the massive expansion of telecommunications, marked by the breakup of the AT&T monopoly (Warf 1989: 259).

The progress made by linking informatics and telecommunications, with the franchising made possible by deregulation, "allowed traders to intervene in real time, twenty-four hours a day, at any point on the globe" (Brie 1993: 28) and made continuous functioning of the major financial markets possible.

The mechanism described above is strongly supported in the financial system, which has changed substantially now that the new technical and political conditions offer new mediums for the circulation of money. Finance is the principal lever for international economic activities. Through the processes linked to multinationalization and transnationalization (Santos 1993b: 54), finance becomes global. Multinationalization occurs as the financial system penetrates every country through their commercial networks. These operations transcend borders with actions and obligations that in the United States went from 9.3 percent of the GDP in 1980 to 93 percent in 1992 and in Germany from 7.5 to 90.8 percent during that same period (Chesnais 1994: 209). The bank loans that provided places for international movements added up to more than $324 billion in 1980 and more than $7.5 trillion in 1991 (Defarges 1993: 43). Transnationalization is marked by the emergence and growth of new financial markets and centers on every continent, including off-shore markets and fiscal paradises (Warf 1989). The planetarization of the stock exchanges (Beteille 1991) adds another degree of importance to this evolution. Japan's arrival on the scene (Gauthier 1989: 182) completes this process of financial globalization (Kebabdjian 1994: 27). In 1990, the rest of the world owed Japan something like $400 billion.

The growth of the financial sector is spectacular. One billion dollars moves daily through a financial market that is now located on every continent. In 1985, it was only $250 million (Defarges 1993: 43). With this growth, financial activity has gained an autonomy that seems justified by its volume, which is many times greater than that of trade in commercial goods. For every dollar that passes through commerce, 40 dollars pass through the financial market. That begs Kebabdjian's (1994: 26) question: What happens to the other 39 dollars?

We also see a simultaneous tendency toward concentration. According to Chesnais (1994: 245), "Thirty to fifty banks and a handful of brokerage houses guarantee the currency markets. This high level of concentration can also be seen in the fact that there are two principle financial centers for the entire planet: 43 percent of the transactions made by the ten biggest banks were made in London and 40 percent were made in New York."

The geographic concentration of transactions is also significant. In 1991 New York City realized 54.1 percent of all of the lending done in the United States, followed by Los Angeles and Chicago, with 16 percent and 12.1 percent, respectively. These three cities and the next three largest

TABLE 8.1 Financial Transactions

	Stock transactions (1991)	Forward market (1991)	Exchange market (1991)
NEW YORK	29.91%	8.81%	15.0%
LONDON	10.9%	12.04%	17.0%
TOKYO	16.19%	—	5.8%
CHICAGO	—	53%	—
PARIS	8.2%	7.95%	5.0%
FRANKFURT	7.53%	—	4.2%
OSAKA	2.71%	7.09%	—
SINGAPORE	—	—	11.2%
HONG KONG	—	—	11.0%
ZURICH	7.12%	—	7.4%

lending cities (San Francisco, Atlanta, and Miami) together represented 92 percent of all of the lending in the country (Ó hUallacháin 1994: 215).

This geographic concentration can also be seen on a world scale. In 1991, three financial centers—New York, London, and Tokyo—were responsible for 56 percent of transactions, for 74 percent of the futures markets, and 38 percent of the exchange markets (*La Croix,* Paris, 2 October 1992), even while new locales are also being established or strengthened (Beteille 1991: 7–8).

The financial sector thus becomes the true regulator of the international economy (Badie and Smouts 1992: 137) and threatens the managerial role previously held by States (Warf 1989: 265).

While the bank develops the capacity to unify different types of surplus value, surplus value itself globalizes [*mundaliza*], benefitting from improvements in the existing process of self-regulation (Schon 1973: 68), now made more effective with introduction of mechanisms based on real-time information into financial activity. Examples include "the global system that electronically links the Chicago Exchange to that of Europe, or Asia, or Sydney" (Beteille 1991: 4) or the SWIFT System (Society for Worldwide Interbank Financial Telecommunication), which in 1977 interlinked 519 banks in 21 countries and today brings together more than 2,000 in more than 50 countries (Swedeberg 1990: 278).

According to Pages et al. (1979: 249), commenting on an apparent paradox, the new "invisible hand" is even more hidden than it was before—and the economic imperative is even less apparent—but, simultaneously, it is more secure and effective than ever.

FLEETING SURPLUS VALUE, A SINGULAR MOTOR

In these circumstances, the imperative for growth and expansion asserts itself, and the search for them becomes constant. On the global scale, the primacy of the market creates the expectation for the performance of increasing growth, guaranteeing growing accumulation and profit (Cooke and Wells 1992: 73).

The purpose of this mode of economic activity, as Peter Dicken (1992: 120) reminds us, is ostensibly to enable a firm to pursue a variety of objectives beyond simple profit, "but in the long term nothing is more important than the search for profit itself," which constitutes the primary barometer of its corporate "health." And this will always drive it toward competition, to propose and realize new mergers and, in doing so, to leave its competition behind.

This is how large organizations function at the world scale, and it is only these organizations that drive the hegemonic techniques of the production of information and finance, through intermediaries who gain control over hegemonic time and realize hegemonic surplus value.

This control happens both through intermediation in direct production, and through its elements that are not strictly technical—in other words, through the political aspects of production and in the areas of circulation, of distribution, and consumption. These political aspects are just as relevant here as the techniques: financial, fiscal, and monetary politics, politics of commerce, markets, and services, employment politics, the politics of information—all of these politics are today operating at the global level.

In this system old forms of competition give way to new ones (Best 1990). When "the planet constitutes, at the end of this century, the only field of competition" (Defarges 1993: 53), a new word becomes part of the vocabulary of economy and politics: *competitiveness*. This, turned into a sort of axiomatic truth and recommended to all corporations and all countries as the only way to salvation, already has many critics, among whom we can count Petrella (1995) and Garelli and Linard de Guertechin (1995). There have also been some recent deserters from the camp of its former defenders, such as the case of the rupture among those charged with formulating the economic program of the electoral campaign of Bill Clinton.[2]

The contemporary situation compels us to repeat Raphael Célis's (1992: 97) beautiful formula: "The imperative that drives this character of the world as an automatic circuit today has the irresistible force of a law of nature."

Everything that serves the production of globalization also serves competitiveness among corporations: technical, informational, and organizational processes, norms and deregulations, places. Everything that contributes to reconstruct the process of globalization, as it actually exists, also contributes such that the relation among corporations—and, by extension, among countries, societies, and people—is founded in an all-out war. Because this is the law of production and circulation of global firms: each moment more surplus value seeks to surpass itself. The supreme irony is that this fleeting surplus value cannot be measured, and, at the same time, it becomes the principal lever, if not the *singular motor*, for the actions most characteristic of the global economy.

9

Objects and Actions Today
Norms and Territory

OBJECTS TODAY

We live in the time of objects. As Baudrillard (1970: 18) puts it, "We live according to their rhythm and according to their incessant succession," and therefore the physiognomy, physiology, structure, appearances, and relations of space are constantly changing. The speed of these changes depends primarily on the array of vectors that cross through space—on how fast they replace one another, on the novelty of the forces that they carry within them, and on their influence over objects, which themselves, regardless of how new they are, rapidly change, are revalorized or devalorized.

In the face of the banality and mystery of contemporary technique, the technical object inspires metaphor. We are shocked and intrigued by Baudrillard's (1973: 62) assertion that objects are actors, because we are accustomed to thinking only of people as actors. In *L'imagination,* Sartre (1969) also wrote that the contemporary object is an object turned subject. This object-actor exhibits behaviors because it itself is a system, a mechanism that only functions according to its own predetermined rules.

The major distinction between the present and the past is that in the past there were fewer objects: they existed alongside of us and were subordinated to us as part of the union of society and individuals that we might call, as Jacques Attali did (1981: 200–1) in *Les trois mondes*, a "living object." Today we live with technical objects that empower our daily lives, but our interaction with them is more instrumental than profound. Marx's idea of alienation is particularly useful for explaining the relative inanity of our opposition to contemporary objects. To that end, Ollman (1971: 46) argues that one of the primary causes of contemporary alienation is that today the producer is subordinated to the produced object rather than vice versa.

In *Mundialização e cultura*, Renato Ortiz (1994) argues that all metaphors are figurative stories in which what we gain consciousness about what is being explained we lose in conceptual precision.[1] The metaphor can be useful, but it cannot substitute for concept, theory, or explanation. In other words, metaphors are useful stylistic resources that can help us to understand a situation, but they cannot take the place of explanation. Explanation must emerge from an analysis of the workings of situations or of things.

When we lack sufficient explanation, we find ourselves unable to understand our surroundings and therefore destined to repeat, as Georges Bernanos (1936) put it, "chimeras, [where] we do not know anything about this world; we are not in the world."

While the contemporary technical system has many characteristics, particularly important principle aspects include: 1) universality and self-expansion; 2) systemic life; 3) concreteness; 4) information content; and 5) intentionality.

Contemporary technical objects can be found in almost every latitude and longitude. The common repetition of objects makes many different places seem familiar. This universality is also based in the fact that the technical system itself is global. Systemic life and self-expansion are correlated, because corresponding activities tend to be broadly disseminated through competition.

Today we are surrounded by technical objects whose production is based in research rather than in occasional discovery, and in science rather than experience. In other words, scientific production precedes material production, and, as a result, objects today are scientific-technical and informational.

The object is scientific by nature of how it is conceptualized, technical due to its internal structure, and scientific-technical because its production and functioning do not separate technique and science. The object is also informational because, on the one hand, it is used to carry out precise work—producing a type of information—and, on the other hand, it functions on the basis of information. In today's cybernetic era, an object can transmit information to other objects. Automatons ensure a chain of causality through a system of objects that transmit information from one to the other, even if people are not present, at least at the beginning of the process.

In other words, objects are not only animated by information; they are forms of information themselves. To take a rather banal example of what Paul Claval (1993: 179) calls a "banal object," an electric razor that only functions with electrical current is dependent on a specific form of information in that it cannot respond to a stimulus other than the one it was created for.

Because objects only function when information directs them, they have become forms of information themselves. Specialized information has two sides—information *for* objects and information *in* objects. All modern objects emerge bearing information indispensable to those who engage in forms of hegemonic work and in the service of hegemonic capital, which is to say in forms of work that are the most economically productive.

This completely redefines the spatial system. Objects deliberately created for the market are animated by scientific information, but they are created through a system of actions subordinated to global surplus value. Alongside these objects we also find other objects animated by a system of actions that is less information-based and demands that are less determined by surplus value. This coexistence creates the conditions for more and different flows, which make space denser and more complex.

Jacques Prades (1992: 11) argues that the technical object is the outcome of methodical production. It is the result of an encounter, a synthesis, in which human intelligence seeks to materially produce an instrument to carry out a given desired function. In other words, it is about the search for an arrangement of material and form that makes possible a function through which society can be fully realized. The technical object is born through a series of intellectual, technical, material, social and political operations that come together for its production in what Simondon (1989) calls "operations of convergence."

In the past, the kind of material used in production determined the kind of object that would be fabricated. Today it is the reverse—the form of the object is conceived in the mind of its creator, and laboratory production processes and the desired function of a given object determine the material that will be used to produce it (Parrochia 1993: 26). For example, space ships and planes, and on a smaller scale, the car, and even buildings drive the creation of materials adequate to produce the object that an engineer or architect might want to make. As such, the history of air and space travel is the history of the production of a material capable of withstanding different temperatures, of entering and leaving the atmosphere, and of holding up under high speeds.

This is the first phase in world history where objects have been created to carry out a particular predetermined function, to reach a clearly defined objective, through an intentionality that is scientifically and technically produced and is fundamental for that object's effectiveness. Each object is also created in a form adequate to produce the desired results.

The intentionality underlying contemporary objects led the sociologist Michel Maffesoli (1989) to lament that "objects no longer obey." In other words, in the past, objects conformed to the logic of the places in which we were located and in which they were therefore created. Today, objects no longer necessarily respond to our particular places, and because they tend to be created according to a logic that is foreign to us (e.g., that of the market), they actually become a new source of alienation. Their functionality is extremely specific, and their ultimate objectives may often be unclear to us. The intentionality underlying contemporary objects is commercial and often also symbolic. In fact, in order to be marketable, it is often necessary for objects to be symbolic first. When we say, for example, that hydroelectric dams will bring to a given region or country the hope of economic salvation, progress, and integration into the world economy, such concepts are symbols that allow us to accept the rationality of the object (e.g., the dam), which in reality, to the contrary, can wreak havoc on our relationship with nature and produce inequality.

In addition to the symbolic, there is also the relationship between objects and needs—the game of call and response explored by Moles (1971b: 86). Because of the interdependence among science, technique, and production, today's technical object is increasingly effective (Akrich 1987: 50). Lucrécia d'Alessio Ferrara (1989) demonstrates how industrial design functions as an intellectual mechanism for creating greater precision and more fully functioning objects. Simondon (1989: 246) argues that to construct a technical object is to create what we might call an availability (for use). In other words, just because an object is produced does not mean that it will be utilized immediately. It might be at rest for days, weeks, months, or years, until social energy incorporates it into the movement of life.

New technical objects are "concrete" in the Simondonian sense, meaning that they tend to be more perfect than nature itself. The further they are from the natural, the more concrete or perfect they are, because they can be intentionally designed to carry particular kinds of information—they both deliver information and need information in order to function. But objects' "pure" (i.e., pre-designed) information is only internal, and other particular kinds of information, "momentary" information, is only acquired through use, that is, when an object is occupied and animated by events. Simondon (1989: 247) calls this *information événementielle*. Concreteness and content in information are, taken together, another way to describe the intentionality of objects' conception. That is, they are the result of the attempt at finding adequation between the structure of an object and its intended function. Being highly adapted to a planned action is what makes possible the exactitude and efficiency often present in today's technical objects. But these also depend on the spatial arrangement in which an object is located.

Concrete, universalized, systemic, informed, intentional technical objects are more numerous and diverse today than at any other moment in history. The number and quality of flows that cross them is exponentially greater than what has previously existed. The contemporary territorial division of labor, based on a multiplicity and differentiation of places, is therefore more extensive and demanding than ever before.

Recent progress in science and technology, and, more precisely, the formidable advances in informatics, has produced a world where infinitely small objects and incommensurably grand ones exist side by side and work together. Jean Chesneaux calls this the era of both miniaturization and gigantization. David Hamilton's "microscopic world" (1973: 47–52) is simultaneously the driver and tributary of mega-objects and mega-machines (Gras 1993; Joerges 1988). In a sense, Siegfried (1955: 171) foretold this present reality when he said that "we are lost in the infinitely large, on the one hand, and in the infinitely small on the other, and we can ask ourselves if we live, as Pascal argues, neither one nor the other."

The technical object is inserted into the broader system, the system of objects. Richard Martin Stern's (1973) book *The Tower* illustrates this point. In it, he erected a 125-story building as his primary actor. He describes the building as breathing during the day through the functions that go on inside of it and sleeping at night when the people sleep. The different pieces of the whole carry out tasks that sometimes appear completely separate from one another but that are complementary.

Each object is a system and functions as part of a system. For example, a shopping center could not exist if it were not served by highways, adequate accessible parking, public transportation systems with regular hours; and if, inside, the activities were not coordinated. This is also true for large buildings, warehouses, silos, and so on. Ports, highway systems, and especially railways are examples of complex and systemic objects.

Since the beginning of human history people have created objects that have held intentionality. But in the past these objects had an instrumentality that was multiple, reversible, that contained a certain degree of freedom and fantasy. The technique underlying the objects was invented by groups of people and worked in their service—to produce what was necessary for subsistence.

As changes intensified, techniques developed allowing groups to participate in commerce, or to adapt to avoid loss in market-associated forms of cooperation that were increasingly unequal. In this scenario, the transfer of techniques tends to be a way to increase productivity and production, and in doing so to escape from an inferior state. The number of techniques—that is, of combined forms for utilizing local resources—is therefore reduced. At the same time, objects for work, such as the means of production, circulation, or distribution, increase in complexity and sometimes also in size, becoming increasingly specialized, nonreversible, nonexchangeable, and less and less equipped with geographic mobility, more immovable, fixed to the earth, their functioning dependent on other objects.

Prior to human existence, natural objects responded to other natural objects through the exchange of energy in its brute form. We might say that natural systems are constituted without any particular goal. Human action determined the purpose of the first social objects (and, also, mechanical objects). We might call this the "socialization" of natural objects. These polyvalent objects constituted a system based in their capacity for social use. They became part of a system through *social choice* and the ideas of both power and scarcity were linked to these choices.

Today technical objects primarily communicate among themselves and achieve a purpose determined by their creator, although they may be appropriated for other types of uses. Their energy is information.

Before, things and objects occurred together in places. They were collections rather than systems. Today, objects tend to appear as systems, and simultaneously, with every passing day, they become more technical. The materiality of territory emerges from objects with a technical origin, a technical content, and that through both their production and their functionality participate in the condition of technique. These contemporary technical systems are made up of extremely specialized objects. This is particularly true for objects that constitute hegemonic systems—those created for the realization of hegemonic actions within a society.

There has never been such an invasive technical system in the history of the world. No previous system has spread as powerfully—with such tremendous capacity to impose and disseminate—as the contemporary system. And while it is widely disseminated, today's technical system also tends toward unity. For the first time in history people have only one technical system regulating all human activity. It is, however, also true that it is never possible, even today, for a single technical system to impose itself on the totality of places and people. While a certain percentage of hegemonic agents use the newest technical subsystems, which is what makes them hegemonic, there are also nonhegemonic actors that are using hegemonized technical subsystems in the same locations. They all constitute part of a whole. In other words, while there may be diverse logics at work, there is a common logic that comes from the hegemonic system that presides over all of them.

The technical systems of the contemporary world tend to have a greater capacity than previous technical systems to use territory instrumentally. In this sense we might say that a territory like Brazil has spaces that are utilized according to rationalities that are hard, precise, and dense, and other spaces are utilized according to rationalities that are soft, tolerant, and tenuous. In these latter spaces, the instrumental rationality tends to be weak or spasmodic, while in other areas, such as most of the state of São Paulo, such rationality is a permanent and necessary presence. This is the difference between spaces that are "dumb" and those that are "smart." In "smart" spaces there is a greater need for and density of information; in "dumb" spaces information is less present and less necessary. Smart spaces, rational spaces, coincide with the parts of territory that are marked by the use of science, technology, and information.

Existing objects are made to seem old by the appearance of more technologically advanced objects of superior operational quality. This creates a certain tension among that group of objects, which runs parallel to the tension in a society between hegemonic and nonhegemonic actions. This situation is different than it was in the past, when lower-order actions were not necessarily hegemonized. Now there is a clear hierarchy of actions that is transferred to the objects that implement them. This is not a technical process; however, it is a historical one.

A different history, less concerned with speed and with rapid changes, would allow for the useful life of objects—from an economic and social point of view—to last longer. Technique does not make situations become old, politics does. For this reason, we ought to consider a world where we are not obligated to think of recently produced objects as "old."

The doctrine and practice of competition is responsible for this rapid aging of our technical patrimony. Competition induces accelerated use and the rapid substitution of new-new-new objects and new-new-new forms of organization.

A world that resisted the contemporary concept of competition would, unquestionably, make possible different types of relationships among people, places, and even businesses. The frenetic pace of competition emerges from politics, not from technique. Technique does not demand that countries, businesses, or places compete with one another; rather, the politics produced by global actors—multinationals, global banks, global institutions—does.

ACTIONS TODAY

Actions today bear the same hallmark; like objects, they are based in science and technique.

Here we are referring to action that contains information that allows us better to understand its outcome—due, precisely, to this science- and technique-based content. Information makes coordinated action possible by indicating the moment and place of each gesture and suggesting the temporal series and territorial arrangements that are most favorable for generating the maximum return for a projected endeavor. Such encoded action is managed through a formalized reason; it is nonisolated action that has a dragging effect, occurs in a system, and has a fundamental role in the organization of collective life and in how we conduct individual life.

Encoded action draws on its own discourse, which has become compulsory, and on objects' discourse. Where Habermas saw that "language coordinated action," Jacques Attali (1982: 184) sees a "language that structures order." This is how action expresses the "formalized reason" discussed by Horkheimer (1974: 24) when he complained that a mathematical, cold, and calculating language was being imposed to the exclusion of emotiveness and surprise. Action would be in large part subject to abstract logic, through which the "theoretical knowing-doing included in machines implies, reciprocally, a rational way of thinking," which results in an "abstract formalization of knowledge" in a user-turned-client, an instrument that is much more than an actor (Gras 1993: 220–21).

These rational actions are animated by a rationality that follows the logic of the instrument being utilized; it is action deliberated by others, inflated action. For the majority of humanity, this information is not endogenous; it is external. Such actions, then, are pragmatic, in the spirit of Horkheimer's "pragmatic intelligence," which replaces meditation, scares off any chance for spontaneity.

Pragmatic intelligence limits the horizon of action to the immediate moment (Horkheimer 1974: 103). As a result, activities are divided up into parts, which division is both a means and an end. The fragmentation of activity helps to explain why people today lack the capacity to correctly and fully evaluate and understand who they are (i.e., to see the whole). The contemporary division of labor among individuals, businesses, and institutions is premised on accepting this form of alienation.

Today's world gives primacy to rational and instrumental action over symbolic action. This form of action is nurtured in the logic of the instrument, a technical reason that is adequate to its environment and unconcerned with theology. Ágnes Heller (1982: 80) makes this point, arguing that in "modern society, rational actions concerned with outcomes completely 'devour' the actions concerned with value."

Knowledge of the planet obtained through techniques of detection and measurement allows for the "global" discovery of places and for the usefulness of those places to be evaluated by the bearers of actions.

Today's world exists in what is called a "real-time" scenario, where information can be transmitted instantly, allowing for actions to occur in a given place, and also at the right time to achieve the maximum effectiveness, highest productivity, and greatest profitability possible for those who control them. The popular idea of *just in time* [English in original] should be complemented by the idea of *just in place* [English in original] in order to account better for the precision of the actions that today's world depends on for efficiency. Productivity is also linked to the fact that actions can be immediate, putting the idea of "real time" into practice. Indeed, the possibility for immediate action creates the possibility for global action.

The current technical systems make possible unified action on the planetary scale in a way that was not previously possible. So-called real time gives actors in different locations the potential to act, in the here and now, through the state, international organizations, transnational firms, and most importantly, the financial institutions responsible for the circulation of universal surplus value.

Differentiated actions require coordination, which may be difficult to discern or may even be invisible but which is what allows individual actions to become part of globalized actions. As Cassirer (1965: 3:30) puts it, human action is discrete, but each person's action contributes to larger, even global, changes. Interaction is made possible through systems of actions based on technique, such as forms of telecommunications, which Max Pages et al. call "the new invisible hand" (1979: 249).

Different, distant points can be reached simultaneously by a decision-making center that can efficiently transmit messages and orders. However, in many places the current possibility for the worldization [*mundialização*] of a large number of actions creates the problem of the superposition of actions at different scales, which themselves are the bearers of different contexts with diverse geographic reaches and active or reactive forces.

We are far from an absolute territoriality of action, since telecommunications became possible. In *Le métier de géographe en pays sous-développé*, we proposed to make a methodological assumption that there is a difference between the scale of a given action and the scale of its impact (Santos 1971b). This would mean that there could be a global variable that has a local action. In other words, the event that happens in a place is one thing, but its motor or fundamental cause could be another.

As a result, global actions become more effective and are characterized by extreme fluidity and extreme substitutability, a succession that can be mind-boggling because of the combination of choices made through the universal intelligence of businesses and banks, of telecommunication, and of competitiveness. Each place is a theater for fleeting combinations whose change factor is this global data itself. Each place and each moment is subject to a process of devalorization and revalorization, in which demands of a global nature play a fundamental role.

But local data does not disappear. The materiality of things and the objectivity of society allows, metaphorically, for the so-called time of the world to exist in every place, alongside other times that it seeks to dissolve. But such dissolving is always incomplete because the inherited materiality of previous times adapts to new actions.

Thus devalorized, this inherited materiality that does not fully conform to the imposed modernity can be the object of new use by "devalorized" people, who give their "devalorized" commands, and carry out their "devalorized" actions, in these "devalorized" pieces of space, where these practices create forms of life where calculation is not necessary and where emotion is possible. These are territorialized forms of life that are inserted into broader contexts or forms, be they localized (the integration of the metropoles), proximate (complementary areas), or distant. Adapting to modernity does not mean that they submit to absolute laws.

In these conditions, the old materiality dissolves the new time; the times of places dissolve the time of the world.

In this way, materiality—objects and bodies—is ultimately the only guarantee in each place against the complete imposition of calculative modernity. That is how place encounters, within its own fabric, a *raison d'être*, a principle of equilibrium, however relative and precarious—because no place exists in isolation.

Rhetoric is another key element of contemporary action—a fundamental fact in the movement of the world. New objects, which transport systems of technique, require a discourse. Until recently objects could speak directly to us; today we look at them and they tell us nothing, if there is no possibility for translation. The instructions that used to be indispensable for us to understand details about, for example, medications are today ubiquitous for even the simplest items for everyday use. Even the razor comes with instructions, and it is nearly impossible to use more complicated instruments without discourse. This leads to the creation of specialists in specialized discourses at the same time that it weakens our generalized capacity to produce a discourse of everything, that is, to understand history and to propose a new history.

Objects have a discourse that emerges from their structure and reveals their functionality. It is the discourse of use but also of seduction. There is also a discourse of actions to legitimize those objects. This legitimation is necessary for a proposed action to become acceptable and to take on more importance in social life.

As discourse becomes embedded in the everyday, it becomes present everywhere that modernity is established. That is why, for example, areas of modern agriculture and the cities proximate to them are home to many people trained to understand agricultural technical systems—they are true translators. There is a tremendous amount of intellectual labor involved in helping to form new tertiary sectors, but the actors involved have far from a complete understanding of what they do. We see a trend toward an increase in the number of people who are literate but a decrease in the number of people who are learned.

The discourse of actions and the discourse of objects sometimes complete one another as the basis of disinformation and misinformation rather than as information itself. For example, sometimes the discourse of objects is used to legitimize an action, but without revealing its actual hidden properties; or discourse can be the basis for an action that is imposed from the outside, that leads to the creation of a story through inverted praxis.

Because the world is inventing something new on a daily basis, each day there are new things that we are ignorant of and whose value we do not understand. This daily production of ignorant people also leads to entire regions ignoring who they are, given that they do not know the how and why their respective objects and actions function as they do. The less that they understand these, the less their ability to control their own evolution and the more driven by external forces they tend to be.

This is a great truth of our time. Simply by being alive new innovations are constantly calling on us to learn new things. Never before has there been such a great need for competent knowledge so that we can reinterpret the lessons of the objects that surround us and the actions that we cannot escape from.

Today space is the theater of the encounter of two systems: the system of objects impels and conditions the system of actions. Technical systems tend to influence behaviors and therefore to create a certain typology of relations, beginning with relations of capital and work.

Frequently, the superposition of these two systems generates selective use and creates shortages, which are local interpretations of distance, of costs and prices, of general norms, and of accessibility, through which they are always redefining the spatializations and totalization.

The fact that the system of objects conditions the system of actions does not mean they have an automatic relation. There are mediations, which include law, norms, custom, religion, and inherited or learned representations. But human interaction can also forge new relations, creating surprise and imposing newness.

Indeed, the force of place comes from the less pragmatic and more spontaneous actions that are often based in objects that are technically less modern and that allow for the exercise of creativity.

NORMS AND TERRITORY

In such conditions, today, the "organization" of "things" becomes fundamental data. From there stems the need for, on the one hand, objects disposed to participate in this order and, on the other, rules of action and behavior subordinated to the logic of instrumental action. According to Godelier (1972), "Unrelated objects constitute a reality devoid of existence," while social life is organized around "explicit principles" and "intentionally created norms." In a globalized world, this means that in order to understand space we must go beyond an analysis of how norms are locally exercised to consider too the distant and planetary-scale reasons for their creation. Like actions, norms are classified according to the scale at which they are located and where they act.

Global order is increasingly normative and increasingly standardized. This happens in response to technique in all aspects of social life, such that even technical phenomena are becoming normative and standardized (Séris 1994: 71), due in part to the "order of material," as theorized by Jean-Claude Beaune (1994).

The demands of international exchange gave birth to a "*lex mercatoria* based in the laws of the market and their juridical corollaries" (Badie and Smouts 1992: 36) and where, "alongside national rights and international public law, private operators—more or less in agreement with the State— organize and progressively impose their system of norms." Alongside the proliferation of juridical norms, in the realm of social relations (Laidi 1992: 32), we see a tendency toward uniformity that can be seen, more specifically, according to Jean-Louis Margolin (1991: 97), "in the realm of management, technology, consumption, and the modes of living."

The rules that govern the functioning of business do not regulate or plan productive processes, the circulation of results, the accounting process, or the planning of these processes.

Warneryd (1968: 136–37) has distinguished between an "internal flow" and an "external flow." The existence of norms regulates the different flows between agents, creating "contact flows," where the reunited internal and external flows encounter a more extensive terrain of operation and influence.

Business norms are, today, one of the drivers that demonstrates their profitability. Such norms may relate, internally, to their technical function or, externally, to their political behavior—their relationships with government or with other firms, whether they are relationships of competition or collaboration. An analysis of a business's dynamism would allow us to see that even the norms for technical order are actually also political norms. The so-called internal norms of the business environment, which regulate things such as vacation time, hours of operation, costs and prices, taxes, and so on, also directly or indirectly reach the social and geographical order in which they are situated.

According to Alain Lipietz (1978: 1778), business performance depends on two types of mediation: juridical and technical. These would be "provided by the system of transport and telecommunication that moves or transfers (commodities, information, etc.), and is often called 'infrastructure.'" Marc Guillaume (1978: 59), discussing the urban milieu, considers the "so-called collective" facilities to be a key element of the "normalizing mode." Juridical and technical mediation are complementary administrative norms. Because of its technical content, space is a regulator, but it is a regulated regulator, because it is administrative norms (beyond the internal norms of businesses), in the final analysis, that determine behavior.

Hence to say that, "thanks to normalization, time and space are no longer important," as Séris (1994: 84) claims, is not really true. General norms are differentially effective, depending on where they are situated, but the technical and informational content of each area plays a fundamental role in the behavior of actors.

The totality of modern actors is subject to a large network of interdependent rules that ultimately constitute what Pages et al. (1979: 50) call a "gigantic administration," a relational field in which the set of activities of every individual is codified by a system of rules. According to Ellul (1964: 173), the logic of norms, which has become essential, is integrated into a plan.

Territory and market become conjoined concepts in their condition as systemic sets of points that constitute a field of interdependent forces. In this sense, we can confirm that the norms they are subject to are "dynamic and self-regulating" (Pages et al. 1979: 50).

These norms structure reality in the sense proposed by Franck Tinland (1994: 27), where order means "interdependence among elements that mutually condition one another and whose interactions give rise to new modalities of relations which . . . inscribe their own rhythms of change in the movement of the world."

The territory as a whole becomes a datum of this forced harmony between places and the actors that live within them, by virtue of a greater intelligence that is situated in the key centers of the movement of information. The power of these centers comes from their differential capacity to receive information from all of nature, to evaluate it, classify it, valorize it, and place it into hierarchies, before redistributing it back to the same points from which it came, although now in the service of the interest of the center. Such intelligence, usually controlled by the major corporations and states, is not, however, the only one. At lower levels, the phenomenon reproduces itself, albeit with less market efficiency.

René Passet (1979: 277) defines this order as "the quantity of subjection established within a system: the constraint of position, for example." For him, a system's order increases as the number of determined positions that it contains increases. The greatest order occurs when each element occupies a single position.

That, according to Remy and Voyé (1981: 55), is how a formal order is created, founded in the generalization of "points of calculation and therefore of autonomy, and points of control and therefore of dependence." But less formal orders and even informal orders are also formed, where norms are recreated according to tastes that are determined locally.

Points of calculation and control are two aspects of the localization of the same current—that of the mercantile system with territorial bases.

Through standardized actions and technical objects, regulation will increasingly be imposed on the economy and territory once the technically fragmented and geographically dispersed productive process requires a permanent reunification in order to be effective. The deepening of this phenomenon, which results from the division of labor, imposes new and more elaborate forms of cooperation and control. New needs for complementarity emerge in parallel to the need to surveil them, accompany them, and regulate them. These new needs for regulation, strict control, and distance constitute a difference between past and present complementarities.

Simultaneously, significant parcels of geographic space situated in the cities (especially in the major cities of underdeveloped countries), escape the rigors of rigid norms. Old objects and less informed and less rational actions build, in parallel, a fabric in which life, inspired in relation to people more direct and more frequent, and less pragmatic, can be lived in emotion, and in which the exchange among men is the creator of culture and economic resources.

10

From the Natural Milieu to the Technical-Scientific-Informational Milieu

INTRODUCTION

Wherever societies are located, the history of so-called nature-society relations is a history of replacing a natural milieu, *given* for a determined society, with an increasingly artificial milieu, which is to say one that is progressively more *instrumentalized* by that society. Across the entire surface of the earth, the path that connects the former to the latter is unique—the "natural" and "artificial" components change, as do the ways they are arranged.

Our premise is that history of the geographic milieu can be broadly divided into three stages: the natural milieu, the technical milieu, and the technical-scientific-informational milieu.

Some authors prefer the term *pretechnical* to *natural*. We would argue, however, that the very notion of the geographic milieu is inseparable from that of technique. The conditions of labor in any milieu are directly related to a specific mode of constituting nature

(Moscovici, cited in Busino 1991: 73), and the lack of more complex arti-facts or machines does not mean that a given society does not have access to techniques. We reserve the term *technical milieu* for the phase following the invention and use of machines, because, when coupled with land, these machines give the geography a completely new dimension. The technical-scientific-informational milieu is the current geographic milieu, in which more dominant objects are elaborated in response to the demands of sci-ence and provide an informational technique with the high coefficient of intentionality with which they serve diverse modalities and diverse stages of production.

THE NATURAL MILIEU

When the milieu was entirely natural, people would select for the parts or aspects of nature that they considered fundamental to the functions of life. They valued things differentially according to their places and cultures.

People utilized this generalized natural milieu without significantly transforming it. They carried out their techniques and work with the gifts of nature, which they related to without mediation.

We argue that this period cannot be strictly defined as "pretechnical" because the methods that people utilized to transform natural things were, in fact, techniques. For example, the domestication of plants and animals is a key moment in the history of this milieu, and, clearly, in this moment people changed nature and imposed laws on it.

During that period, technical systems had no autonomous existence. Their symbiosis with nature was total (Berger 1964: 231; George 1974: 24, 26), and we might say that the possibility for creation was immersed in the determinism of function. People's motivations for using techniques were, above all, based in localized needs, although the role of exchange in social determinations did grow during this time. Local society drove the development of useful tech-niques and commanded social time and the limits of their utilization. The social-spatial harmony thus established, was, therefore, respectful of the exist-ing, or what we might call inherited, nature while also creating a new nature. As it produced the things for life, territorial society also produced a series of behaviors whose underlying logic was the preservation and continuity of the milieu of that life. Examples of this include, among others, the fallow lands, crop rotation, or shifting agriculture methods, which constituted social and territorial rules that tended to align with the use and the "conservation" of nature so that it could be utilized again. These *technical systems without technical objects* were not, then, aggressive, simply because they were inseparable from nature, which they helped to reconstitute through their operation.

THE TECHNICAL MILIEU

The technical period saw the emergence of mechanized space. The objects that formed the milieu in this moment were cultural and also technical. The material component of space in this period was increasingly formed by the "natural" and the "artificial," but the number and quality of artifacts varied. Areas, spaces, regions, and countries began to be distinguished according to the extent and density of the substitution of natural and cultural objects by technical ones within them.

Technical, mechanical objects added their own instrumental logics to the existing natural logic, creating, in the effected places, conflictive hybrids or mixes. Technical objects and mechanized space were loci of "superior" actions, able to dominate through their triumphant superposition onto natural forces. Such actions were also considered superior because of the particular beliefs that people hold regarding these new powers—most importantly, that they had a prerogative to confront both natural and socialized nature from the previous period with new instruments that were no longer extensions of the body but that instead represented the extension of territory, acting as true prostheses. Using new materials and transcending distance, people began to fabricate a new time in work, in exchange, and at home. Social times tend to be superimposed on and counterposed to natural times.

The international component of the division of labor tended toward exponential growth. The motivations driving the use of technical systems were therefore increasingly external or foreign, coming from outside of local logics or even national ones; and the importance of change in the survival of the group also grew. For success, commerce depended in a large part on the presence of efficient technical systems, which were increasingly ubiquitous. The logic of commerce presided over that of nature. In other words, the very existence of commerce became increasingly indifferent to preexisting conditions. Pollution and other environmental offenses were not yet recognized as such, yet there was evidence nevertheless that they increased significantly in the nineteenth century in large European cities. For example, people protested the arrival of trains in the countryside. That, along with the resistance to machines among different Luddite groups and the social struggle against urban miasmas, prefigured today's environmental struggles.

These phenomena were, at the time, limited to the few countries and regions where technical progress was established, and those technical systems were geographically circumscribed such that their effects were far from generalized.

THE TECHNICAL-SCIENTIFIC-INFORMATIONAL MILIEU

The third period began just after the Second World War and began to include countries in the Third World beginning in the 1970s. This phase, which Richta (1968) called the technical-scientific period, can be distinguished from previous periods by the profound interaction between science and technique, to such an extent that some authors use the term *technoscience* to highlight the current inseparability of the two concepts and practices.

The union between technique and science in this phase occurs under the aegis of the market, which itself becomes global precisely because of this union. The changes occurring in nature are also subordinated to this logic. In order to encounter a new interpretation of the ecological question, we must therefore consider the ideas of science, technology, and the global market together.

In this period, technical objects tend to be both technical and informational. That is, given the extreme intentionality associated with their production and their localization, they emerge already containing information within them, especially given that the type of energy necessary for their functioning is itself also information. Today, when we discuss the geographic manifestation of new kinds of development, we no longer refer to the technical milieu but rather to the production of something new—what we are calling the *technical-scientific-informational milieu*.

The same way that they affect the creation of new vital processes and the production of new animal and vegetative species, science, technology, and information form the basis for the production, utilization, and functioning of space.

In the past, only large cities were considered to be empires of technique, objects of modification, suppression, and growth that were increasingly more sophisticated and populated by artifacts. Today, this artificial world is also increasingly rural, marked, as Dorfles argues (1976: 39), by the presence of "plastic materials, fertilizers, and dyes that do not exist in nature and from an organoleptic, tactile, and chromatic perspective, we have a clear sensation that they do not belong to the natural world." In an entry in the 1981 *Universal Encyclopedia* dedicated to the French peasant, Bernard Kayser shows that their investment in the means of production—land, buildings, machines, fertilizers, pesticides, and so on—grew from 20 to 50 percent.

This creates a real "technocosmos" (Prades 1992: 177), a situation where natural nature, where it still exists, retreats in ways that can be extreme. Ernest Gellner (1989) argued, "Nature has ceased to be a significant part of our environment." Antonio Labriola's (1947) idea of an artificial milieu provided evidence for this assertion. Technique that is produced in an increasingly dense space, according to Rotenstreich (1985: 71), becomes the milieu of existence for a large part of humanity.

We can therefore speak of a scientification and of a technification of the landscape, but we must also note that information is not only present in the technical objects that form space, but is also necessary for the action that acts on those objects. Information is the fundamental vector in the social processes and territories that are equipped to facilitate the circulation of such objects. Sergio Gertel (1993) refers to this as the inevitability of the "informational nexus."

Above all, such redeveloped spaces serve the interest of hegemonic actors in economy, culture, and politics and are fully incorporated into new global currents. In other words, the technical-scientific-informational milieu is the geographic face of globalization.

It differs from previous forms of the geographic milieu precisely because the global logic imposes itself on all territories and on each territory as a whole. As a result, "the space in which people have survived for more than fifty thousand years . . . tends toward functioning as a unit" (Maurel 1994: 40). Because it is technical-scientific-informational, the geographic milieu tends toward universalism. And its particular manifestations secure the functioning of processes linked within it to what is called globalization.

As in all other periods, the new is not disseminated in a generalized and total manner. However, technical-informational objects do have a more generalized and more rapid diffusion than previous families of objects. Even though their presence is particular, they mark the totality of space, which is why we characterize the geographic space of the present world as a technical-scientific-informational milieu (Santos 1992; Santos 1996d).

The more "technically" contemporaneous that objects are, the more they are subordinated to global logic. Today, the association between modern objects and hegemonic actors has become less ambiguous in that both are principally responsible for the contemporary processes of globalization.

As the importance of fixed capital and constant capital increases, the need for movement also increases, which results in the growing number and importance of flows, particularly financial flows, and a growing emphasis on relations.

Preexisting equilibria are broken and new, more fleeting ones—in terms of the quantity and quality of the population and of jobs, of utilized capital, of forms of organization and social relations—take their place. Geographically, areas reserved for direct production become circumscribed while spaces for other types of production, circulation, distribution, and consumption expand. Marx anticipated this reduction of areas necessary for production of the same amount of goods, calling it the "reduction of arena." Advances in biotechnology, chemistry, and organization have made it possible to produce much more per unit of time and space.

The process of respatialization, creating separate areas where production of certain products is more advantageous, increases the need for exchange, which now happens across greater spaces—a phenomenon that Marx called the "expansion of area."

As exchange value is increasingly produced, respatialization is soon followed by the need for more circulation. This role in the transformation of the production of space becomes fundamental. One of its consequences is the deepening of productive specializations that then convoke more circulation. This vicious—or virtuous?—circle depends heavily on the fluidity of the networks of flexibility of regulations.

The technical and organizational possibilities for moving products across distances makes it possible for these productive specializations to co-occur across the world. Some places in both the country and the city tend to become specialized due to the technical and social conditions of natural resources. For example, the new fruit production in the Central Valley of the Rio Negro causes what is called the "big bang" [English in original] of investment in Chimpay in Patagonia, Argentina (Correa et al. 1993: 6).

KNOWLEDGE AS A RESOURCE

The expression *technical-scientific milieu* can have a more specific meaning if we recognize that technique and science give people the ability to accompany the movement of nature, and through technologies such as remote sensing make it possible to apprehend phenomena that occur across the surface of the earth.

Satellite photos record the earth's surface at regular intervals, allowing us to see, rhythmically, how situations evolve and, in many cases, to project the succession of events into the future. Increasingly powerful and precise meteorological radars then make it possible for these forecasts to be made at smaller and smaller intervals. Theoretical and applied scientists use these recording and predicting instruments to improve their understanding of the laws of nature, to anticipate its behaviors, and, with this precise information, to more efficiently implement economic and social activities. Such instrumentation affords its users a greater degree of certainty and success in carrying out their activities because they know, for example, in many cases in agriculture and industry that certain steps in the productive process are more profitable when undertaken in favorable meteorological conditions. Preparing land, planting, and applying fertilizers or herbicides are more or less effective depending on the weather. Having such information tends to favor business owners when they have better advance knowledge in advance of the meteorological for planning their work and capital investment.

In general, we could say that the parts of territory that are instrumentalized in this way offer greater possibilities for success than do other zones that are equally rich from the point of view of natural resources but that lack the same knowledge resources. Between two regions with the same physical potential, the one that is better equipped scientifically will have a more favorable relationship between investment and outcome, thanks especially to the just-in-time use of material and human resources. In a region that does not have the means for predictive knowledge of the movements of nature, the mobilization of technical, scientific, financial, and organizational resources will be comparatively mediocre.

For example, the meteorological radar at the Bauru University in the State of São Paulo, Brazil, which for a long time was the only one in the country, has a virtual radius of 400 km, but its signal capture is economically effective in a 300 km radius. This means that the businesses located within this perimeter—and which can therefore benefit from its information—can operate more efficiently than those in other places. The sectors that most take advantage of this are sugar cane and orange production (Ellias 1996). The data produced by the radar itself is generic, so each firm or group of firms (as is the case with agricultural cooperatives) must rework the data for their specific objectives.

This differential knowledge introduces a new dynamic of differentiation in territory. First, zones served by this kind of information are differentiated from those that are not. And within the "knowing" areas, businesses can be distinguished according to their capacity to use the information. It is possible for spatial and socioeconomic selectivity to create rapid changes in the territorial division of labor: the firms with greater technical and financial resources are more likely to locate areas of higher profitability, leaving the rest of the territory, even if it has same natural potential, for less powerful firms. The same logic would lead us to see that, in similarly instrumentalized areas, the different opportunities among producers tend to grow rapidly and aggressively after new technical-scientific resources are established. The rearrangement of activities and respective economic power would therefore be double: on the scale of the instrumentalized area and in the region where that area is privileged.

Knowledge therefore strongly exercises its role as a resource, participating in the capitalist system in the classic manner, in which those who own resources have a competitive advantage over those who do not.

THE NATIONAL SPACE OF
THE INTERNATIONAL ECONOMY

Now, hegemonic actors, armed with adequate information, can take advantage of any networks and use any territories. They generally prefer networked space, but their influence also extends to the most hidden, banal spaces.

National territories are transformed into a *national space of the international economy*, in that transnational firms are better able to take advantage of the most cutting-edge engineering systems created by each country than the nations themselves are. This calls the concept of territoriality into question, and many thinkers have even described this phenomenon as deterritorialization (Ianni 1992: 94; Margolin 1991: 100). These writers attribute great significance to such processes, describing them as, for example, driving the suppression of space by time (Virilio 1984) or creating the crisis of what they call "non-place"(Augé 1992).

Analyzing the United States and Latin America, Armen Mamigonian (1994: 1) argues that globalization "seeks the indiscriminate opening of national markets along with the break-up of market reserves, deindustrialization, and the diminishing of sovereignty." Along these lines, other authors discuss the emergence of a space without borders (Ellul 1977: 17; Masuda 1982: 90) and a "capitalism without borders" (Cicciolella 1993), where multinational businesses circumvent states (Andrade 1994; Petrella 1989), exercising what Paviani and Pires (1993: 125–36) call the "external management of territories."

Such action by major corporations "above states" allows us to imagine that "presently markets are triumphing over the politics of governments, while control of the market is being appropriated by the businesses that are able to take advantage of the most current technologies" (Cooke 1992: 205). Globalization, according to Veltz (1993: 51), should be understood as "a global management of multiple differentiated territories."

From this perspective, businesses govern more so than governments (Laszlo 1992), and, with the globalization of technology and the economy, states function in the service of multinational corporations (Petrella 1989). Under such conditions, Warf (1989: 265) and Michalet (1994: 19) argue, the state is no longer needed to manage international transformations.

This would be a true "erosion of national sovereignty" (Schiller 1986: 21–34), but it would be a mistake to believe that the state had become unnecessary. Instead, the emergence of multinational firms and organizations has accentuated the role of the state, which has become more important than ever before (Boismenu 1993: 13; Giddens 1984a: 135; Groupe de Lisbonne 1995; Silver 1992).

As Michel Beaud (1987: 50) argued, "even if today capitalism has international, multinational, and world dimensions, it also has not lost its national dimension." According to Hirst and Thompson (1996), "We do not have a completely globalized economy, but rather an international economy whose responses are determined by national policies." For Peter Dicken, who cites Hirst and Thompson, "States continue to be important actors, because they have the ability to encourage or inhibit global integration or are responsible on the national level for confronting the designs of transnational business" (1994: 103, 146).

Signaling this passage from an international economy to a global one, Savy and Veltz (1993: 5) invite us to "rethink the relation between entities that correspond to the national territory, and the strategies and organizations in the process of globalization [*mundalização*]." Scholars have envisioned different solutions to the emergent problems, from strengthening regional blocks (Arroyo 1994; Cicciolella 1994; Geiger 1993: 104–6;) to creating confederations of semiautonomous states (Barber 1992: 19). John Whiteman (1990) draws on different examples to argue for the need for intervention in the strategic sectors; Jacques Delcourt (1992) argues that the state is essential to secure social well-being in an era of globalization; and S. Picciotto (1991) foresaw the ineluctability of an international popular response that would legitimate the emergence of the elaboration of a national project (Neves 1994: 275) for each country that would seek to have some control over the process of their insertion into the newly emerging global order.

The same line of postmodern thinking that theorizes the end of territory and the existence of nonplace also negates the idea of the region, when there really is no subspace on the planet that escapes the combined processes of globalization and fragmentation—that is, of individualization and regionalization.

Throughout the unfolding of the history of civilizations, regions were configured through organic processes and expressed through the absolute territoriality of a given group, where that group's exclusive and circumscribed identity characteristics were expressed without mediation because that group was the only one present [in a given place]. The differences among areas occurred through the direct relationship that different peoples had with the places where they were located. We could say that the solidarity characteristic of a region occurred almost exclusively as a function of local arrangements. The speed of global transformations in this century, and especially in the post–World War II period, brought on the collapse of past regional configurations.

Just as today some say that "time obliterated space," one could also argue that the expansion of hegemonic capital across the entire planet has eliminated regional differentiation and made it nearly impossible to continue to imagine that regions exist.

To the contrary, we would argue that: first, accelerated time actually accentuates the differentiation of events and therefore increases the differentiation of places; and second, just as space becomes global, the world itself is redefined, and the phenomenon of region is actually further extended to all inhabited places. Regions provide the bases and conditions for global relations that would otherwise go unrealized. It is precisely in this moment that we must therefore turn our attention to regions, even while we recognize them as a space of expediency and even if we call them by a different name (Leite 1994: 14).

We are accustomed to the idea of region as a subspace that has long existed as stable infrastructure. In today's globalized world, marked by the growth in the international division of labor and the exponential growth of exchange, we also see movement accelerating and changes that are more frequently repeated in the form and content of regions. Regions are not defined in terms of the longevity of their structures but by their functional coherence, which distinguishes one region from another, whether or not they are neighbors. Ephemerality, in other words, does not change the fact that a territorial division exists.

Contemporary conditions may continually transform regions and shorten the durations of their structures, but this does not eliminate the region as such; it only changes its content. The density of the event increases, in the face of a greater volume of events per unit of space and per unit of time. The region continues to exist, but at a level of complexity previously unseen.

SPATIAL PRODUCTIVITY AND
THE WAR AMONG PLACES

The new subspaces are not all equally able to capitalize on production. Each combination has its own logic and makes possible different forms of actions specific to particular economic and social actors. We have seen, for example, that hegemonic actions are established and realized through hegemonic objects that privilege certain areas. Therefore, just as in a system of systems, other spaces and actions are called on to collaborate with the hegemonic ones.

Places can differentiate themselves according to their differential capacity to offer a return on investments. This profitability depends more or less on the local technical (machinery, infrastructure, accessibility) and organizational conditions (local laws, taxes, work relationships, work traditions). Market effectiveness is not, however, generalized for a place; rather, it tends to refer to a particular product produced in that place (see also Moraes and Costa's [1984] discussion of the valorization of space).

In the same way that we might talk about the productivity of a machine, a piece of land, or a business, we might talk about *spatial productivity* or geographic productivity—an idea that can also be applied to a place but, as mentioned above, only in terms of a given activity or set of activities. Here we are talking specifically about productive space, about the "work" of space. Without minimizing the importance of natural conditions, we recognize that artificial conditions tend to be more important in evaluating spatial productivity, as they are the expression of technical processes and of geographic bases of information. This begs the question: are we facing a new kind of determinism, a neodeterminism of artificial space?

A given place's productivity cannot go unchallenged for very long, however, because another place could easily begin to produce the same product with some different localized comparative advantage. In this context, Richard

Walker's (1978: 26–27) idea of "the reserve army of places" takes on new meaning. Here we could use it to mean an actual professional army of sorts, in which each member would be better and better prepared to carry out a particular function. In this sense we might say that we live in a world where places display a tendency toward rapid aging (from a technical and socio-economic perspective) and that different and unexpected rhythms occur in different places.

Places become specialized according to their natural virtualities, their technical reality, and their advantages in the social order. This specialization also responds to capital's growing demands for security and profit, which emerge from an always intensifying competition. This dynamic generates a marked heterogeneity among territorial entities that manifests in a more profound division of labor and a more intense life of relations (Mlinar 1990: 58).

Alongside the search for better business sites, there is also, within those sites themselves, an open search for new infrastructure and attention to the existing infrastructure (Sánchez 1991: 150; Smith 1984: 128–29). David Harvey (1989:12) argues that "many of the innovations and investments designed to make particular cities more attractive as cultural and consumer centers have quickly been imitated elsewhere, thus rendering any competitive advantage within a system of cities ephemeral." The idea of a dual strategy pursued by business and the public authority, that Julie Graham (1993) mentioned in relation to machine-tools, applies to many other branches of economic activity and can be used to shed light on the metaphor "war among places."

This war becomes even more dramatic around the question of employment. The move by the American group Hoover from Dijon, France, to Glasgow, Scotland, is only one of the many examples of how Europe's technical-economic and geographic time has been changing en route toward unification. This particular battle was conducted by central planning agencies, the French DATAR and the Scottish LOCATE, the latter of which, in this case, gave them a better deal. The entire operation cost the British coffers about $8 million.

To the extent that the business possibilities held by places are more easily discerned today on a world scale, their selection for implementing any given activity becomes even more precise. And further, that selection is contingent upon the business success. This is how places become "competitive." The dogma of competition, then, is not only imposed on the economy but also on the geography.

The unicity of techniques produces a certain similarity among many different objects, to the extent that we see similar-feeling landscapes emerge in many different places. Relph (1976: 114, 134) describes this attenuation of morphological difference among places as the expansion of standardization and banalization across cultural landscapes (Cunill 1994). City centers are the most visible example of this tendency towards sameness; as Parkes and Thrift (1980: 132) point out, not only do cities today look architecturally similar, but they function on a similar rhythm. Anthony King (1990: 128–29) examines this phenomenon by analyzing the global diffusion of the built environment through two key examples: the bungalow and the skyscraper.

In 1956, the North American geographer James H. Johnson was so shocked by the proliferation of skyscrapers that he wrote an article about their geography. Since then, the number of tall buildings has grown substantially, especially in the United Sates, and banalized cities across the world, even in underdeveloped countries. Authors have written about this phenomenon in São Paulo (Souza 1994), among other places. Kenneth Frampton (1985: 39) described this type of metropolitan development in underdeveloped countries as a testament to "the victory of universal civilization over locally modeled culture," marked by the presence of smart buildings and expressways in central neighborhoods.

In many so-called backward countries where the process of modernization was slow, successive generations have passed on forms of life based in productive activities, labor relations, and forms of consumption based in their own history. Among these societies, even when some of the goods were exported from their production and imported for their consumption, the social mechanism did not fundamentally change. In most of these countries, *technical civilization* has only been established in the past few decades, with major consequences for the meaning of territory as a whole and for each of its parts in regional cities and productive zones. Furthermore, current scientific and technical revolutions and globalization has a greater impact in countries that have more recently been structurally integrated into the movement of the international economy.

The less involved a country has been in previous technical innovations, the more brutal the destructuring effect of technology. These social, economic, political, and cultural—and especially spatial and geographic—effects provoke a reorganization of territory through a redistribution of functions that include altogether new *roles* [English in original] that are foreign to the entire territorial society. The fact that the transformations happen simultaneously—in transport and communication networks, productive structures, consumption habits, forms of exchange, labor relations, monetarization, forms of control, and so on—has cumulative and accelerated effects on all of the processes of change, while simultaneously causing profound disequilibrium. Although these new relations extend only to parts of the economy and territory, and take hold incompletely across society, they are strong enough to cause fundamental transformations. Phenomena like mercantile spatial disparity take on new dimensions in this context.

The new forms, created to respond to renewed needs, become more exclusive, more materially and functionally hardened, and more rigid, both in terms of the techniques involved and their localization. We thus move from a plastic city to a rigid one.

The hardening of the city happens alongside a growing intentionality in the production of places, which take on specific and precise values that are different from their preestablished uses. These places transmit value to the activities that happen there, and in doing so give rise to a new modality, creating scarcity, and new segregation. This is the final outcome of the combined exercise of science and technique, and of capital and power, in the reproduction of the city.

This rigidity has consequences for the urban form, affecting the size of the city and amplifying the tendency toward functional spatialization through the commercial devalorization and premature aging of certain sectors of urban space. This also renders existing systems of movement increasingly anarchic.

In the countryside, the constant capital necessary for production includes infrastructure and improvements added to the land, including chemical additives. In an economy dominated by circulation, improving roads and communications networks also builds the stock of fixed capital, whose form is qualitatively and quantitatively adapted to the purposes of production in the moment that they are established.

Regardless of whether they are located in dispersed or concentrated locations within space, the presence of monopoly or transnational businesses that tend to occupy entire territories determines which dormant capitals are mobilized and thus make national space in the image of their own interests. They use their political force to impose what is often called the modernization of territory. We call this process the "corporatizing territory" (Santos 1993).

To the extent that production depends on particular needs, the development of the density and organic composition of capital creates material conditions that are always more rigid than the exercise of living labor.

This rigidity manifests in new, convergent techniques and the forms of labor that these technical means imply. Flexibility and flexibilization are often lauded as the greatest aspects of production and labor today, but they actually create an expanding demand for rigidity. You could also say, without being paradoxical, that one can only arrive at fluidity through the production of more fixed capital, which is to say, greater rigidity.

THE ENVIRONMENTAL CRISIS

The dynamics of spaces of globalization presuppose that forms and norms are constantly adapting. Geographic forms, meaning the technical objects necessary to optimize production, make optimization possible by establishing and applying juridical, financial, and technical norms that are themselves adapted to the needs of the market. While norms are created at many different geographic and political levels, global norms created by supranational organizations and the market tend to configure norms at other scales; and market norms tend to configure public norms. As a result, and because of competition, the current tendency toward the use of techniques and the objects they produce tends to be more and more anarchic.

These modern (or postmodern) objects range from infinitely small microsystems to very large objects, such as large hydroelectric dams and cities—whose very presence accelerates the predatory relationship between people and environment and imposes radical changes upon nature. Both large dams and large cities have become central elements in the production of ecological crisis, which cannot be analyzed without attention to the types of and motivations for technical objects within the current historical period.

The search for surplus value at the global level makes it such that the location of the productive impulse (which is also destructive, to use an old expression from Jean Brunhes) is stateless, extraterritorial, and therefore indifferent to local and environmental realities. This explains why environmental crisis emerges in this particular historic period, when the power unleashed by forces in a given place exceeds the capacity to control them. The global condition has its national repercussions.

On the other hand, the production of the technical-scientific milieu demands a *qualitative* reinterpretation of public investment, in that circles of cooperation are established on a higher level of complexity and a much larger geographic scale of action. The resulting flows are more intensive, more extensive, and more selective. Public investment might increase in a given region, but the flows of surplus value that investment produces may benefit particular firms of people that are not necessarily local. This contradiction between the flow of public investments and the flow of surplus value make possible the increasing regional appropriation of constant capital while local society is decapitalized. Similarly, environmental vulnerability can also grow alongside local economic growth.

These phenomena may parallel a local political "emptying," with direct or indirect repercussions at the regional or national level. To the extent that recently arrived actors can create perturbations, an event in a given fraction of territory begins to follow an extralocal logic, with an often profound break with the local nexus, which Mattos (1990: 224) calls the "deterritorialization of capital." Given the similar way that techniques moved by distant interests can produce local environmental risks, perhaps we might also speak of the deterritorialization of ecological disaster.

THE EXPANSION OF CONTEXTS

Our current moment is also marked by what we might call the expansion of contexts—where new possibilities for fluidity emerge in the formidable expansion of exchange. The number of incidences of exchange grows exponentially and occupies a greater number of places on every continent, multiplying the number and complexity of connections (Fischer 1980: 27) such that they cover practically the entire surface of the Earth.

What Chesneaux (1983: 16) calls the "hegemony of circulation," the need for displacement, or what Jean-Pierre Dupuy (1975: 768) calls the "explosion of individual space," will ultimately result in what Daniel Bell (1976: 142) has described as a situation in which "all classes and all regions are at play."

On one hand, the division of labor grows, extending to many more spaces; and on the other hand, it becomes more profound, incorporating a much greater number of points, places, people, and businesses in every country. To the extent that interdependencies multiply and the number of actors involved in any given process grows, we might say that the dimension of contexts both extends further and becomes denser.

In the course of history, we move from a situation of relatively autonomous subspaces to increasingly interdependent ones; from a local interaction with regional society and nature to a sort of capitalist socialization that is territorially expanded; from local circuits that encompass few products and very few producers to the predominance of more extensive circuits. The deepening of the division of labor imposes new and more elaborate forms of cooperation and control at the world scale, marked by the centrality of the role of engineering systems that can assure the fluidity of hegemonic elements and a greater regulation of productive processes through the mechanisms of finance and speculation.

THE TECHNOSPHERE AND THE PSYCHOSPHERE

The geography of flows also depends on the geography of fixes. Technique appears as a true "universe of milieus" (Ellul 1977: 48) in the spaces that people utilize. The "urbanization of the countryside" emerges as a controversial and increasingly common idea: it marks a process of change in social relations and also in the material content of territory. In this concept, the "urban revolution," proposed by Giairo Daghini (1983: 23) as a strategy for creating second nature, meets the contemporary technoagricultural revolution. We come to see the world as a total metropole (Sottsass 1991: 39–40); and second nature tends to become total (Subirats 1988: 23).

In reality, however, the old distinction made by a certain Marxism between first and second nature should today be understood as less rigid: nature modified by people can also be considered "first nature." In cities today, production is no longer the action of labor applied to nature, but rather labor applied to labor. If on the one hand geographic space increasingly offers itself as an abstraction to be interpreted, on the other hand it serves as the basis of an economic and social life that is increasingly intellectualized as a result of the complexity of production and its role in providing services and information (Britton 1990). As "our environment is today constituted only of other people and of meanings . . . what we call labor is actually the manipulation of meaning and other people" (Gellner 1989).

At the same time that a technosphere dependent on science and technology is established, a psychosphere is also created on the same foundation. The technosphere is adapted to the mandates of production and exchange, and therefore often reflects the different interests at play. From the moment that it is established, replacing the natural or technical milieu that preceded it, it becomes a local fact and conforms to its given place like a prosthesis. The psychosphere, the domain of ideas, beliefs, and passions, and the place for the production of meaning, constitutes this environment, this area of life, providing rules for rationality or stimulating the imagination. Both the technosphere and the psychosphere are localized, but they are products of a society that exceeds any given place. Their inspiration and their laws have greater and more complex dimensions.

A. C. T. Ribeiro (1991: 46) argues that the relationship between "the organization of the productive structure of a country and the creation of a technical and economic base for modern communication processes" includes the modern system of communication "as part of the institutional infrastructure created for developing strategies of control over territory, in its economic capacity as articulator and expediter of markets." This "psychosphere" consolidates "the social base of technique and the behavioral adequation to modern interaction between technology and social values," which is why the psychosphere "supports, accompanies, and at times, precedes the expansion of the technical-scientific milieu."

The technosphere and the psychosphere are reducible to one another. The technical and scientific content of the contemporary geographic milieu conditions new human behaviors that increase the need to utilize technical resources that constitute the operational base of new social automatisms. The technosphere and the psychosphere are the two pillars through which the scientific-technical milieu introduces rationality, irrationality, and counterrationality into the content of territory.

FROM THE REALM OF NEEDS TO
THE REALM OF FREEDOM

The spaces of globalization are thus defined by the joint presence of a technosphere and a psychosphere that function as a single entity. The technosphere is the world of objects; the psychosphere is the sphere of action. Natural and artificial objects are hybrid—as Rotenstreich (1985), Latour (1991), and Gras (1993) have argued—in that they have no real existence or valuation without actions. Each space and subspace is defined as much by its corporal existence as by its relational one.

The spaces of globalization have different roles for technical, informational, and communicational content, and as a result places are defined by their technical, informational, and communicational density. These different aspects penetrate one another and are characterized and distinguished by that merging. These three categories can be easily identified in empirical reality.

Technical density comes from various degrees of artifice. The limits of the concept are, on one side, a natural area untouched by people—a wild ecology—and, on the other side, an area that contains only what Simondon

(1989) called mature technical objects, such as in a business center in a large city, where smart spaces are available to quickly respond to the intentions of those who conceive of and produce objects that are more perfect than nature.

Informational density derives, in part, from technical density. Objects that are constitutionally rich in information can still be "non-acting," inactive and awaiting an actor. Information is put into motion with action, on whose intentionality it depends. Informational density indicates the degree to which a given place is exterior, and whether its tendency to enter into relation with other places (privileging particular sectors and actors) has been realized. Univocal information that follows the rules of a hegemonic actor tends to intervene in space in a vertical manner, ignoring the local environment and putting itself in the service of whoever is in command.

Communicational density results from what Gaston Berger (1964: 173) called "the human character of the time of action," where the event can be seen as intersubjective praxis (Petit 1991) or transindividual praxis (Simondon 1989: 248). This plural time of the shared everyday is also the conflictual time of copresence. As a place of solidarity events, this banal space of geography (not the special, particular, or adjectival space of the economist, anthropologist, psychologist, or even of an architect or philosopher) mandates interdependence and solidarity, through face-to-face situations (Schutz 1967: 60). For this interdependence to occur, it is essential that "you and I share an environment," where "only in this situation . . . is it possible to assume, more or less certainly, within the directly lived (experimented) reality, that the table that I see is your table, and it is the same in all of its situational possibilities."

While technical and informational relations can be "indifferent" to the social environment, communicational relations are a direct outcome of it. The first two are more dependent on the sphere of materiality, of the technosphere, even if the techno- and psychospheres are always integrated. The communicational relations that are created *in place* have more of a *geographic flavor* than others, irrespective of the potentially distant origin of the objects, people, and orders that move them.

In the contemporary conditions, informational relations are the bearers of the realm of needs, while communicational relations can point toward the realm of freedom.

Today places tend to come together vertically, and everything everywhere is oriented around making this possible. For example, international credit is made available to the poorest countries so that modern networks can be established there to serve big capital. Places can, however, also come together horizontally, reconstituting the basis for life in common, creating local and regional norms that can ultimately affect national and global norms.

In a vertical union, the vectors of modernization are entropic. They bring disorder to the regions where they are established because the order that they create is meant for their benefit alone. They work in the service of the market and tend to produce a horizontal cohesion that serves civil society taken as a whole.

But the effectiveness of this vertical union is always negotiable; and it only persists through the creation of rigid norms—rigid despite the fact that they may be associated with liberal discourse. At the same time, horizontal unions can also be expanded through their own new forms of production and consumption. One example is how rural producers come together to defend their common interests, allowing them to move from a purely economic alliance, necessary for their respective production projects, to a political alliance that is locally defined. We should bear this in mind in thinking about the construction of new horizontalities that will allow us, beginning from a base in territorial society, to encounter a path that would point toward a perverse globalization and bring us closer to the possibility for constructing another globalization altogether.

In the meantime, place—regardless of its dimension—is spontaneously the site of (sometimes involuntary) resistance within civil society, but it is possible to imagine elevating this movement for higher purposes and to greater scales. This is why we must insist on the need for a systematic knowledge of reality through the analytic treatment of territory, interrogating the purpose of its constitution in the current historical moment.

Territory is the site of opposition between the market, which singularizes, and the techniques of production, the organization of production, the "geography of production," and civil society—all of which generalize and therefore involves everyone, without distinction. With the present democracy of the market, territory and the support networks transmit verticalities, which are selfish (from the point of view of hegemonic actors) and utilitarian rules and norms, while horizontalities account for the totality of actors and of actions.

11

For a Geography of Networks

INTRODUCTION

Antoine-Laurent Lavoisier's work in chemistry at the turn of the nineteenth century marks the appearance of "the true science of connection and communication among substances," which required the "theoretical instruments originating in the scientific concept of 'networks'" (Parrochia 1993: 21).

Today the concept of the network is in vogue in the social and natural sciences and in everyday life, but this popularity comes at a cost. The pervasive polysemy of the word has rendered its meaning vague and created imprecision and ambiguity in its analytic application, as can certainly be seen in geography.

WHAT IS A NETWORK?

What, then, is a network? While different definitions and conceptualizations of the term proliferate, the analyses generally fall into two primary categories: the first only considers appearance, or the network's material reality; and the second tries to account for its social content. The first approach can be formally defined, as Nicolas Curien argues (1988: 212), as addressing "all infrastructure that allows for the transport of material, energy, or information that is inscribed onto territory and characterized by the topology of its points of access or termination, its arcs of transmission, and its nodes of bifurcation or communication."

But the people, messages, and values that use it determine a network's social and political content. Without accounting for this social content, regardless of the nature of the materiality through which it imposes new meanings, a network remains a mere abstraction. Perhaps this is why the geographer Olivier Dollfus (1971: 59) proposed that the use of the term *network* should be limited to describing systems created by people, while natural systems should be classified as "circuits." In other words, social content is essential to understanding networks, because such systems take on meaning and value through human action.

The idea of a reticular space [*espace maillé*], found in the work of the psychologist G.-N. Fischer (1980: 28) and the geographer Claude Raffestin (1980: 148–67), is based in this deliberate construction of space as a framework for life that responds to stimuli created by production in all of its material and immaterial forms. Through networks, "the point is not to occupy areas, but to activate points and lines, or to create new ones" (Durand, Lévy, and Retaillé 1992: 21).

In Pierre George's renowned *Dictionary of Human Geography* (1970: 336–68) the concept of the network has at least two, and maybe even three, distinct meanings (Bakis 1993: 4), including: 1) the polarization of points of attraction and diffusion, which is the case of urban networks; 2) an abstract project, such as the meridians and parallels in the cartography of the globe; 3) a concrete project to draw lines of relations and connections, including things like hydrographic networks, technical territorial networks, and even the Hertzian telecommunications networks, despite the absence of existing lines and the fact that its structure is physically limited to nodes.

THE PAST AND PRESENT OF NETWORKS

To understand how networks relate to territory, we can either analyze their genealogy or contemporary expression. In the former they are seen as a process and in the latter as an element of current reality. The genealogical study of a network is necessarily diachronic—networks are made up of sections, established in different moments, on different dates, and the many previous networks that may no longer be present in a given territory were likely displaced at different times. The succession of networks, however, is not random. Rather, every movement operates in a particular, appropriate moment when the movement of society demands a morphological and technical change. The reconstruction of this history is therefore a complex task, but it is also fundamental to our understanding of the evolution of a place as a totality.

The contemporary study of any given network is necessarily premised on a description of that network's present elements. This study might include, for example, a statistical analysis of the network's technical quantities and qualities, and also an assessment of the relations that the elements of the network maintain with all aspects of social life, which is to say, the way that the network provides material support for everyday life.

A contemporary view of networks involves knowing the age of objects in the network (here considering the "global" age of the respective techniques involved), their longevity (the "local" age of the respective objects), their quantity and distribution, their use, the kinds of relations they maintain with elements outside of the area being analyzed, and the modalities of control and regulation for their use.

These two approaches are not hermetic and, in fact, it would be impossible to carry them out separately. Rather, they must be brought together in our analysis, especially given that each phase of the process can also be seen as a separate situation; and each situation can be seen as a division in a movement that is unequal, if we consider only one element or another. Seen through geographic space, diachrony and synchrony can only be understood as two faces of the same phenomenon—or better, two ways of seeing a unitary movement.

In broad strokes we can identify at least three different moments in the production and life of networks: a long, premechanical period; an intermediary, mechanical period; and the current period.

In the first period, there is a sort of "empire" of natural facts and human ingenuity that was limited by and sometimes subordinated to the contingencies of nature. Under these circumstances, spontaneity was a major factor in the formation of networks.

In the second moment, which coincided with the early days of modernity, networks were named such because of the deliberate character of their creation. Colbert, Luis XIV's minister in France, provides a paradigmatic example of this explicit desire to "correct" and "improve" territory through networks. The development of techniques is a new phase in this second moment. Gras's (1993: 26) "networks of steps" takes on a functional unity with new forms of energy.

So-called postmodernity, the technical-scientific-informational period, marks a third moment in this evolution. Network carriers in this moment can be found partly in territory, in the natural forces dominated by men (e.g., the electromagnetic spectrum), and partially in the forces recently elaborated through human intelligence and contained in technical objects (e.g., the computer). Thus, when the phenomenon of the network becomes absolute, the fact that it retains the name *network* is misleading. In reality, there is no actual network; its carriers are only points.

In the first moment, the existing networks served a small life of relations. The consumption spectrum was limited. With a few exceptions, local societies met their needs locally. Traded items and actual trading were limited, and most of the time competition between territorial groups was practically nonexistent. People lived time slowly.

In the second moment, consumption grew, albeit moderately. Technical progress had limited utility. Commerce was directly or indirectly controlled by the state. Although a given socioeconomic formation may have extended beyond the oceans, such expansion was limited to a few key goals. The "world market" was the sum of colonial markets. Colonization created a "closed" international commerce. Networks sought to globalize, and did so physically, but their function continued to be limited for some time. Borders were a political, and also an economic, financial, fiscal, diplomatic, and military fact.

The role of spontaneity in network creation is the major distinction between the networks of the past and present. The more advanced material civilization is, the more it deliberately imposed its character on the constitution of networks. With the recent progress in science and technology and the new possibilities opened to information, the creation of networks presumes that we can anticipate the functions a network could exercise and can plan its material form—such as the rules of its management—accordingly. That is how Bakis's (1990: 18) "space of transition" was created, as part of the total space whose technical content allows for permanent, precise, and rapid communication among the principal world actors. Michel Fouquin (1993: 3) argued that the current technical revolution, dominated by telecommunications and computers, allows for the structuration of a set of economic activities happening across the entire world, twenty-four hours a day.

According to Musso (1994: 256), "Networks deposited a 'geologic' layer to supplement 'earth-history,' increasing topology to 'topography' and giving birth to the 'contemporaneous [space] of the current moment.'" The idea of the network can also be applied the world economy (Margolin 1991: 96), and its configuration transcends national borders (Ominami 1986: 176).

It is in this sense that we must understand that this space of connectivity is organized by discourse, drawing on Claudette Junqueira's (1994) discussion of a reticular space presided over by a distant sociability. Discourse, in this situation, is the language of norms and orders that distant actors impose instantly and as imperatives on other, distant places. Such networks are the most effective transmitters of the process of globalization that we see today.

FAST TIMES AND SLOW TIMES

To refine historical inquiry, Fernand Braudel proposes a distinction between the *long durée* and the *short term*, with the latter referring to the conjuncture and the former to an analysis of structure—the movements of the base—which cannot be fully comprehended in shorter periods. This analysis transcended the field of history and spread to the other social sciences, seduced the natural and exact sciences, and colonized geography, even if geographers, with a few rare exceptions (such as Hägerstrand) only apply this idea mechanically. Derwent Whittlesey's (1929) idea of sequential occupation could be revisited and developed in order to account, spatially, for this process in which synchronies and diachronies cooccur.

Today, however, Braudel's (1979) distinction between the *long durée* and the *short term* becomes less effective—in geography and in other territorial disciplines—if it is not supplemented with another concept that, we argue, could also be expressed in terms of two opposing terms: the idea of a *fast time* counterposed to a *slow time*. Here we are talking about relative quantities—what we call "slow time" is only slow in relation to fast time, and vice versa; their denominations are not absolute. This quantifiability of time lived by people, businesses, and institutions differs from place to place, making "absolute time" impossible. In fact, it is also true that "intermediary times" temper the rigor of the concepts of fast time and slow time, but the advantage of our proposed framework is its objectivity. The time considered here, however, is not the time of machines, or of instruments in and of themselves, but rather the time of the actions that animate technical objects: machines are what offer possibilities and set limits.

In the past, slow time and fast time could be juxtaposed within the same subspace, occurring in parallel without being superimposed on one another. For example, J. H. Boeke's (1953) portrayal, in the years following the end of World War II, of a parallel evolution in the modern and traditional sectors across Indonesia might have been inspired by this duality of time present within a single place. We might argue that temporality, considered as a particular interpretation of the social time of a group or a person, would be a more accurate term than "time."

Fast time does not cover the totality of territory or extend to all of society. In each area, there are multiple degrees and forms of combination.

The local effects of globalization make it such that slow times refer to fast times, even when that fast time is not directly exercised on places or social groups.

A SPACE THAT IS NONHEGEMONIC AND UNSTABLE

Just as there is no homogeneity in networks, there is no homogeneity in space. When people speak of "homogeneous distribution" or of "ubiquitous, instantaneous, and simultaneous services" (Dupuy 1991; Remy 1991: 167–68), they are generally talking about existing networks and services, not about territory or its subspaces as a whole. As Begag, Claisse, and Moreau (1990: 189) put it, homogenization is a myth; its perception is the result of an "analytic delirium" that associates the existence of spatial indifference with the idea of spatial revolution. Bakis (1990: 25) argues that space remains differentiated, and that therefore the networks established within it are equally heterogeneous.

In fact, and first of all, everything is not a network. Examining any representation of the surface of the earth, we can see that there are numerous and vast areas that escape the reticular design that is present in nearly all developed countries. These areas are magmas, or zones of lower intensity.

The networks that do exist are not uniform. Networks can be superimposed on one another within the same subspace and may include primary networks, tributary networks, constellations of points, and traces of lines. Their social utility and use is uneven, and different actors take on different roles in their control and regulation.

Today, flows become even more important for understanding a given situation, because circulation takes precedence over actual production in the global process of production. The geographic pattern itself is defined by circulation, because circulation is more common, denser, and more extensive and therefore controls the changes in the value of space.

In a situation where the virtualities of each localization are constantly changing, what we might best call "the war among places" occurs. That is to say that in this context, places should use their existing comparative advantages, and also create new ones, to attract promising activities for jobs and resources. In the battle to make themselves attractive, places take advantage of both material resources (such as structures and tools) and immaterial resources (such as services). And each place seeks to highlight its virtues by deploying its inherited or newly created symbols in order to use the image of a place as a magnet.

Advanced activities are more sensitive, which generates inconsistency in the value of space that is due both to the incessant renewal of products and to the ongoing incorporation of new materials and methods. They have significant requirements in terms of the content of their immediate area (Fischer 1990: 12). But the lower-performing businesses that work in "externalized networks" are very dependent on access to professional information and services (Ganne 1993: 115).

This real instability made R. Lobato Correa (1993: 31) ask, "To what extent [do] large corporations, structured organically and spatially in the form of a network, alter the territorial division of labor, that is, the productive specificity of different areas and the urban centers that existed previously?"

THE GLOBAL AND THE LOCAL

Networks for production, commerce, transport, and information are increasingly global as a result of technical progress and contemporary forms for realizing economic life. Kayser and Brun's (1993: 1) work demonstrates that "space in places like rural France and its zones that appear to be marginal is actually completely integrated into the socioeconomic global system." But the most complete and effective form of the network is created by finance (Goldfinger 1986; Retaillé 1992: 118), one made possible by the dematerialization of money and its consequent instantaneous and generalized use. The idea of a global network emerges during this phase of history.

Networks would be incomprehensible if we tried to understand them based solely on their local or regional manifestations, despite the fact that these manifestations are indispensable for understanding how networks function on the world scale. Building on Braudel (1979: 57), if we start from the privileged movement that we are trying to understand, we can describe global movement through the movements of particulars, given that "all of these cycles are contemporaneous and synchronized; they coexist, mix, and add or subtract their movements in response to oscillations of the whole."

Within networks we can broadly discern three types or levels of solidarity and just as many levels of contradictions: the world level, the state territorial level, and the local level.

The first totality that appears is the world, empiricized through networks. This production of a totality that is both concrete and empirical is the major innovation of our times.

The second totality is territory, or the social-spatial formation of a country and a state; it is the result of a contract and is delimited by borders. The globalization [*mundialização*] of networks, however, weakens both borders and fidelity to that contract, despite the fact that states continue to control different forms of regulation and networks.

The third totality is place, where fragments of the network take on a unique and socially concrete dimension as the result of the contiguous occurrence of socially aggregated phenomena based on solidarity events that are the outcome of diversity and of repetitive events that may include an element of surprise.

Networks are vehicles of dialectical movement where, on one side, world is opposed to territory and place and, on another, it encounters place and territory taken as a whole.

We should revisit J.-M. Roux's (1980) idea from the late 1970s: he dedicates one strong paragraph of his book to what he calls "networks against regions," arguing that regions will be made obsolete by reticulated territory.

The existence of networks is inseparable from the question of power. The territorial division of labor that emerges from networks gives particular actors a privileged role in the organization of space. According to Martin Lu (1984), this integrating role is both functional and territorial, because integration drives the intensification of spatializations, new spatial divisions of labor, a greater intensity for capital, the more active circulation of markets, messages, values, and people, and a greater asymmetry in the relations among actors. For Lu, "Integration could be understood as a process of unification of the space of decision-making, with all consequences taking place at the level of markets for intermediate and final factors and products."

Taylor and Thrift (1982: 1604) pointed out an interesting path by remembering that the power systems inherent to the action of large organizations play an important role in building of organizational structures. They failed to add that the very structure of space itself constitutes a fundamental condition for the exercise of power, as well as for the local or regional nature of this power. The word *power* should here be recognized as Taylor and Thrift define it, as an organization's capacity to control the resources necessary for the functioning of another organization.

To what extent can this idea can be approximated through Rainer Randolph's (1990: 13) assertion that "the logic of activities of big business becomes *objectively* incomprehensible when observed on the scale of actuation of most agents, because of the lack of territorial congruence between this scale and the spatiality of macroeconomic logic?" Or when Pierre Veltz (1993: 66) refers to the creation of what he calls the "network-metropole," with the tendency to pass from a polarized zone to a networked one. In support of his argument, Veltz argues that there is a "growing disconnect, that is statistically measurable, which may lead to strong divergences between economic dynamics of the primary cities and their retro-country or their regions (in the case of France)."

NETWORKS AND THE DIALECTICS WITHIN TERRITORY

On the other hand, when confronting a reality defined by networks that are simultaneously global and local, there is a great temptation also to counterpose a local and national society, a local and national territory, and a local or regional socioeconomic formation and a national one.

How do we define, then, the category of national society, national territory, or national socioeconomic formation, and the category of local society, territory, or socioeconomic formation? How can we approach these themes analytically?

We believe that the concept of the division of labor, which is both a reality and an analytic category, can help us in this discussion. Our first question should be whether we can say that local society does local work, while national society does general or national work. But this question raises a prior question of how to understand "national work." What is it? How is it expressed other than statistically? What is the role of a national territorial configuration?

Configurations carry different weight in different places, depending on their material content. Through the given mechanisms of power, national society distributes technical and functional content within a country, allowing places to become obsolete or making their modernization possible. Through the general relations directly or indirectly imposed at each location within the country, through legislative or budgetary means, national society imposes its political weight upon the local geographical configuration and the corresponding local piece of society by controlling the use of immovable and lasting materiality.

National decisions interfere with forces occurring on lower levels of territorial society through the geographic configuration as a whole, but they only take on meaning within each place.

Local work depends on both locally existing infrastructure and the national division of labor. The local territorial configuration conditions the direct process of production and its demands for labor, time, and capital. National labor—that is, large-scale productive and sociocultural production—implies a division subordinated to resources, opportunities, and competencies and the submission to general norms of internal and external relations.

To what extent, then, does local labor depend on local society? Local society primarily controls the technical aspects of local labor. Its control over the political aspects of local work is residual and incomplete. Political control tends to come from different institutions at greater scales and distances. Today, the center of decision making tends to be foreign.

Local cities exercise this technical command linked to what, in the territorial division of labor, comes from production proper. Distant cities that hold higher positions within the urban system (and global cities, above all) control politics through orders, the availability of surplus value, and the control of movement, all of which guide circulation, distribution, and regulation.

We can further demonstrate the dialectic of territory through the local control of the technical aspect of production, alongside a remote control of the political part of production. The technical part of production allows for local or regional cities to have a certain power over the portion of territory surrounding them, where the work that they control is carried out. This control is based in the technical configuration of territory, in its technical density, and also in the functional density that we can also call information density. Distant control, locally realized, over a political portion of production comes from global cities and reaches into different territories.

The result is an accelerated alienation of spaces and of people, of which one key component is the current significant individual mobility. Today that maxim of Roman law—*ubi pedis ibi patria* (the homeland is where the feet are)—either loses or changes its meaning, especially given that neither local nor international laws have made it possible to concede the right to participate in the political life of a place to someone who was not born there but who lives or works there.

NETWORKS, COMPETITIVENESS, AND THE IMPERATIVE OF FLUIDITY

The contemporary world demands fluidity for the circulation of money, ideas, messages, and products that are of interest to hegemonic actors. Technical networks form the basis for fluidity by acting as key supports for competition and by functioning as the points from which the insatiable search for ever more fluidity emanates, which in turn drives the search for new and more effective techniques. Fluidity is simultaneously a cause, a condition, and an effect.

We see the creation of objects and places that favor fluidity, such as pipelines, canals, freeways, airports, and telecommunications infrastructure, and the construction of telematic buildings, smart neighborhoods, and technopolises. These objects create value for the activities that use them, as if these objects and places were flows themselves.

For objects to effectively meet our desires for acceleration, we must have advance knowledge of when they will be used, how fast they can move, at what frequencies, and at what cost. By standardizing objects, we can measure and predict their performance. Without standardization, the mass production of cars, boats, and planes would be impossible, as would the creation of their bases of operation—gas stations, ports, and airports adapted to this new frenzy of velocity. New scientific developments in chemistry, biotechnology, and cybernetics also make it necessary to develop new objects for use in the production of these complex machines.

Constantly increasing fluidity causes brutal changes in the value of objects and places. Fluidity, however, is always relative—we can compare any given flow to another flow, or even to itself in a previous moment. The greater the existing gap between a given place and its competitors, the greater the technical shift necessary in that place to attract new competitive activities. In these conditions, there is a tendency for subspaces that cannot increase their fluidity to become obsolete quickly. In cities, for example, we see that processes of rapid obsolescence are more accelerated in some neighborhoods than in others. As we discussed earlier, such shifts in the value of space often leads people and businesses to migrate out of particular spaces and into others.

We can analyze the volume of goods that economic actors can produce or move in order to distinguish among those who create flows and those who merely create volume—in other words, those who create a mass of things but cannot turn that mass into a flow. That is to say that today it is not enough simply to produce. Production must be set into motion, because production no longer directs circulation. Rather, circulation shapes production.

It is as if the dominant economy is compelled to enter into an untiring and wild search for fluidity. Only the fastest people or entities can piece together the conditions for survival in a world defined by galloping innovation and wild competition. Hence, we see a generalized desire to overcome every obstacle to free circulation of the market, information, and money, often on the pretext of guaranteeing free competition and assuring the primacy of the market, which has itself turned global.

Fluidity is not, however, only a technical category, it is a sociotechnical one. Contemporary technical innovations are only possible through the creation of new norms of action, beginning, paradoxically, with what is called "deregulation." In other words, the contemporary economy cannot function without a system of norms adequate to new systems of objects and new systems of actions designed to make the functioning of those objects more precise. Norms constituted in different interdependent subsystems must be constantly monitored and guaranteed by a world legislation, world tribunals, and a globalized police force. Contrary to popular imagination, deregulation does not transcend norms. Rather, to deregulate means to increase the number of norms.

Contemporary fluidity can therefore be understood as a result of the combined realization of three possibilities: 1) perfect universal forms; 2) new universal norms resulting from universal deregulation; and 3) universal information that is also the base of a universal discourse.

As we have seen, perfect forms are created through a new step in technical evolution toward informational technique. Perfect forces supported by instant and ubiquitous information are the conditions of possibility for creating and imposing norms at a global scale. The phenomenon of the network, which defines this moment, rests on these perfect forms and perfect forces.

Existing objects are not all perfect, however, and perfect objects are not distributed homogeneously throughout the planet. Further, norms are not all universal, nor do they have equal geographic reach. Information also occurs differently at different scales.

Fluidity is produced through a combination of public and private sectors. The state, either directly or through concessions, together with supranational organizations, provide the territory for the technical macrosystems that techniques need in order to function. Businesses work together or separately to establish private networks whose geography and functionality correspond to their own business interests and through which they circulate, often exclusively, the information, specialized data, and commands that structure production. Our discussions of fluidity must therefore also account for the mixed and ambiguous nature of networks and what they disseminate.

In fact, fluidity is selective. Even economic agents do not use flows equally. In England, 300 businesses create 60 percent of the data traffic, and in Norway only 25 firms are responsible for 50 percent of all data circulated (Hepworth 1989: 65). An analysis of influence by private business on public power in the creation of infrastructure adds new dimensions to our understanding of telecommunications.

We should therefore distinguish between the production of an expectation of fluidity—which is to say, the creation of the conditions for its existence—and the use of fluidity by an agent, or its empirical effectiveness.

DISPELLING AMBIGUITIES IN THE CONCEPT

Networks are simultaneously virtual and real. Like all technical objects, the independent material reality of networks exists as a future promise, which is why we can say that "the network pre-exists every demand for communication and only realizes communication that is solicited" (Pinaud 1988: 70). In this sense, the network's first characteristic is that it is virtual. It is only really real, really effective, historically valid, when it is utilized in an action.

Networks are technical and social. Parrochia (1993: 39) argued that they are both material and alive, if we understand being alive, as Andre Lwoff (1969: 25) and François Jacob (1970: 87–145) argue, as a doubly ordered system that is simultaneously structural and functional. In the first decades of the nineteenth century, in his "Exposition du systèm de la Méditerranée," Michel Chevalier (1832) said that "industry [the economy] is composed of centers of production linked together by a relatively material link, transport nodes, and a relatively spiritual link, the banks" (cited in Ribeill 1988: 51).

We tend to imagine networks almost exclusively as flows, and flows are, in fact, what animate them, but networks remain connected to the fixes that constitute their technical bases, even when these fixes are fixed points. This combination of fixes and flows makes networks stable and dynamic. Fixes and flows are interconnected and interdependent within the networks. Although networks are active rather than passive, they themselves do not actually contain the primary force that moves them, which is social.

Their movement is influenced by dynamics that are local, distant, and even universal, moved by large organizations. Because they are both local and global, networks are singular and multiple, or "single and immediately plural" (Parrochia 1993: 6). The world provides the original unity of the network and also creates plurality in the different ways that networks are made manifest through functionalization and historicization.

Where Barber (1992: 4) sees an evolution that tends toward either uniformity or fragmentation in the network, a geographic view of the network sees a tense crisis between the forces of globalization and localization (Dicken 1992: 144). The resulting regionalization is as much an effect of regulated supranational organization as it is of the local, subnational forces unleashed under the aegis of the market by the process of globalization. As Yves Berthelot (1994: 13) noted in his analysis of nascent economic communities, the paradox is obvious.

According to Jacques Ellul (1977: 123), "Regionalism is a product of technical society, despite the appearance to the contrary that technique is always a centralizer"; or, as Edgar Morin (1965: 71) put it, "The world on track toward homogenization, unification, and organization is simultaneously on the road to heterogeneity, disorganization, conflict, and crisis."

The expansion of contexts that network efficiency makes possible is also an outcome that Marx predicted regarding territory: the reduction of the arena of production and the extension of its area. The technical and scientific progress that has created massive increases in productivity has also made it possible to concentrate production in a smaller space (reduction of arena). This same progress, especially in telecommunications, also makes effective exchange possible over greater areas. This also magnifies changes in the social division of labor (which divides) and cooperation (which unifies).

Networks, then, are concentrators and dispersers, conductors of centripetal and centrifugal force. It is common for the same matrix to perform both of these functions. The vectors that, from a distance, ensure the presence of a large business, act as centripetal forces for the businesses but as centrifugal forces for the many preexisting activities in the area of their impact.

Through networks there is a parallel, effective creation of territorial order and disorder, because networks integrate and disintegrate, destroy old spatial configurations and create others. When seen exclusively on the side of the production of order, of the integration of the constitution of spatial solidarities of interest to particular actors, they appear as part of a process of homogenization. The other side—heterogenization—might be hidden, but it is equally present.

The fact that the network is global and local, one and multiple, stable and dynamic, makes it such that its reality, seen in its movement as a whole, reveals the multiple overlapping systemic logics, the mixture of different rationalities whose changes are directed by the market and the state but above all by the sociospatial structure.

The idea and reality of the network create a sense of ambiguity if we fail to account for its definitive character as a hybrid or a mix. The role of mixes, in the words of Bruno Latour (1991: 166–67) is specifically to bring together the four "regions" created as different states of being—the natural, the social, the global, and the local—in order to avoid "all conceptual resources [being] accumulated at the extremes," such that "we poor subject-objects, humble societies-natures, we modest locals-globals, [are] literally quartered among ontological regions that define each other mutually but no longer resemble our practices" (Latour 1991: 167).

Geography ought to work with an idea of space that has a content-form and that considers technical systems as a combination of time and material, stability and history. In this way, we can overcome the dualities that are also, directly or indirectly, the matrices of many of the ambiguities within the discourse and method of geography itself.

12

Horizontalities and Verticalities

The words *horizontal* and *vertical* have long existed in geography and other disciplines, but they are generally used to mean something other than what we plan to elaborate for them here.

Our analysis will draw on the work of three theorists: the Dutch geographer Gerben de Jong, the Russian sociologist Pitirim Sorokin, and the French philosopher Henri Lefebvre. De Jong (1962: 27) makes two types of chorological differentiation: 1) "the integration of things and their respective phenomena at any given point on the earth," which he calls *vertical interrelation*; and 2) "relations among things and their phenomena at different points or places in the world, based on their relative localization," which he called *horizontal integration*. De Jong developed these definitions before technological progress was generalized at a planetary scale, yet he was able to foresee the effect that "foreign things" would have on localities and therefore to demonstrate how the intersection of these phenomena would generate geographic diversity (1962: 75).

Sorokin studies horizontal and vertical forms of communication among people as a way to study the circulation of cultural objects, phenomena, and values. For him "the paths that people follow and use to communicate are also the paths of cultural values and objects" (1964). He writes, "A trail through the mountains, a caravan trail in the desert, a big staircase for carts, animals or cars, rivers . . . maritime routes . . . railroad or plane routes . . . the telegraph, the telephone, the radio . . . are the primary roads through which values move, circulate and propagate themselves horizontally."

In his article "Perspectives de la sociologie rurale," published in *Cahiers de sociologie*, Lefebvre (1953) argues that when we analyze the rural world, we must consider two forms of complexity: superimposed forms and interactive forms. *Horizontal complexity* is based on the life of a human group and their relations with place, as mediated by techniques and the social structure. *Vertical complexity* can also be called *historical complexity*, or the influence of past facts on contemporary existence. In *Search for a Method*, Sartre (1968: 52) explains that through this conceptual development Lefebvre sought to unite sociology and history, and Sartre expresses regret that other Marxist intellectuals were not followers of Lefebvre.

Regional economist Martin Lu (1984) explores the concepts of functional and territorial integration in a way that resembles our analysis. For Lu, functional integration is the outcome of productive processes whose flows run hierarchically through space: "The process of functional integration . . . controls the process of accumulation and the reproduction of capital in time and in space" (14). Territorial integration results from consumption processes, which also hierarchize space according to the potentialities of supply and demand.

Based on these two forms of integration, Lu develops the concepts of *functional surroundings* and *territorial surroundings*, emphasizing that there is no necessary link between the processes of functional and territorial integration (15). He therefore also insists on differentiating between a functional (or sectoral) hierarchy and a spatial (or territorial) one. He then argues that the more the two distinct forms of integration coincide within a given region, the more developed that region would be. His point of departure is economic space, or the space of firms. We, on the other hand, prefer to begin our analysis in banal space—the space of all people, all businesses, and all institutions—which we have previously described as a system of objects animated by a system of actions. Our goal is to create simple analytic categories that can account for the inseparability of the "functional" and the "territorial."

TWO ARRANGEMENTS AND TWO SEGMENTATIONS

Today spatial arrangements are not only made up of figures formed by continuous and contiguous points. Alongside these spots, or above them, are constellations of discontinuous but interlinked points that define a space of regulatory flows. The segmentations and partitions that exist within space make it such that we must recognize at least two types of divisions: *horizontalities* are made up of aggregated continuous points, as in the traditionally defined region; and *verticalities* are points in space that are separate from one another and assure the global functioning of society and the economy. Space itself is made up of some of these dynamics, and they are inseparable from one another. Our new analytic categories must be developed based on these new subdivisions.

While horizontalities are primarily the factory of production itself and the locus of a more limited cooperation, verticalities primarily account for the other moments in the production process (circulation, distribution, and consumption) and function as the vehicle for a broader economic, political, and geographical cooperation.

We can see these dynamics at play in the relationship between the city and the country, where rural subspaces with different functionalities relate to one another in order to serve the production process, and the city, especially in the areas that have been most modernized, regulates agricultural work. In the verticalities—such as interurban relationships—solidarity is created through circulation, exchange, and control.

To underscore our point, we could paraphrase Baudrillard in *System of Objects,* who writes that "'functional' in no way qualifies what is adapted toward a goal, merely what is adapted to an order or system" (1968: 63). We pass from a "natural" (spatial) structuration, based in the exchange of energy among its constituent elements (both as they are and as they are available), to a structuration in which things are valorized through the intermediary of organization, which controls its functional life. Instead of the organic solidarity that defined regions in the past, today we have organizational solidarities. In other words, today regions exist because organizational arrangements are imposed on them that create an organizational cohesion based on rationalities that—while originating externally—become one of the bases for regional existence and its definition.

Verticality creates interdependencies that become more numerous and attenuated as the need for cooperation among places expands. As Gilles Paché has argued (1990: 91), this "new geography of product flows" creates a "system of reticular production" based on territorial foundations that are widely redistributed and that assure the cohesion of the production process.

These interdependencies tend to be hierarchical and to create a particular order. The hierarchy itself is created through technical, financial, and political controls that form the basis for the functioning of the system.

Information—which serves the interest of hegemonic economic forces and the state—is the primary manager of the actions that define new spatial realities. An incessant process of entropy unmakes and remakes the contours and contents of subspaces, in accordance with the dominant forces, imposing new maps on existing territory. The expansion of hierarchy also gives rise to processes of homogenization, and homogenization demands a form of interdependent integration that refers to a point in space that may be within or outside of the country (or place). The incorporation of these external nexuses and norms has a disintegrating effect on locally existing solidarities, which leads to a correlating loss in the local capacity to manage local life.

Cities are a good example of points of intersection between verticalities and horizontalities. Studying the difference between modernized and nonmodernized places on the Argentinian highlands of northern Patagonia, Maria Silveira (1994: 75–77) describes the processes of production and circulation, explaining that "these logics cross cities and produce a territorial arrangement" in which they superimpose horizontal and vertical links. Verticalities are vectors of a higher-level rationality and pragmatic discourse through which hegemonic sectors create an obedient and disciplined everyday. Horizontalities are both the place of finality imposed from the outside, far away, and up above, and also the counterfinality that is locally generated in response to such imposition. Here we can see the existence of an everyday that conforms but that is not necessarily conformist, that can be simultaneously the place of blindness and discovery, of complacency and revolt.

Centripetal and centrifugal forces also cross territory as tendencies that are simultaneously contrasting and confluent, acting at different levels and scales.

Centripetal forces are based in economic and social processes, and they may also be subordinated to the regularities of the process of production and to the surprises of intersubjectivity. They are forces of aggregation and factors of convergence. They act in the country, in the city, and in between. They operate as factors for homogenization in the city, agglomeration in the country, and of cohesion between the country and the city.

In the contemporary technical-scientific milieu, the cohesion between the city and the country has become greater and stronger. For example, modern agriculture—based in science, technology, and information—demands a productive consumption that can usually be found in the closest city. The specialization of tasks that occurs within the interurban division of labor reduces costs, thereby increasing the productivity and profitability of individual agents and strengthening the given group of cities overall.

Centrifugal forces can act as a disaggregating factor when the commanding elements are located outside of and far away from a given region. We could argue that centrifugal forces have a destructuring effect relative to a previous moment of equilibrium. If, however, we examine the forces from the point of view of the current moment, we might instead understand them as restructuring. External factors that give rise to local tensions include international commerce, the demands of big industry, the need for urban and capital infrastructure, and public policies imposed in national or foreign metropoles.

Centripetal forces drive processes of horizontalization, and centrifugal forces drive verticalization, but, in all cases, centrifugal forces act on centripetal ones. Centrifugal forces occur at different scales, the largest being planetary, where they function as what Uribe and Lopez (1993: 172) call "universal flows." Regions and superregions, as well as national and continental scales, exist between the global and the local. Because these scales are superimposed on one another, any explication of what is going on in a given area must necessarily account for forces acting at higher scales. The solidarity within a subspace created by centripetal forces is constantly perturbed by centrifugal forces and therefore must be constantly remade.

VERTICALITIES, HORIZONTALITIES, AND POLITICAL ACTION

There is a current trend toward the vertical integration of places. For example, international credit is made accessible to the poorest countries and regions so that financial networks can be established there that serve big capital.

The vectors of modernization within this vertical integration are entropic. They bring disorder to the subspaces where they take root and create new orders that serve their own interests. And the vertical union—or rather, unification—is constantly evolving and cannot survive without rigid norms.

But places can also be horizontally strengthened, rebuilt through local actions that form the basis for a form of life that strengthens civil society in the service of the collective interest.

The functional specialization that happens within subspaces tends to generate a homologous everyday life that expresses this horizontal interdependence. The information needed in order to work on a common activity can be disseminated more rapidly and increase local productivity. This is true both in the formation of production areas of one or more combined agriculture products in the country and in cities that specialize in a particular kind of industrial production or in services.

We might also argue that this homologous everyday life allows for a more effective politics. Techniques of production and the market render information common. These interests create an active solidarity that can be seen in forms of common expression that generate political action. The emergence of local media, for example, is a testament to this phenomenon where forces arising from the local, from horizontalities, can actually counter the tendencies of verticalization. One such example can be found in the local media of São Carlos in the state of São Paolo, Brazil (Bernardes 1995).

This political action can, in many cases, be directed toward some particular and specific interest, often that of the hegemonic one in that place. But this often only happens at first. Activities that, complementary or not, have a logic that differs from the hegemonic logic tend to be driven by concerns that conflict with that logic and therefore to ultimately inspire debates that address the interest of local society as a whole. This in turn drives the search for a system of broader demands, adapted to the contingencies of the common, in horizontalized space.

13

Spaces of Rationality

INTRODUCTION

Referring to Weber's introduction of the concept of rationality, Habermas (1973: 3) argued that rationalization means, first and foremost, extending the areas of society subject to the criteria of rational decision making. Our central assertion here is that, after having (successively) extended to economy, culture, politics, interpersonal relations, and individual behavior, the march of the process of rationalization is now, at the end of the twentieth century, taking root in the milieu of people's lives—which is to say, in the geographic milieu.

The crucial question is whether we can speak of a rationality of geographic space, and whether we can do so with the same language that we use to discuss the rationality or the rationalization of other facets of social reality.

IS A RATIONAL SPACE POSSIBLE?

As an introduction to a more substantive discussion of a capitalist economic rationality, and in order simultaneously to banalize and to delimit the concept, Maurice Godelier (1974: 38–58) examines the figures of the rational businessperson, the rational worker, and the rational consumer. But might there also be room in this discussion to refer what we would like to call "rational space?"

Godelier argues that there are two forms of rationality: an intentional and an unintentional rationality. The first refers to the economic actor's behavior, and the second refers to the economic system of which they are a part. If we apply this conceptualization to geographic space, its *current* existence would be located under the rubric of unintentional rationality, while its (future) planning and management would be part of its intentional rationality.

If we accept the distinction that Karl Mannheim (1935: 54) poses between a *substantial* and a *functional* rationality, geographic space would be categorized as the latter. Functional rationality involves a reorganization that tends to allow for a series of actions to extend to previously designated objects, calculated in advance (Mannheim 1935: 55). Along the same lines, we can also apply Usher's (1954: 67) concept of "weak determinism" to characterize the effect that instrumentalized territory has on the actions of individual people, businesses, and institutions.

Habermas (1973: 32–33) distinguishes two parallel and interdependent tendencies: rationalization that is executed or brought about from *above* and from *below*. This results in "a cumulative progress of productive forces . . . at the level of an entire territory," with a "horizontal extension" of subsystems of rational action. Economic crises result from "permanent pressure" on these traditional structures, a pressure arising from the transformations imposed "on the infrastructure of a society obligated to modernize itself." In this Habermasian model, the rationalization of geographic space amounts to a rationalization from *below*.

What would be the conditions for rationality in the material environment? The response is exceedingly simple: those conditions that tend to facilitate so-called rational actions. From this perspective, rather than considering space itself as "rational" we can see it for what it really is—a field of instrumental actions. We might, like E. A. J. Johnson (1970), argue that the rationality of space began at the moment of mechanization. But the railroad, the car, and the telegraph really only created a relative fluidity of territory; their actual geographic area of action was relatively limited. It is only at the end of the twentieth century, with the development of new techniques for disseminating and collecting information, that we can say broadly that territory has fluidity. That is also why now the idea of the rationality of space now becomes clearer and more extensive.

The reality of this "rational space" would not be possible if technique did not take the form, as it does today, of *informational technique*. In other words, geographic space adds the additional attribute of information to the existing technical content that has characterized the last two centuries, and that today is itself becoming denser and more complex.

Simondon (1989) proposed the concept of the concrete technical object in order to express how a tool could be created that embodies the most perfect convergence between technology and desired function. This movement of technique toward perfectibility cannot be achieved by nature alone. Through this process, fabricated things can attain the condition of *hypertely*—another key word in Simondon's vocabulary—meaning the maximization of intentionality. These perfect objects offer maximum efficiency and results to equally perfect actions.

This novelty emerges at the same time that informational objects are diffused within territory. As technical objects, they embody the essence of technique, which is to say that they can be equipped with the rationality of technique. Because they are also informational objects, they can be used for informed actions which then also become the bearers of rationality.

Such objects are informed by their specific role in intentionality, and they only function based on specific information. This "informationalization" of space is a result of both the objects that make up its material skeleton and the objects that traverse it, that give it life. Fixes and flows are therefore rich in information.

Would this, then, be rationality as an instrumental condition within things, confronting a rationality of the subject with informed actions? A first objection to this formulation might take the form of a tenacious question: Rationalization encounters and places limits on an object, but is rationality itself attributed to the actor or to the "acted upon?" Our first impulse might lead us to refuse to ascribe a category of action to an object. But do they not speak extensively, in both philosophical and technical discussions, of the rationality of machines and the rationality of technique?

So, what would this rationality of things be? Or would it, perhaps, be a rationality *in* things? The latter proposition again raises the initial problem of distinguishing between actor and acted-upon within the same object of action. In any case, creating this dichotomy would not eliminate the problem. What would this rationality in things be—or, for our particular problematic, this rationality in geographic space?

Would asking this question be reinforcing the second argument, that there can only be a rationality *in* space, while a rationality *of* space could only be, at best, a metaphor?

Here the discussion becomes both more complicated and more simple. Following the divergent epistemologies of geographic space, we would find ourselves at a dead end, based in a dualistic vision of phenomena: i.e., material-immaterial, physical-human, social-natural, and so on. Habermas

(1973: 3) uses the description "the urbanization of the mode of life" to refer to the domain already penetrated by rationalization, in parallel to the "technification of changes and communications." But the city and urbanization, seen globally, go unmentioned. Instead, why not consider urbanization—which is to say, urbanization of the mode of life—and the city as a unitary whole, as the urban phenomenon? To separate them would be to engage a "purified" epistemology, as Latour has put it, which proclaims a unity of parts but, like frying two eggs, treats them separately. Space, however, is a mixture, a hybrid, formed, as we discussed previously, from the indissociable union of systems of objects and systems of actions. The systems of objects, the space-materiality, form territorial configurations, where the action of subjects, whether rational or not, is established to create a space. This space—geographic space—is more than the social space of sociologists because it also includes materiality.

The condition of rationality is not exclusive to the "social space" of the sociologists. Rationality cannot be fully exercised without the necessary technical conditions. In the words of Barry Hindess (1987: 151), the domains that have meaning in social life for rational action are represented as a field of instrumental action. Geographic space is one of these fields of rational action. This comes from technique, present in things and in actions—what simultaneously characterizes geographic space today and makes it a space of rationality.

THE PRODUCTION OF A RATIONALITY OF SPACE

That is how "landscapes of reflection and reason" (Relph 1976: 125) are created across the surface of the earth. We refer not only to reflexive and rational landscapes but also to something more, to spaces of reflection and reason, because we are no longer encountering only a materiality (the result of a past action) but also the combination of present action and objects of action. In the second chapter of his famous book *The Organization of Space in Developing Countries*, E. A. J. Johnson (1970: 58–71) calls this the "rationalization" of American landscapes. In that chapter he explores how the introduction of techniques for transport, and the adoption of geometric, often rectangular models that had previously been experimented with only in New England, changed conditions for planning human occupation in the Midwest. He calls this process the "pragmatic improvement of spatial organization" (70), because the occupation process begins spontaneously, which is to say irrationally, in relation to the desired outcomes for this new economic phase. Johnson compares the cities, the "central places" of the

Midwest, with those of the Third World. For him, central places "are unable to offer an inter-related system of exchange that offers the incentives necessary for the intensive use of work, capital, and *savoir faire*." He concludes, "The experience of the American Midwest demonstrates that, in order to realize a tolerable degree of satisfaction of regional productivity, the model of central places and their functions must be progressively restructured and rationalized." Stephen Salsbury (1988: 56–60) also argued for the need for standardization and uniformity, beginning with the birth of the railroad system in the United States.

We discuss this example here because the history of modern rationality is increasingly assimilated into the history of machines and mechanization, a history often associated with the work of military engineers and strategists toward the re-creation of the geographic milieu on technical foundations (Druet, Kemp, and Thill 1980: 36).

G.-N. Fischer recognized this vocation. He explained the spatial needs of industrial business as "space that seeks to be rational" and that therefore needs an "instrumentalized space" that appears "as a guarantee" for business needs (1980: 31). This space should be "a milieu subject to the rules of a science transformed into technique" and equipped with "a technological desire to eliminate randomness" (31). In a broader sense, in *The Great Transformation*, Karl Polanyi (1957: 57) described "complicated machines" that serve as the material base for a self-regulating market. These references to the industrial milieu, understood as the "instrumentation of reality," can be applied to geographic space, transforming rationality into territory. It is clearly in this spirit that one could read the third chapter of Fischer's book, entitled, "Space, an Instrument of Rationality" (1980: 29–34). Equipped with "a specific organization . . . rationalized space is a space that can be manipulated as if it were a thing" (34).

Techniques, in all of their domains, authorize actions. The degree of intentionality of any object is derived from this situation. We might therefore imagine that a space tends to become more rational as its level of artificiality increases.

What is commonly called the "space of flows" does not actually extend to all of space. This term refers to a subsystem, formed by points or, maximally, by lines and spots, supported primarily by artifacts that facilitate fluidity and authorize the movement of the factors essential to the globalized economy.

And, indeed, this idea of a space of flows is often thought to be broad but is, in fact, quite restricted, and is frequently accompanied by the idea of homogenization. The invasive character of technique, today, attributes possession and therefore governance (of places, actions, objects, and so on) to vertical territorial divisions, but the dependent actions are actually governed by active points that reign over heterogeneous planes. Such actions seek to make these planes adapt, to impose an order, without altering their heterogeneity.

The only idea of homogeneity that could be reasonably applied here would be the conceptualization put forward by Georges Bataille. Marc Guillaume (1978: 107–8) explained Bataille's idea thus: "Industrial society tends toward a universal measure of generalized homogeneity," in which "everything is useful to everything else, and nothing has value in and of itself." So-called homogeneity comes from "productive value." And, according to Bataille (1968: 342), its common measure, based in money as a fixed norm, is possessions. Territorial divisions are made hierarchical based in their technical requirements and, today, also, their informational requirements. Information and money have been treated as synonyms for centuries, at least since Genoa had commercial hegemony at the dawn of the modern age. What, then, are the implications of this for the current moment, when the genuine territories of globalization are marked by the presence of automation, whose cybernetic systems constitute, in the words of J. Rose (1978: 31), "an intentionally designed decision-making machine?" The simultaneous diffusion and inseparability of the territorial networks of computers connected with new technological advances in telecommunications increases the effectiveness of information. The generalization at the world scale of the money-form had to wait for the arrival of the cybernetic age.

The effectiveness of any action depends on the degree of certainty with which it is exercised. This is precisely why the ideas of *just-in-time* and *just-in-place*, which are now indispensable to successful economic functioning, ceased to be an ambition and became a reality. According to Henri Laborit (1971: 15), "The less random any message is, the more likely it is to provide information"' or as Joel de Rosnay (1975: 170) put it, "Information increases when uncertainty decreases."

Under contemporary conditions, the most effective use of territory by hegemonic actors largely depends on information, which itself is a consequence of the technical level of available machinery. One needs to "discover the places where information concretizes" (Ferrara 1990: 76). Or as Gras (1993: 18) put it, "The more artificial that space-time is, the more secure." He argues that the contemporary technical systems "associate their objects with an information technology that then takes on a consistent presence within them." Accordingly, all of the respective territorial points function as points of regulation. As a result, the goal of "predicting and commanding risk" (Fischer 1980: 30) that was present in the technical milieu becomes redundant in the technical-informational milieu.

The central bank of the Soviet Union (Gosbank) used cybernetic technology to understand and control all financial operations within its territory (Brender 1977: 198). Gosbank's 4,000 agencies, the 600 Strojbank (investment bank) agencies, and the 80,000 Caixa Economica offices were the links in this enormous and precise chain of information.

It is ultimately through technique that we see the realization of the "progressive objectivization of rational activity relative to a goal" that Habermas discussed and which, moreover, Gehlen took as proof of the relation between technique and rational activity.

Technique rendered as a "sort of principle for all activity, for everything" is, in and of itself, "a principle of rationality," according to Marc Humbert (1991: 54). Invested in objects, it appears as a "logic, thanks to the engineer, written into the nature of things" (Gras 1993: 218; Latour 1989: 21). Therefore, the prior determination of a rationality, "a predetermined form of action on nature," exists within the technical object as a result of "the immediate connection of technology with the practical activities of life" (Leiss 1972: 147). Likewise, as Sartre (1960: 184) taught us, "Praxis inscribed in the instrument by past labor defines behaviors *a priori*."

Technology constitutes a sphere of reality and an ordering of reality; it has its own rationality (Rotenstreich 1985: 147). Technical innovations encounter history on their own terms, and all other possibilities are expected to submit to those terms. According to Langdon Winner (1980: 30), "Options tend to strongly fix themselves within the material apparatus," and, accordingly, "the original flexibility is expended for practical purposes, both economic investment and social habits." It is as if the technical innovations circulated as law. Each technical period therefore tends to correspond to a general change in social relations.

Today, the infrastructure is localized through a planning process that serves the hegemonic actors in society and economy. Horkheimer (1974: 67) explained that, "just as the process of rationalization is no longer a result of the anonymous forces of the market, but is decided in the consciousness of a planning minority, so the mass of subjects must deliberately adjust themselves: the subject must, so to speak, devote all of their energies to be 'in and of the movement of things' in the terms of the pragmatic definition." Rogério Hasbaert (1995: 55) studied this in the Brazilian Cerrado, and it can also be seen in many other places.

This ordering of technique is transferred to technicized space. This order is visible in forms, but things are merely "the surface of an abstract order" (Guillaume 1978: 101), the product of invisible relations that are based in the technicity of objects themselves. In reality, this produces a double order: "that which is the product of the technical existence of each object, a material order" (Beaune 1994); and that which is the outcome of their form, their arrangement. In both cases, this order encompasses objects and actions and results from the systemic nature of techniques.

Rational space presumes a rapid response that is adequate to the demands made, that allows for the intended action and available object to encounter one another, and that occurs with maximum efficiency. It depends on the technique contained both within things and actions. The commercial value of any given technique depends on its ability to guarantee that, once an action begins, it will follow a particular trajectory and deliver the programmed results. The norms of action are therefore important because they make it possible for actions to live up to the ideal of a useful rationality (Stiegler 1994: 106). Human actions are fully adapted to the demands of material artifacts (Werlen 1993: 182–83).

RATIONAL SPACE

The contemporary emergence of this rational space makes it appear that Saint Simon's prediction in *Catéchisme des industriels,* that a government of things would eventually replace a government of men, is finally being realized. In this sense, "the administration of things" would be progress. The implication was that things, by their nature, could drive people's behavior. Leibniz (1994) proposed a similar idea of utopia, hypothesizing an "absolute synchronicity of psychic and physical events," similar to what Carl Jung (1984: 64) described as a situation that would open the road toward the "universal harmony" of their dreams.

Spaces of rationality function as a regulating mechanism, where each part convokes the other parts and sets them in motion through a kind of centralized command. This is the logic of an artificialized nature that seeks to imitate and surpass natural nature (Sottsass 1991). This artificial milieu is another dream become reality, one which functions as a perfect laboratory that replaces the very nature it is built upon. Georges Sorel (1947: 284) explained that "each day it becomes clearer that science seeks to superimpose onto nature an idealized studio [*ateliê*] made up of different mechanisms that function with mathematical rigor that seeks to imitate, with great approximation, the movements of natural bodies."

This passage—from a world of approximation to a world of precision, a passage that Alexandre Koyré (1957), G. J. Whitrow (1993), and Calvino (1991: 71–94) also described—also achieves, with the "implacable rigor" predicted by Halévy (1948: 64), "the mathematicization of people that began in the seventeenth century" and that continues today with the "obsessive temporalities" satirized by D. S. Landes (1992: 102).

Following this logic, we would be facing the passage that Antoine Augustin Cournot predicted, from a "post-historic" epoch, from the domain of the vital to the domain of the rational, given that "man finds himself, little by little, absorbed by the very force of the products of his reason, his institutions, his techniques. Within him, nothing of the *vital* remains" (cited in Friedmann 1949: 47). Cournot declared the entire nineteenth century as "the general era of mechanization," in which history would be replaced by statistics in the study of social events. Veblen (1932: 174–75) foresaw a situation in which thought would be subordinated to machine processes rather than natural causes, where impersonal facts would dominate and generate mechanical effects in rational space (148).

Gras (1993: 21) argued that large technical systems "physically illustrate a dimension characteristic of the modern representation of the world, that defines it as a mathematical space that they materially embody."

This "real existence originating in ideas," according to Friedrich Dessauer's (1964: 244) formulation, is what Carl Mitcham (1989: 47–48) calls "existence outside of essence." Simply put, the current technological innovations that are "rationally materialized" (Séris 1994: 157) take the form of simple objects, machines, and spatial configurations whose conception, production, and inception tend to be shaped by a pragmatic desire to follow the logic of instrumental goals.

Queau (1987: 5) described this situation as one where "the images of synthesis surpass, at times, the strict framework of their military applications and become widespread instruments of knowledge and action, as well as of creation. Even further, they reawaken the desire for ancient philosophical questions, and offer original approaches to them."

These new realities, taken separately or as a whole, point not only to what Friedrich Schiller in his 1788 poem "Die entgötterte Natur" called the "disenchantment of nature," but also to a "disenchantment of geographic space," which today tends to be completely rationalized, subject to preestablished rules that include their own essence.

According to Condorcet (cited in Séris 1994: 160) in his *Éloge de vau-canson*, the genius of mechanics is that it "mainly consists of different available mechanisms in space that can produce a given effect and that serve to regulate, distribute, and manage the driving force." For Séris himself (1994: 160), this idea should be placed alongside that of Henri Bergson, who defines space as "the framework for our possible action on things" (1991: 628).

In truth, with the advent of rational space, space itself becomes a true machine whose energy is information and where the things themselves constitute the framework of our possible action.

In the historic evolution of geographic space, the technical-scientific milieu represents the arrival at the level of calculability, according to Weber, necessary to impose capitalist law "on anything as if with a machine."

This technical-scientific milieu is made up of objects that incorporate technical knowledge and support hegemonic knowledge, while other spaces become mere spaces of doing.

Through new actions and objects, regional relationships that had previously been called "dependent" take on this new rationality as their content. There is also a new form of centrality dependent on this rationality, one which is unevenly distributed. New information-laden central spaces replace the previous concept and function of the "core," as defined by Friedmann (1963) and Boudeville (1964). In this new configuration, there are rational spaces marked by science, technology, and information; and there are other spaces. There are spaces that command and spaces that obey. This systemic rationality does not, however, occur in a complete and homogenous way. Zones exist where it has a lesser presence or where it is even nonexistent, where other forms of expression exist with their own logic.

THE LIMITS OF RATIONALITY IN
THE COUNTRY AND THE CITY

With globalization, agricultural specialization based in science and technique inserts the field of modernization into a competitive logic that accelerates the arrival of rationality into all aspects of productive activity, from the reorganization of territory to the models of exchange, and even into interpersonal relations. Competition leads to the deepening of new technical relations and new capitalist relations that become the bases for the expansion of cooperation and, therefore, of the social and territorial division of labor. This expansion of context also creates a new deepening of context that brings corresponding areas into an intensifying process of rationalization that tends to establish itself in all aspects of life.

This process generates a rural world that is practically without mystery, where each action and each outcome ought to be predictable in a way that ensures the maximum possible productivity and profit. Plants and animals are no longer passed down over generations but rather are created through biotechnology; the techniques that serve production, storage, transport, and the transformation of products and their distribution all respond to a global model and are calculated to achieve pragmatic objectives that become more attainable as the calculation of their selection and implantation becomes more precise. This creates strange nexuses within local and also national society, which play particular roles and present themselves as cause and consequence of technical and organizational innovation. The whole is moved by the (external) force of commercial myths, this logic of the market that imposes itself as the motor of consumption and production.

These conditions in the countryside mimic industry in the unending search for increasing precision. Benjamin Coriat's (1982) parable is emblematic of this dynamic. He used the example of the "*ateliê* and the chronometer" to describe Taylorism, which we might reinterpret today as "the countryside and the chronometer." In this domesticated rural world, an empire of measured time takes hold in pursuit of new regularities. Many such regularities only become possible when the desire to eliminate natural laws triumphs. The traditional respect for natural conditions (land, water, and so on) is displaced, in different proportions and depending on which products and regions are at play, by a new agricultural calendar based in science, technique, and knowledge.

This world of invasive techniques is also the world of invasive technological capital that seeks to, and does, infect different rural undertakings. In the process, it expands the domination of this hegemonic capital into the country, with its demands for rationality imposing new uses and definitions of social time. Together, new techniques and new capital cease to be exclusive to one particular domain of activity and spread to the entire social body, thus becoming some of the key regulators of social time.

They create new models of action and new sociabilities that are also at the root of new forms of urbanization: cities become depositories for new components of agricultural work and poles for their regulation. On the one hand, we see the presence of technological capital that must be on hand to attend, in the precise moment, the requirements of each step in the production process. On the other hand, we see financial capital destined to provide, at the proper time and place, the necessary financial resources. There is also knowledge capital, which an agriculture based in science cannot do without. If we also take the possible stores of education, health, leisure, and security that the consuming population require into consideration, it becomes clear how cities have taken on such substantial capitalist content. Their adaptation to the modernized countryside is more obvious as they are better able to respond to the demands of rationality in rural areas.

In the city, the expanding division of labor intensifies capitalist socialization dominated by exchange value. Today the expansion of urbanization and the importance of the urban phenomenon serve as a basis for more rationalization, which increases with greater articulation with the technified and modernized country and the more complex interdependencies between cities. Within these, modern activities tend to be increasingly subject to the realm of hours, clocks, norms, regulations, and prohibitions. This is not only a privilege of industry; it also extends to services.

Technical macrosystems, indispensable in this phase of globalization, play a crucial role in explaining the tendency toward the rationalization of cities, as do domestic techniques, which are the invisible techniques that play a role in ordering people's everyday life. Every aspect of life, however, is not colonized by modern techniques. The different parts of the city distinguish themselves according to their respective differences in technical and informational density. Technical objects somehow form the foundation of the use-values and exchange-values of different parts of the city. It could be said that, taken in their technical reality and their regular uses, infrastructure "regulates" behavior and therefore "chooses" or "selects" possible actors. Certain spaces of production, circulation, and consumption are where "rational" actors operate, while other actors are content to operate within parts of the city that are less equipped with information and technique. Human action is compartmentalized according to levels of the rationality of material.

Plans for economic adjustment that respond to a demand for rationality intensify the situation described above, because the imperative for competition accelerates the modernization of certain parts of the city to the detriment of the rest. The creation and use of social resources and collective goods becomes irrational. Globalization, therefore, has a determining role in the production of "irrationality" and the irrational use of the urban machine.

In fact, the city has been created by its excluded people and their irrationalities. The process of globalization is accelerating this tendency. It generates a simultaneous demand for productivity by privileged actors and a production of irrationality for the majority of people.

In the country and in cities, the understanding and critique of hegemonic rationality happens through the use of technique alongside experiences of shortage.

The modernized countryside is the location of new monocultures and new productive associations that are anchored in science and technique and dependent on an information without which no profitable work is possible. The diffusion of this information across a continuous space assures that a given area has a certain set of common concerns, even if the interests of different actors located there may be diverse. That solidarity frequently manifests as a particular way of exercising politics, in defense of particular interests, linked to the day to day of products and producers. This activity takes many different forms, from the defense of prices to the demand for tools and the guaranteeing of markets. Concerns that were originally economic therefore become political.

To the extent that local rural or urban agents of agricultural production have a limited power of control over what is produced locally, the knowledge of relations between local production and the global aspects of exchange accelerate this political production, therefore appearing as a limit on rationality, a desire to counter it, or the wish to superimpose other objectives onto it.

Adaptation to imperatives of globalized modernization is more challenging in the city than it is in the country. In the city, it is more difficult to rebuild the physical infrastructure than it is in the rural world. The city's fixed capital is more durably fixed in place in ways that make it rigid, such that it resists a more rapid and broader diffusion of contemporaneous rationality. While new objects are established (smart buildings, rapid travel passes, infrastructure) in some urban areas, most of the urban agglomeration consists of objects inherited from other eras.

New objects are expensive. Calls to create them in the name of modernization and economic globalization indicate governmental acceptance of an order of priorities that privileges a small group of actors, relegating everyone else (small businesses, less structured institutions, and people) to a secondary plane and thereby aggravating social problems. It also means that while some actors are able to take advantage of public resources in order to fully realize their goals (fluidity, meeting new technical needs of production), the rest—that is, the majority—have no adequate way to meet their basic needs. In other words, there is a limited production of rationality associated with a greater production of scarcity.

Urban space brings together areas with very different technical and socioeconomic content. This can be seen in the example of biodiversity, or of a sociospatial diversity, located in the sociotechnical ecologies re-created throughout urban history and expanded in the current moment. This diversity assures that cities—especially large ones—can develop different types of activities through different techniques of capital and organization. It makes it possible for cities to house all types of capital and all types of work. This is, in other words, their wealth.

The urban landscape also brings together different types of material time, thereby allowing for different economic and social behaviors. While "luminous" areas are the sites for the vectors of globalizing modernity, the parts of the city that "get old" can operate without being subjected to the dynamics at play in these nexuses, escaping the direct regulation of hegemonic economic and social actors.

Different productive modes, modalities of exchange, and forms of distribution and consumption are established according to levels of capital, of work, of information, and organization necessary to produce a particular good or service. In any given city there are different particular logics enacted at each of these levels of activity. The superposition of these individual and complementary logics produces, in each agglomeration, a unitary urban logic.

Within each city the principle of unity is created by both the market and territory, which unify the different elements of urban life. The urban market and the urban territory are inseparable ideas and interdependent realities that consist of submarkets and spatial subcircuits for specific production, each of which has their own rationality.

We could intellectually construct an explanation of these new urban ecologies—of the relations between the market, institutions, and the so-called built environment—to understand, in each case, the relations between the temporality of doing and the temporality of things, to the extent that they condition the moments and the modalities of that doing through their technical structure and their spatial arrangement.

In the face of the dominant rationality that seeks to take over everything, we could speak, from the point of view of the actors who do not benefit from that rationality, of irrationality, of the deliberate production of nonreasonable situations. In other words, we might argue that from this hegemonic rationality, counterrationalities also establish themselves.

These counterrationalities are located, socially, among the poor, migrants, the excluded, and minorities; economically, within marginal, traditional, or recently marginalized activities; and, geographically, in the less modern and more "opaque" areas, which are rendered irrational for hegemonic use. All of these situations are defined by the fact that they cannot be completely subordinated to the dominant rationality, given that they do not have the means to access contemporary material modernity. This experience of scarcity is the basis for a creative adaptation to existing reality.

What many consider, adjectivally, to be "irrationality"—and, dialectically, "counter-rationality"—constitutes, in fact, other forms of rationality, or parallel rationalities, that are divergent and convergent at the same time. We can echo Godelier's (1972: 312) argument that "there is no rationality in and of itself, nor an absolute rationality." We can also recall Schutz's (1987b: 51) argument that the concept of rationality, "in a strict sense . . . does not refer to actions within the common experience of everyday life in the social world, but rather is an expression of a *particular* type of construction of certain specific models."

Weber himself, in *The Protestant Ethic*, predicted the coexistence of different rationalities when he wrote, "A thing is never irrational in itself, but only from a particular point of view" (1958: 194). Indeed, it is important to bear in mind his other declaration in this same book and in others, where he predicted the loss of reason by society, when the process of the expansion of capitalist rationality became unlimited. The moment in which we are living—and the rationalization of space is this limit—points toward this loss of reason. But, simultaneously, and happily, it also points toward the possibility of a new sense, based precisely in the elaboration of counter-rationalities that geographic analysis reveals in the daily behaviors in the country and the city.

The fact that the limited production of rationality is associated with the widespread production of scarcity leads actors who are outside of the circulation of the hegemonic rationality to discover and understand their exclusion and to seek alternative forms of rationality that are indispensable to their survival. As such, the dominant and blind rationality ends up producing its own limits.

IV

THE POWER
OF PLACE

14

Place and
the Everyday

In the current conditions of globalization, it appears that Pascal's metaphor has become reality: the universe can be seen as an infinite sphere whose center is everywhere. One could similarly repeat Tolstoy's famous saying that if you want to be universal, you must begin in your own village.

Michel Serres (1990) similarly reminds us, "Our relationship with the world has changed. What used to be a local-local relationship is now local-global." Deploying a more or less geographic framework, he further argues that "today we have a new relationship with the world, because we can see it in its entirety through satellite imagery; we have images of the whole entire earth."

In practice, globalization also means the rediscovery of corporeality. The world of fluidity, the dizziness of velocity, the frequency of dislocation, the banality of movement, and the constant allusions to places and distant things reveal in human beings, in contrast, the body as materially sensitive certainty in the face of a universe that is difficult to comprehend. We might therefore quote Edgar Morin (1990: 44) in saying that "today each of us is like a singular point in a hologram that, in a sense, contains all of the planet which contains it."

Places, from this point of view, can be seen as intermediaries between the world and the individual, according to Mlinar (1990: 57), for whom the logic of the development of social systems can be seen in the union of opposing tendencies toward individuality and globality.

This is a tense reality, a dynamism recreated in each moment, a permanently unstable relationship in which globalization and localization, or globalization and fragmentation, are the terms of a frequently remade dialectic. The demands of the new regime of accumulation create a greater dissociation between different processes and subprocesses, the multiplicity of actions using space to make complex forces and fields, as the result of the individualization and minute spatialization of the elements of space—people, businesses, institutions, the built environment—while it simultaneously deepens the relationship that each of those elements has to the world system.

Each place is, in its way, the world. Or, as M. A. A. de Souza (1995: 65) put it, "All places are virtually global." That is to say that each place is undeniably immersed in a unity with the world, and yet each place can also become exponentially different from all other places. In other words, the largest globality has the correspondingly largest individuality. Benko (1990: 65) called this phenomenon "glocality" and highlighted the challenges to theorizing it. Given that the world can be encountered everywhere, he argued, a "localist" view is insufficient for understanding the changing reality of place. He cautioned that in trying to theorize this situation "we should not risk losing ourselves in a blind simplification" based in an idea of particularity that only accounts for "the general phenomenon created by global social forces" (Benko 1990: 65).

The concrete history of our time makes the question of place a central one, as geographers have emphasized.

Revisiting the question of place in the current world demands that we understand its new meanings. We might do this through a consideration of the everyday (Buttimer 1976; Damiani 1994; García Ballesteros 1992). This category of existence lends itself to a geographic analysis of the lived world that accounts for the variables we have investigated in this book: objects, actions, technique, and time.

RATIONAL ACTIVITY, SYMBOLIC ACTIVITY, AND SPACE

In Weber's widely recognized typology of social action he distinguishes between a rational action with a practical goal and a communicative action mediated by symbols. Habermas (1971; 1973; 1987) and other later authors also took up this question more broadly and deeply to investigate the role of social interaction in the production of social systems. Simondon (1989) had also theorized a difference, based on technical phenomena, between a human action on the milieu, on the one hand, and on the other, a symbolic action on human beings. Without making it explicit, Stiegler (1994: 25) also approximated these two propositions, reinterpreting Gehlen and Habermas to explore the opposition between an interaction mediated by techniques and their rationality, and an interaction mediated by symbols and communicative action.

A given situation cannot be fully understood if, on the pretext of analyzing its objectivity, we fail to consider the intersubjective relations that characterize it. Berger (1964: 173), for example, argued that the "human character of the time of action is *intersubjective*." And Bakhtin (1993: 54), whose position is more similar to ours, argued that the concrete architecture of the contemporary world of realized action has three "basic moments: the I-for-myself; the other-for-me; and the I-for-the-other." In other words, we construct and remake values through a continual process of interaction.

José Luiz Rodrigues Garcia (1994: 75) invites us to establish a clear distinction between information and communication. He argues, "It is possible for us to communicate with the world surrounding us, with others, and even with our own selves, without transmitting any information and without creating or cultivating any social links." For him, "in a communicational experience, dialogic and interactive processes intervene to create, cultivate, and re-establish social ties and sociability between individuals and social groups that share the same frameworks of experience and identify the same historical resonances of a common past."

"Etymologically," Laborit (1987: 38) reminds us, "to communicate means to place in common." This process, in which different interpretations of what exists—objective situations—come into play, is the outcome of a true social negotiation among both pragmatic concerns and symbolic values, "points of view that are more or less shared" in variable proportions, according to Sander van der Leecew (1994: 34). In this formulation, in addition to the subject itself, things and other people are also at play. Or in other words, as Berger puts it (1964: 15), "The idea of others itself implies the idea of a world."

According to Tian-Duc-Thao (1971: 260), the "symbolic sketches" that emerge from the movement of cooperation prolong the activity of the subject itself and encompass the totality of the common task, such that each subject becomes conscious of the fact that universality is the true meaning of their singular existence.

"Praxis also reveals itself as totality," according to Lefebvre (1958: 238), which is why "an analysis of everyday life involves conceptions and investigations at the scale of social experience in general" (Lefebvre 1971: 28)—which also includes, in parallel, what Sartre (1960: 207) called "a profound appropriation and an immediate understanding."

We might say, then, that the world takes on meaning because it is a *common* object, accessed through relations of reciprocity that simultaneously produce alterity and communication. This makes it possible for, as Berger argues (1964: 15), the world to constitute "the means to unite us without confusing us."

Similarly, Simondon's (1989: 248) "trans-individuality" is constituted by the interhuman relations that include the use of techniques and technical objects. Territoriality is also transindividuality, and the sharing of human interaction in space (Raffestin 1980: 146; Sanguin 1977: 53; Soja 1971) is both an element of territoriality and of transindividuality.

The relation of the subject with the "practico-inert" includes its relation with space. *Practico-inert* is Sartre's term to explain the crystallization of past individual and societal experience embodied in contemporary social forms, spatial configurations, and landscapes. Building on Sartre's teachings, we can also say that space, through its geographic material forms, is the most complete expression of practico-inert.

THE ROLE OF PROXIMITY

In space—which is a differentiated whole—the practico-inert unity of multiplicity that André Gorz (1964) discusses, this "exterior unity of the activity of individuals in their condition as the representative of the other," imposes itself more strongly. Space occurs among the group of people who act within it as a set of virtualities of unequal value; they struggle over its use in every moment, according to the power of each individual. We can compare this situation to what Sartre (1960: 210) called the phenomenon of scarcity. As Sartre put it, scarcity can be understood as a situation where each person or group knows that "it functions as an object in the practical field of the other," and "this is precisely what prevents the two movements of practical unification from constituting, with the same environment, two different fields of action."

The idea of sociality that proliferates among sociologists is also further explored by geographers like Di Meo (1991b) and Lévy (1994). According to Schutz (1967) sociality intensifies as the proximity among people increases. Simmel (1903: 47) had already pointed out the difference between extreme spatial distance and social proximity (Werlen 1993: 170). We could say, as Muniz Sodré (1988: 18) does, that "the spatial relation, incomprehensible in the terms of the classical structures of action and representation, is intelligible as a principle of coexistence of diversity" and therefore guarantees the exercise of multiple possibilities of communication.

Economists also concern themselves with this question of proximity, conceiving of distance as a key factor structuring international commerce (Berthelot 1994: 15–16). But the proximity that interests the geographer—as we have argued—is not limited to distance, simply defined. Instead, for geographers, proximity refers to the physical continuity among people in the same area, within the same group of continuous points, living with intense interrelations. In other words, we should not only analyze economic relations in terms of proximity; we should analyze the totality of relations in this way, which will allow us to explain how proximity "can create solidarity, cultural links and also identity" (Guigou 1995: 56).

Jean Duvignaud (1977: 20) addresses role of proximity in the production of consciousness in his discussion of "social density," which he argues is a product of the fermentation of people in a single, enclosed space, an "accumulation that provokes a surprising change," moved by affectivity and passion, and generating a global, "holistic," perception of the world of people. A cursory reading of his discussion of "closed spaces" [*espace clos*; *huis-clos*], could lead one to believe that the situation described above would be limited to fortified places that are marked by a fear of an external enemy and protected behind big walls, such as medieval cities. In reality, because of the structure of their territory and their market—one and multiple—contemporary cities, particularly megacities, which are open to everyone and to global currents, are no less individualized. With their infinite array of situations, contemporary cities are sites of production for numerous, frequent, and dense relations. For example, the number of internal trips made within a city is many times greater than departures made from a city to other places. Under similar conditions, large cities are much more frantic than medium or small ones; there are more encounters and more mobility. The contemporary anarchy of the big city ensures a greater amount of travel and generates greater numbers of interpersonal relations. Movement is compounded in underdeveloped countries because of the enormous range of different personal situations for generating income, the disproportionate size of the megacities, and the lower coefficient of "rationality" in the operation of the urban machine.

Within them, copresence or exchange are conditioned by the existing infrastructure and its norms of use, by the territorially delimited market, and by the possibilities of culturally local life (itself dependent on the existing infrastructure). The division of labor within these cities is not only an outcome of economic factors, but rather of the intersection of all of these different factors.

The idea of copresence has been used by sociology since its founding. This idea, emphasized by Erving Goffman (1961) and then again later by Anthony Giddens (1987), takes on a new dimension when put into conversation with the geographic notion of proximity, or the "residential group," to follow Sartre's (1960) terminology in *Search for a Method*. Shared territory imposes interdependence as praxis, and this "base of operation" of the "community" (Parsons and Shils 1952: 91) constitutes an inevitable mediation for the exercise of the specific roles by each individual (Werlen 1993: 1990). In cities, where people who do not even know one another work together to produce collective results, copresence can be seen even more clearly.

Long ago Teilhard de Chardin discussed what he called the "human pressure" resulting from the accumulation of people in limited spaces, as a factor in the rapid qualitative changes in social relations in the contemporary world (cited in Berger 1964: 249–50). Gaston Berger (1964: 249) also commented on this phenomenon, emphasizing that "agitation, and the ray of actions and relations are simultaneously augmented" among people. He compared this to the physical phenomenon through which the gas pressure grows as temperature increases, which is to say, as the particles become more agitated. It is worth recognizing, as Berger did, that "today masses that were previously stationary are entering the scene."

This phenomenon is even more significant because today popular culture is no longer tied to a particular, restricted geography. Instead, it finds a multitudinous stage in the large arenas and stadiums and the enormous houses of spectacle and diversion, and also because of the ubiquitous special effects created by technotronic multiplier machines. Popular culture takes a sort of revenge on certain aspects of mass culture and is constitutionally destined to suffocate it. A pop culture of the masses emerges, fed by a spontaneous criticism of the repetitive everyday and often preaching change, even if it does not contain a systematic proposal. According to Funtowicz and Ravetz (1993), "The 'permissive' mass culture of the twentieth century extracted a new freedom from a cultural system that was previously repressive and hierarchical."

THE SPATIAL DIMENSION OF THE EVERYDAY

As information and communication have taken on greater roles in all aspects of social life, the everyday of everybody has taken on new dimensions. Among these, the spatial dimension in particular has become more important at the same time that this enriched everyday imposes a kind of "fifth dimension" of banal space—the space of geographers.

By developing an understanding of this geographic content of the everyday we can, perhaps, contribute to the necessary understanding (and perhaps theorization) of the relationship between space and social movements, seeing materially this indecipherable component of geographic space which is, simultaneously, a condition for action, a structure of control, a limit on action, and an invitation to action. We cannot do anything today that is not based on the objects around us.

And while other specialists can choose from the list of actions and the population of objects based on whatever is of interest to their particular specializations, the geographer is obliged to work with all objects and all actions.

Space therefore includes this "materialistic connection of men with one another" that Marx and Engels discussed in *The German Ideology* (1947: 18–19), a connection that "is ever taking on new forms." The current form, as we have discussed, both depends on information and itself constitutes information because of the intentionality of its production. Given that today we cannot do anything without the objects around us, everything that we do produces information.

Locality opposes globality, but it is also confused with it. The world, however, is our stranger. Although it may be able to hide its essence, it cannot hide its existence, which manifests in places. In place, in our surroundings, the axes of succession that transport external time from greater scales, as well as internal times from the axes of coexistence, superimpose themselves on one another dialectically, such that the understandings and realities of space and time merge, are knitted together definitively.

In place—an everyday shared among many different people, firms, and institutions—cooperation and conflict are the basis for life in common. Because each individual firm or institution exercises their own action, social life individualizes; and because contiguity is the creator of communalism, politics territorializes in the confrontation between organization and spontaneity. Place is the framework for a pragmatic reference to the world in which solicitations and precise orders for conditional actions emerge, and place is also the irreplaceable theater for human desires and responsibilities, through communicative action, through the most diverse manifestations of spontaneity and creativity.

With contemporary modernization, all places globalize [*se mundializam*], but global places can be either simple or complex. Simple global places have only a few vectors of contemporary modernity. Complex global places tend to be megacities with a proliferation of different kinds of vectors that range from those that directly represent hegemonic logic to those that oppose them. Different kinds of vectors have different purposes, some of which may even be external, but they are all intertwined in common places. That is why big cities, the most significant of places, are such enormous, banal spaces. All types of capital, labor, techniques, and forms of organization can exist side by side and prosper there. Today the big city is also the space where the poor can survive.

For a long time, the metropolis in underdeveloped countries was understood to be a place where national resources were located and the capitalist density was highest. This organization was the basis for the development of core and periphery theories by thinkers such as Myrdal (1957), Hirschman (1958), Perroux (1961), John Friedmann (1963), and Boudeville (1964). Today, as a result of the proliferation of networks and the subsequent diffusion of modernity across territory, new capital is dispersed much more broadly, more deeply, and more rapidly in the countryside than in the city. In fact, the built environment of the city is itself often an obstacle to the diffusion of new capital. Because of its geographic configuration, the city, especially big cities, appears to have a sociospatial diversity akin to the biodiversity that is today so dear to the environmental movement. As the site of activity for all different types of capital and of labor, the big city can attract and accommodate the multitudes of poor people who have been expelled from the countryside and from medium-sized cities because of agricultural and service sector modernization. The presence of the poor increases and enriches cities' sociospatial diversity, produces different kinds of neighborhoods, and also different types of work and of life. As a result, both people's needs and the forms of the division of labor develop as possibilities and pathways for intersubjectivity and interaction. That is the location where the city encounters its path to the future.

Here we do not intend to reproduce the old, dual (though not dualist) framework for analyzing the urban economy that was first used to analyze the countries of the Third World (Santos 1996c) but that today has been extended to rich countries, recognizing the existence of the so-called informal sector alongside the so-called formal economy. One could, however, recognize that in contemporary conditions—permeated by an infinitude of intermediary situations—there are two situations in all big cities. There is an explicitly globalized economy, produced *from above*, and another sector produced *from below,* which in the poor countries is a popular sector and in wealthy countries includes the unprivileged sectors of society, including immigrants. Each one is responsible for establishing typical divisions of labor. In all cases, the city is a large system, the product of the superposition of different subsystems of cooperation, which creates many other systems of solidarity. In contemporary conditions of globalization, all of these subsystems of solidarity tend to have specializations that are different in nature. We might say that there is a specialization of activities above and a specialization of activities below. But the former is rigid, dependent on implacable norms, the obedience to which depends on its efficiency. We say that these norms are complex because of their scientific and technological content and their search for precision in the productive process. But could we not also say that, in the poorer economy, the divisions of labor considered to be "simpler" by the dominant discourse are, in fact, more complex?

In the big cities, especially in those of the Third World, the precarious existence of a large part (sometimes the majority) of the population does not preclude the production of needs based on the consumption of the wealthiest classes. In response, an imitative division of labor, perhaps a caricature, finds a rationale to establish and reproduce itself. But here the occupational framework is not fixed: each actor is very mobile, able to engage in different activities according to the flavor of the moment without any trauma, depending on the circumstance. These metamorphoses in the work of poor people in large cities create what we have elsewhere (Santos 1991a) called "tropical flexibility." There is an infinite variety of occupations, a multiplicity of combinations in permanent movement, endowed with a great capacity for adaptation and sustained within their own geographic environment, which is understood to be a content form, a hybrid of materiality and social relations. Such different and changing forms of the division of labor are adaptable, unstable, and plastic; their adaptation is driven by internal and external compulsions. Their solidarity is created and re-created in that process, while the solidarity imposed by the hegemonic cooperation is commanded from a point outside of the geographic and social milieus that it affects.

In the first case, relations of proximity are particularly important, guaranteeing communication among participants. In this sense, in urban ghettos more so than in other parts of the city, relations of proximity tend to have a greater communicational content because people there have a clearer understanding of each other's personal situations and a greater sense of shared fate, or of a shared cultural and economic situation.

For centuries, we believed that the fastest people had the greatest intelligence in the world (Virilio 1977: 54). The literature that glorifies power treats velocity as the magical force that allowed Europe to first become civilized and then to impose "its" civilization on everyone else (Valéry 1922: 1014; cited in Beaud 1987: 4 and Pascallon 1986: 23). Now we are discovering that, in cities, the time that commands or that will command in the future is actually the time of slow people. In other words, today what happens in big cities is the complete opposite. Power comes from the "slow people" rather than from those who control speed and who were celebrated by a delirious Virilio, inspired by the work of the dreamer Valéry. Those who, within the city, have the most mobility end up seeing very little of the city and of the world. Their intimacy with prefabricated images is their perdition. Their comfort, which they do not want to give up, comes precisely from their cohabitation with these images. The "slow" people, for whom these images are only a mirage, cannot for long periods engage with a perverse imaginary and discover fantasies.

This is how they escape the totalitarianism of rationality, which is ultimately impossible for the rich and the middle classes. Condemned by a repetitive sociological literature that is oriented to the present, it is the poor in the city can look more fixedly toward the future.

In the "luminous" modern city today, the "naturalness" of the technical object creates a routine mechanics, a system of signs without surprise. This historicization of metaphysics spurs the development of urban areas with a modern flavor that are juxtaposed, superimposed, and counterposed to the uses of city in the spaces where the poor live, in the "opaque" urban areas. These are the spaces of approximation and of creativity, as opposed to the "luminous" zones, the exacting spaces of urban modernity. The inorganic spaces are open, and the regular spaces are closed, rationalized, and rationalizing.

Because they are "different," the poor open a new and unprecedented debate, sometimes quiet and sometimes loud, among the existing populations and things. In doing so they reevaluate the technosphere and the psychosphere in order to find new uses and ends for objects and techniques, as well as new practical articulations and new norms in social and affective life. In the face of technical and informational networks, migrants and the poor are passive, just like everybody else. But in the communicational sphere, they are active, unlike the so-called upper classes.

They are the search for a future, imagined as needs to be satisfied—for material and immaterial consumption, as well for political consumption in the form of participation and citizenship. This future is imagined or glimpsed in the abundance of the other and has its counterpart in the possibilities presented by the world and perceived in place.

Thus, the spell turns against the sorcerer. Consumption that is envisioned but not realized—this "fundamental need" as Sartre put it—produces a creative discomfort. The shock between subjective and objective culture becomes an instrument for the production of a new consciousness.

According to Rimbaud (1973: 283), "The city transforms everything, including inert material, into elements of culture." Culture, or the forms through which people and groups communicate with the universe, is inherited and also relearned through the profound relations between people and their environment.

But: "What culture are we talking about? Are we talking about mass culture, fed by things, or of profound culture, popular culture, fed by people? Mass culture, which is called culture because it is hegemonic, is often a palliative for consciousness. The moment of consciousness occurs when individuals and groups throw off a system of customs, recognizing them as a game or a limitation" (Santos 1992: 64).

The mollified middle classes allow themselves to be absorbed into mass culture and then they rationalize their impoverished existence through that culture. The needy, especially those in extreme poverty, are not absorbed into mass culture in this way, in part because they do not have the resources to acquire the things that would inculcate them into it and assure their participation in it. As a result, cities, which are increasingly unequal, tend to house simultaneously a mass culture and a popular culture that collaborate and clash, interfere with one another and exclude one another, come together and separate themselves in an unending dialectical game.

Mass culture is generally indifferent to social ecology; it tends toward uniformity and nondifferentiation. Popular culture, on the other hand, is rooted in the land where it exists; it symbolizes people and their environment, embodying the desire to confront the future without breaking from place, thereby obtaining continuity through change. Its framework and its limits are the profound relations that establish themselves between people and their environment, and those relations have a global reach.

This search for pathways is itself an illuminated vision of the future that is not bound by a present subalternized by the hegemonic instrumental logic or imprisoned within a stigmatized daily life. It embodies the victory of reinforced individuality that transcends the barricade of repetitive praxis and instead establishes a liberating praxis, or what Lefebvre called an inventive praxis (1958: 240).

MIGRANTS IN PLACE: FROM MEMORY TO DISCOVERY

We live in changing times. In many cases, the mind-boggling succession of events means that we experience not only change, but vertigo. In the past, the subject in place had a long and repetitive coexistence with the same objects, paths, and images, which generated a level of familiarity that was the product of its own history, of local society and of place, where each individual was active.

Today mobility has practically become a rule. Movement overlaps with rest. Circulation is more creative than production. People move from place to place like tourists or immigrants, as do products, commodities, images, and ideas. Everything flies. In this context *deterritorialization* emerges. Deterritorialization is often another word for estrangement, or even deculturation.

To come to the big city is to leave behind an inherited culture in order to encounter a different one. When a person encounters a space that they did not help to create, whose history they do not know, and whose memory is strange to them, that place is the point of a strong alienation.

But, in a world of movement, reality and the idea of residence (Husserl, Heidegger, Sartre) do not disappear. People reside perhaps less, or for much less time, but they still reside: even if they are unemployed or migrants. "Residence," and the workplace, however short their duration, are frameworks for life that carry weight in the production of people. As Husserl said (1975: 26), "The permanent basis of the subjective work of thinking is the vital environment."

According to David Lowenthal (1975), the past is another country. We might reinterpret this to say that the past is another place—or better, in another place. In a new place, the past is not present; we must instead face the future: we may experience perplexity at first, but then we confront the need to orient ourselves. For migrants in this situation, memory is useless. They carry with them a whole body of memories and experiences created in another milieu and that will not serve them sufficiently in their daily struggle. They must create a third way to understand the city. Their lived experiences are left behind and their new residence obliges them to have new experiences. It creates a clash between the time of action and the time of memory. Obliged to forget, their discourse is less contaminated by the past or by routine. They have the privilege, pragmatically and practically, not to utilize the practico-inert (that comes from other places) that they are the bearers of.

After an initial moment of surprise and shock, they reawaken their alert spirit, reformulating the idea of the future based in a new understanding of the new reality in which they find themselves. The lived environment is the place of a change, the matrix of an intellectual process.

In this context, people seek to relearn what they were never taught, and little by little to replace their ignorance of their environment with a knowledge of it, albeit a knowledge that may be fragmented or partial.

The new environment operates as a sort of spark. Its relations with the new inhabitants manifest dialectically as new territoriality and new culture, which intervene in one another, so that territoriality and culture move in parallel, and in doing so, change people themselves. As one comes to understand this synthesis, the process of alienation gives way to the process of integration and understanding, and the individual recuperates a part of their being that had seemed to be lost.

To what extent, then, is "long-term" territoriality more important than "short-term"? Collective memory tends to be regarded as a social glue indispensable to the survival of societies, an element of cohesion that guarantees the permanence and development of the future. This thesis is so powerful that today, in the face of a society and a culture that is in a state of perpetual agitation, the culture of movement is regarded as the primary driver of disaggregation and anomie.

But we also know that events erase existing knowledge and demand new knowledges. Today events are more numerous and unprecedented everywhere such that one's active or conscious reintegration into the framework of local or global life depends less and less on experience and more and more on discovery.

It does not matter that, in the face of contemporary acceleration, and due to the clutter of events, the exercise of rethinking requires a heroic effort. This prohibition on resting, this generalized urgency, this state of alarm demands a motivation, a disposition, and a renewing force from the conscience.

The force of this movement comes from the fact that, while memory is collective, forgetting and the consequent (re)discovery are individual, differentiated, enriched through interpersonal relations, and communicative action. As such, what was thought to be a weakness is actually an advantage.

Contrary to what today's hegemonic theory might lead us to believe, the less securely an individual (the poor, the minority, the migrant) is located within the hegemonic framework, the more easily they encounter the shock of the new and they can therefore more easily discover new knowledge.

The excluded are the bearers of a memory, a sort of congealed conscience, that they bring from another place. The new place obliges new learning and a new formulation.

Memory looks to the past. A new consciousness looks to the future. Space is a fundamental given in this discovery. It is the theater of this renewal because it is, simultaneously, the immediate future and the immediate past, and a present that is simultaneously concluded and inconclusive—marking a process of continual renewal.

The more unstable and surprising space is, the more surprised an individual will be and the more effective the operation of discovery. The consciousness *of place* is superimposed by the consciousness *in place*. The idea of unknown space therefore loses its negative connotation and takes on a positive one, as a product of its role in the production of a new history.

The present is not merely the result or a consequence of the past, just as the future cannot be a consequence of the present, even if this is an "eternal novelty," in the words of Borelli (1992: 80). The past can be better understood as one of the conditions for the realization of the event, but the present itself—understood as the selective conjunction of existing forces in a given moment—is the dynamic data central to the production of a new history. In reality, if, as Sartre said, Man is a Project, then we need to recognize that the future drives the actions of the present.

Universal Order, Local Order
Summary and Conclusion

INTRODUCTION

We have seen how the movement toward the rationalization of society that marked the Enlightenment and the beginning of the industrial revolution, and that then slowly came to occupy all corners of social life, has today reached a new level that we might call the rationalization of geographic space.

We have also seen that this new step in the secular process of rationalization is fundamentally tied to the emergence of a technical-scientific-informational milieu that seeks to replace the natural milieu, and even the technical milieu, in order to produce spaces of rationality and support key globalized actions. We have tried to show how contemporary techniques functioning in the ongoing worldwide revolution drive this process. This technique, now present in all aspects of life, is in itself an order, a *technical order* that is inseparable from a *planetary social order* that sits above it; together they create new relations between space and time, which are today empirically unified.

An examination of the geographic reality produced by these transformations raises a series of questions. In the context of our problematic, we have underscored three in particular:

1 We consider this reconfigured geographic space to be an indissociable set of systems of objects and systems of actions. This question has been addressed in previous chapters.

2 On the global plane, all actions, even "deterritorialized" ones, create use norms for localized systems of objects; while on the local plane, territory itself constitutes a norm for the exercise of actions.

3 Based in these two orders, a global reason and a local reason constituted in parallel are, in each place, superimposed on each other in a dialectical process in which they simultaneously associate with and contradict one another. In this sense, *the place* faces *the world*, but also confronts it because of its own order.

OBJECTS AND ACTIONS

Given that geographic space is always an indissociable set of systems of objects and systems of actions, it manifests differently in different historical moments according to the nature of the objects and actions present in each period. Because technique is also social, the system of objects and system of actions together constitute technical systems, and the succession of those systems makes up the history of geographic space.

The objects that constitute contemporary geographic space are intentionally designed to act in particular ways. The resulting spatial order is also intentional. Technical objects produced using science and technology are meant to have even more functional precision than nature itself. They are therefore more precise than natural objects, and they act as the material bases for actions representative of the current moment.

We live the world of action in *real time*. Because we have the ability to accurately predict the steps of action, temporal order resulting from those steps is associated with a spatial order of objects meant to facilitate greater economic or political productivity. We might call this the possibility of rational action in a rational space. Because space is not homogenous and, in fact, evolves unequally, the diffusion of modern objects and the incidence of modern actions is not the same everywhere. More modernized subspaces can better accommodate actions that serve the interest of hegemonic actors.

A hegemonic subsystem is created within a group of subspaces based on the privileged relations established between these new objects. From these objects, the speed of the world is realized and the clock of the world occurs as a *despotic synchronization*. This despotic time is less technical than social and is only possible through the creation of competition, which is the war machine of a universal surplus value that is impossible to measure. While we can't say that things will always be this way, we can say that, in contemporary conditions, anyone who lags behind, who is not fast enough, is penalized. At the global scale, global surplus value is the implacable motor of innumerable social, economic, political, and also geographic organizations. Its weapon is competition, which in this bellicose world is the most warlike dynamic.

Even if the fact that the new space of business is the entire world (Savy and Veltz 1993: 5) guarantees that hegemonic systems will tend toward universality, what we might call the general coordination among businesses is still not yet global, since each action is directed toward a fact, a factor, an aspect, a partial dynamism.

Just as there is no single global time, only a global clock, there is also no global space, but only spaces of globalization—spaces that are globalized and brought together through networks.

Earlier we explained that networks are mixed; they are made up of materiality and action. Today's globalized technical network is an instrument of production, of circulation, and of globalized information. In this sense networks are global, and they transport the universal to the local. For example, global processes are created through telecommunications, which unite distant points within the same productive logic. This is the vertical functioning of contemporary geographic space.

But networks are also local, and, locally, they create the technical conditions of direct labor just as the global networks assure the division of labor and cooperation through the nontechnical instances of work—circulation, distribution, and consumption.

The order brought about by hegemonic vectors creates localized disorder, not only because it creates functional and structural changes but primarily because it is not the bearer of any particular meaning; given that its objective—the global market—is self-referencing, its only goal is to create the global market. In this sense, the current phase of globalization is perverse for most of humanity.

In the local milieu, the network is practically integrated or dissolved through collective work, which implies a strong solidarity among different actors. This work, carried out both in solidarity and in conflict, also coexists in continuous space, creating the contiguous everyday. We call this territorial division *horizontality* to distinguish it from the other division, which we call *verticality*. In such spaces of horizontality, the target of frequent transformations, a spatial order is permanently re-created where objects adapt to external demands and simultaneously encounter, in each moment, their own internal logic, a meaning that is all their own and is constituted locally. That is how the law of the world and the law of place come face to face.

A GLOBALIZATION OF SPACE?

Is it possible, then, to imagine a globalization of space in the sense that its management and actualization are the responsibility of the world?

The world today is primarily activated through big businesses; these global corporations produce their particular norms privately, and the duration of those norms is generally determined by factors "indifferent" to the contexts in which they operate. For their part, "global" governments like the World Bank and the International Monetary Fund care for "global" interests, but corporations and institutions rarely have a "global" force.

We might say that the World Bank exercises this role when they intervene, directly or indirectly, in the creation of infrastructure. But however significant their interventions might be, they are also topical, despite the fact that they may have profound and generalized impacts over larger and larger spaces. Thus, while the "World" intervenes in space and transforms it unilaterally, in order to respond locally to so-called global but exclusive imperatives—such as transnational interests—the complexity of spatial organization is aggravated as a collective problem.

The struggle for the use of space places big business in an active position and reserves a passive and subordinated position for everyone else. This is a conflict to be maintained, attenuated, or suppressed, depending on the circumstances—but in any case, to be regulated. The World does not have its own respective instruments of regulation; this role falls to the national and local agencies at their respective levels.

Although in the World only the global matters, in national territory everything matters. Businesses and institutions at very different scales (i.e., not only big business) coexist in conflict: coexistence is necessary, and conflict is inevitable, and, the more unequal a society and its economy, the greater the conflict. This can be seen quite clearly in underdeveloped countries and particularly in their major cities. In this context, all conflicts demand regulation, which is to say, the production of norms. While they may not always have the capacity to actually attenuate or supplant global norms, territorialized norms do confront the world, even when they adhere to global interests.

Different businesses regulate their productive needs according to the rules and processes within the firm itself, as can be seen in their vertical and horizontal relations. But the fact that such norms have become indispensable to the productive process has led to their widespread proliferation and has generated conflict among norms that the market is unable to resolve.

Many such conflicts move from the private realm into the public one. The use of space itself is a prime example of this. How can one attain a coordinated use of space when the law of competition suggests that use of space must be increasingly privatized?

One example would be speed of circulation, which is subject to local norms. For example, it is in the interest of big corporations to economize time by speeding up circulation, but the opposite is often true in the case of local communities and local businesses. Regulations regarding public road use, for example, must respond to this conflict by either finding common ground among those interests, or privileging one or another of them.

Conflicts also happen around the allocation of public resources for infrastructure. With the corporatization of territory, public resources are increasingly directed to meet the geographic needs of large companies. This shift ends up affecting the whole society because public expenditures are less and less commonly used to address social and local problems. But when the public budget, as a norm, is used to resolve a distributive conflict in favor of the globalized economy, it aggravates other, more localized conflicts because the budget itself is not global; it is national, territorialized.

The national social formation functions, therefore, as mediation between the world and the region, or place. Place is also a mediator between the world and territory.

But the sociospatial formation, more so than the socioeconomic one, does this work of mediation: this mediation is not performed by territory alone, but through territory and its use in a given moment. This presupposes that natural geographic forms and those transformed by humans have, both a material existence and juridical or customary (formal or informal) norms of use. The way that businesses utilize places depends on both of these elements. In other words, forms and norms function as an indissociable set.

And even when customary forms governing the use of national or local territory are not explicitly formulated, territory functions as a norm in and of itself because of its structure and function.

Therefore, norms and forms both come together and confront one another—with two polar situations figuring globalized action as a norm or local territory as a norm, along with a variety of intermediary situations.

There is no global space; there are only spaces of globalization. The world manifests primarily as a norm, which produces the spatialization, at different points, of its technical, informational, economic, social, political, and cultural vectors. We can say that they are "deterritorialized" actions, in that through tele-action they can separate causes from their final effect.

The world is, therefore, only a set of possibilities whose realization depends on the opportunities provided by places. This fact is fundamental today, when the competitive imperative demands that places of action be global and preselected according to which places can offer the highest level of productivity to a given production process. In this sense, the exercise of any given action is dependent on the existence, in any given place, on the local conditions that can guarantee efficient production processes.

As a result, territory becomes a key point of mediation between the world and national and local societies, because the material expression of the "world" is dependent on the mediation of places, according to their capacities for particular uses. In any given moment the world selects particular places and rejects others, and in doing so it modifies the set of places, and space as a whole.

Place is the potential site for the effective realization of the world's movement. To become space, the world depends on the virtualities of place. In this sense we might say that, locally, territorial space acts as a norm.

The two extreme situations referenced above are, then, a global deterritorialized norm and a normative local territory.

Between these two extremes, there are intermediary situations created between universality and individuality. The *universal* is the world-as-norm, a nonspatial situation but one that nevertheless creates and recreates local spaces; the *particular* is made by the country, that is, normalized territory; and the *individual* is the place, the territory-as-norm. The intermediary situation between the world and the country is an outcome of supranational regions, and the intermediary situation between the country and the place are infranational regions, legal or historical subspaces.

In each case, different combinations of norms and forms exist. In the case of the world, the form is above all a norm; and in place, the norm is above all a form.

The global order seeks to impose a single rationality on every place. And the places respond to the world according to the different modes of their own rationality.

The global order serves a sparse population of objects regulated by this single law, which constitutes them in a system. The local order is associated with a contiguous population of objects, brought together by territory and as territory.

In the former, solidarity is the product of organization. In the latter, organization is a product of solidarity. The global order and the local order constitute two situations that are genetically opposed, even while they each affirm aspects of the other. Universal reason is organization; local reason is organic. The former emphasizes information, which is also a synonym for organization. The latter emphasizes communication.

The global order creates scales that are higher than or external to that of the everyday. It is defined according to parameters of technical and operational reason, the calculation of function, mathematical language. The local order creates the scale of the everyday and is defined by copresence, closeness, intimacy, emotion, cooperation, and socialization based in contiguity.

The global order is "deterritorialized" in the sense that it separates the location of action and the source of action. Its space is unstable and inconstant, formed by points whose functional existence are dependent on external factors. The local order that "reterritorializes" comes from banal and irreducible space (Dos Santos 1994: 75), which brings together all of its elements in the same internal logic: people, businesses, institutions, social and juridical forms, and geographic forms. The immediate everyday, lived locally—and the commonality of all of this information—guarantees communication.

Each place is simultaneously an object of global and local rationality, lived dialectically.

Notes

INTRODUCTION TO THE ENGLISH-LANGUAGE EDITION

1   L. Melgaço, "Thinking Outside the Bubble of the Global North: Introducing Milton Santos and 'The Active Role of Geography' Organisers: Lucas Melgaço and Tim Clarke," *Antipode* 49, no. 4 (2017): 946–51; and F. Ferretti, "Geographies of Internationalism: Radical Development and Critical geopolitics from the Northeast of Brazil," *Political Geography* 63 (2018): 10–19.

2   Ferretti, "Geographies of Internationalism."

3   J. Cañizares-Esguerra, "How Derivative Was von Humboldt?," in *Nature, Empire, and Nation* (Palo Alto, CA: Stanford University Press, 2006), 112–28; N. Safier, "Global Knowledge on the Move: Itineraries, Amerindian Narratives, and Deep Histories of Science," *Isis* 101, no. 1 (2010): 133–45; N. Safier, "Itineraries of Atlantic Science: New Questions, New Approaches, New Directions," *Atlantic Studies* 7, no. 4 (2010): 357–64; F. Nunes, R. Rajao, and B. Soares, "Boundary Work in Climate Policy Making in Brazil: Reflections from the Frontlines of the Science-Policy Interface," *Environmental Science and Policy* 59 (2016): 85–92.

4   Melgaço, "Thinking Outside"; F. Ferretti and B. Viotto Pedrosa, "Inventing Critical Development: A Brazilian Geographer and His Northern Networks," *Transactions of the Institute of British Geographers* 43, no. 4 (2018): 703–17.

5   J. Holston, *The Modernist City: An Anthropological Critique of Brasília* (Chicago: University of Chicago Press, 1989); J. C. Scott, *Seeing Like a State* (New Haven, CT: Yale University Press, 1998).

6   Scott, *Seeing Like a State*; T. J. Finan and D. R. Nelson, "Making Rain, Making Roads, Making Do: Public and Private Adaptations to Drought in Ceara, Northeast Brazil," *Climate Research* 19, no. 2 (2001): 97–108; D. Ekbladh, "Meeting the Challenge from Totalitarianism: The Tennessee Valley Authority as a Global Model for Liberal Development, 1933–1945," *International History Review* 32, no. 1 (2010): 47–67; E. Buckley, *Technocrats and the Politics of Drought and Development in 20th-Century Brazil* (Chapel Hill: University of North Carolina Press, 2017).

7   E. da Cunha, *Os sertões* (Rio de Janeiro: Laemmert, 1902).

8   The Caatinga forests are a semi-arid, highly diverse environment adapted to the intense periodic droughts associated with El Niño weather events.

9   B. Latour, *Science in Action* (Cambridge, MA: Harvard University Press, 1987).

10 A. Metcalf, *Go-Betweens and the Colonization of Brazil* (Austin: University of Texas Press, 2005); P. Robbins, *Political Ecology* (New York: Routledge, 2011); P. Descola, *Beyond Nature and Culture* (Chicago: University of Chicago Press, 2013); S. Jasanoff and S.-H. Kim, *Dreamscapes of Modernity: Sociotechnical Imaginaries and the Fabrication of Power* (Chicago: University of Chicago Press,); E. V. d. Castro, *The Relative Native: Essays on Indigenous Conceptual Worlds* (Chicago: Hau, 2016).

11 J. J. Reis, *A invenção de liberdade: O negro no Brasil* (São Paulo: Companhia das Letras, 2003).

12 S. Hecht, *The Scramble for the Amazon and the Lost Paradise of Euclides da Cunha* (Chicago: University of Chicago Press, 2013).

13 J. J. Reis and F. dos Santos Gomes, *Liberdade por um fio: História dos quilombos no Brasil* (São Paulo, Editora Companhia das Letras, 1996).

14 D. M. d. Albuquerque Júnior, *A invenção do Nordeste e outras artes* (São Paulo: Cortez, 2011); S. E. Blake, *The Vigorous Core of Our Nationality* (Pittsburgh, PA: University of Pittsburgh Press, 2011); J. De Castro, *The Geography of Hunger* (New York: Little, Brown and Company, 1952); N. Arons, *Waiting for Rain: The Politics and Poetry of Drought in Northeast Brazil* (Tucson: University of Arizona Press, 2004); P. R. Pessar, *From Fanatics to Folk: Brazilian Millenarianism and Popular Culture* (Durham, NC: Duke University Press, 2004).

15 T. E. Skidmore, *The Politics of Military Rule in Brazil, 1964–85* (New York: Oxford University Press, 1988).

16 Arons, *Waiting for Rain*; J. N. B. Campos, "Paradigms and Public Policies on Drought in Northeast Brazil: A Historical Perspective," *Environmental Management* 55, no. 5 (2015): 1052–63; J. A. Marengo, R. R. Torres, and L. M. Alves, "Drought in Northeast Brazil: Past, Present, and Future," *Theoretical and Applied Climatology* 12, nos. 3–4 (2017): 1189–1200.

17 This document is published in *Antipode* 49, no. 4, and is introduced by Lucas Melgaço. Melgaço, "Thinking Outside."

18 M. Santos, "A revolução technologica e o território: Realidades e perspectivos," *Terra Livre* 9 (1991): 7–17.

19 F. H. Cardoso and E. Faletto, *Dependency and Development in Latin America* (Berkeley: University of California Press, 1979); P. B. Evans, *Dependent Development: The Alliance of Multinational, State, and Local Capital in Brazil* (Princeton, NJ: Princeton University Press, 2018).

20 L. Melgaço and C. Prouse, *Milton Santos: A Pioneer in Critical Geography from the Global South* (Cham, Switzerland: Springer, 2017); Ferretti, "Geographies of Internationalism"; Ferretti and Viotto Pedrosa, "Inventing Critical Development."

21 M. Davis, *Late Victorian Holocausts* (London: Verso, 2001); D. Chakrabarty, "The Climate of History: Four Theses," *Critical Inquiry* 35, no. 2 (2009): 197–222; G. Wood, *Tambora: The Eruption That Changed the World* (Princeton, NJ: Princeton University Press, 2015).

22 Buckley, *Technocrats and the Politics of Drought*; Ferretti, "Geographies of Internationalism."

1. TECHNIQUES, TIME, AND GEOGRAPHIC SPACE

1 Translator's note: I have translated *man* as *human* or *humanity* to avoid distracting the reader with outdated writing conventions.

2 Translator's note: The original French is "techniques d'encadrement" and is used by Gourou to refer to the different forms of social, cultural, and political organization in society.

3 In Pierre Musso's (1994) edited volume, he writes in the introduction, "Technical Innovations and Space," that with new techniques, we encounter an attempt to understand space that seeks to separate these new techniques from preexisting ones by abstracting them from the space that they all share. This method can be useful for understanding the potential uses of these new techniques, or as a sales strategy, but it is insufficient to address the idea of geographic space, banal space. Such an approach, which has already been utilized for analyzing railroads and later highways, is reductive and actually places us even further from the construction of an epistemology of geography that is adequate for understanding the role of technical phenomenon in the construction of banal space.

3. GEOGRAPHIC SPACE, A HYBRID

1 For Claude Raffestin (1979: 103), it is not possible to assimilate landscape and space. For him, they are two very distant things, two signs that communicate different messages to the same geostructure.

7. THE CURRENT TECHNICAL SYSTEM

1 Translator's note: For Santos "the current century" refers, of course, to the twentieth century.

8. UNICITIES

1 Chesneaux (1983: 258) discusses the four laws of Partant, the fourth of which is the "law of planetary banalization, . . . in which progress in the techniques of production is realized in one place in a particular point, to

which the rest of the world must then align itself in order to remain competitive. In this sense, it is in this era that Marx's statement from the *Communist Manifesto* becomes true, 'the bourgeoisie creates a world after its own image.'"

2 See the debate in *Foreign Affairs* between Paul Krugman (1994), who strongly doubts the truth of the concept, and his former colleagues (S. Cohen 1994; Prestowitz 1994; Scharping 1994; Steil 1994; Thurow 1994).

9. OBJECTS AND ACTIONS TODAY

1 Translator's note: In Portuguese, *mundialização* is derived from the French term *mondialisation*, of which the English equivalent is globalization. Here, however, Santos's use of *mundialização* is drawn from Renato Ortiz, who argues that the word *mundialização* tends to correspond to cultural phenomena and *globalization* to more economic and technical phenomena. Ortiz translates *mundialização* to English more literally, as mundialization. In this chapter I have translated it instead as *worldization* both to make it more legible in English and to highlight that Santos uses the word specifically to emphasize processes that emanate "from below," as opposed to globalizing forces "from above."

References

Akrich, Madeleine. 1987. "Comment decrire les objets techniques?" *Techniques et Culture* 9 (June–July): 49–64.

Alexander, Samuel. 1963. "The Historicity of Things" (1936). In *Philosophy and History*, edited by R. Klibansky and H. J. Patton, 11–25. New York: Harper and Row.

Anderson, James. 1985. "Ideology in Geography: An Introduction." *Antipode* 3, no. 5: 1–6.

Anderton, Ronald. 1971. "Technological Change: The Impact of Large Technical Systems." In *Technology Today*, edited by Edward de Bono, 108–36. London: Routledge and Kegan Paul.

Andrade, Manuel Correia de. 1994. "Territorialidades, desterritorialidades, novas territorialidades: Os umites do poder nacional e do poder local." In *Território: Globalização e Fragmentação*, edited by Milton Santos, Maria Adelia Aparecida de Souza, and Maria Laura Silveira, 213–20. São Paulo: Hucitec-Anpur.

Arendt, Hannah. 1981. *A condição humana* (1958). Rio de Janeiro: Forense.

Aristotle. 1979. *Aristotle's Metaphysics.* Translated by Hippocrates G. Apostle. Grinnell, IA: Peripatetic Press.

Arroyo, Monica. 1994. "Mercosul, discurso de uma nova dimensao do territorio que encobre antigas falacias." In *Território: Globalização e Fragmentação*, edited by Milton Santos, Maria Adelia Aparecida de Souza, and Maria Laura Silveira, 308–14. São Paulo: Hucitec-Anpur.

Attali, Jacques. 1981. *Les trois mondes: Pour une theorie de l'apres-crise.* Paris: Fayard.

Attali, Jacques. 1982. *Histoires du temps.* Paris: Fayard.

Augé, Marc. 1992. *Non-lieux: Introduction à une anthropologie de la surmodernité.* Paris: Seuil.

Augé, Marc. 1994a. *Nao-lugar: Introdufifo a uma antropologia da supermodernidade.* Translated by Maria Lucia Pereira. Campinas: Papirus

Augé, Marc. 1994b. *Pour une anthropologie des mondes contemporains.* Paris: Aubier.

Bachelard, Gaston Louis Pierre. 1932. *L'intuition de l'instant.* Paris: Gonthier.

Badie, Bertrand, and Marie-Claude Smouts. 1992. *Le retournement du monde, sociologie de la scene internationale.* Paris: Presses de la Fondation Nationale des Sciences Politiques-Dalloz.

Badiou, Alain. 1975. *Theorie de la contradiction.* Paris: Maspero.

Bailly, Antoine, and Hubert Bégion. 1982. *Introduction a la geographie humaine.* Paris: Masson.

Bakhtin, E. 1993. *Toward a Philosophy of Act.* Austin: University of Texas Press.

Bakis, Henry. 1984. *Géograpie des télécommunications.* Paris: Presses universitaires de France.

Bakis, Henry. 1987. *Géopolitique de l'information.* Paris: Presses universitaires de France.

Bakis, Henry, ed. 1990. *Communications et territoires.* Paris: La Documentation Francaise.

Bakis, Henry. 1993. *Les reseaux et leurs enjeux sociaux.* Paris: Presses universitaires de France.

Balandier, Georges. 1991. "La technique en jeu: Tecnophiles et tecnophobes." *Revue Europeenne des Sciences Sociales* 29, 91: 5–10.

Barber, Benjamin R. 1992. "Djihad vs. Mcworld: mondialisation, tribalisme et democratte." *Futuribles* 170: 3–19.

Barnes, Hazel E. 1968. "Introduction." In Jean-Paul Sartre, *Search for a Method*, vii–xxxii. New York: Vintage Books.

Barre, Remi, and Pierre Papon. 1993. *Economie et politique de la science et de la technologie.* Paris: Hachette.

Barthes, Roland. 1967. *Système de la mode.* Seuil: Pais.

Bataille, Georges. 1968. *Œuvres completes, Volume IV.* Paris: Gallimard.

Baudrillard, Jean. 1968. *Le système des objets.* Paris: Gallimard.

Baudrillard, Jean. 1970. *La societe de consommation.* Paris: Denoel.

Baudrillard, Jean. 1973. *O sistema dos objetos.* São Paulo: Perspectiva.

Baudrillard, Jean. 1996. *The system of objects.* Translated by James Benedict. New York: Verso.

Baulig, Henri. 1948. "La geographie est-elle une science." *Annales de Geographie* 57: 1–11.

Beaud, Michel. 1987. *Le systeme national mondial hierarchise.* Paris: La Decouverte.

Beaufret, Jean. 1971. *Introduction aux philosophies de l'existence.* Paris: Mediations de noel gonthier.

Beaune, Jean-Claude. 1994. "L'ordre et ja matiere." In *Ordre biologique, ordre technologique*, edited by Franck Tinland, 48–71. Paris: Champ Vallon.

Beaver, S. H. 1961. "Technology and Geography." *Advancement of Science* 73, no. 18: 1–13.

Begag, Azouz, Gerard Claisse, and Patrick Moreau. 1990. "L'espace des bits: Utopies et realites; Teleinfornatique, localisation des entreprises

et dynamique urbaine." In *Communications et territoires*, edited by
H. Bakis, 187–217. Paris: La Documentation Francaise.

Bell, Daniel. 1976. *The Coming of Post-industrial Society: A Venture in Social Forecasting*. New York: Basic Books.

Benetti, Carlo. 1974. *L'accumulation dans les pays capitalistes sous-developpes*. Paris: Anthropos.

Beniger, James R. 1986. *The Control Revolution: Technological and Economic Origins of the Information Society*. Cambridge, MA: Harvard University Press.

Benko, Georges B. 1990. "Local versus Global in Social Analysis: Some Reflexions." In *Globality versus Locality*, edited by A. Kuklinski, 63–66. Warsaw: Institute of Space Economy, University of Warsaw.

Bense, M. 1971. *Zeichen und Design. Semiotische Ästhetik*. Baden-Baden: Agis.

Berdoulay, Vincent. 1978. "The Vidal-Durkheim Debate." In *Humanistic Geography*, edited by D. Ley and M. S. Samuels, 77–90. Chicago: Maaroufa Press.

Berger, Gaston. 1964. *Phenomenologie du temps et prospective*. Paris: Presses universitaires de France.

Bergson, Henri. 1991. *L'évolution créatrice*. In *Oeuvres*. 5th ed. Paris: Presses universitaires de France.

Bernardes, Adriana. 1995. *Os jornais locais: O caso de Sao Carlos, São Paulo, Brasil*. São Paulo: Universidade de São Paulo.

Bernanos, Georges. 1936. *Journal d'un curé de campagne*. Paris: Plon.

Berry, Brian J. L., and D. F. Marble. 1968. *Spatial Analysis*. Englewood Cliffs, NJ: Prentice Hall.

Berry, Brian J. L., and V. L. S. Prakasa Rao. 1968. *Urban-Rural Duality in the Regional Structure of Andhra Pradesh: A Challenge to Regional Planning and Development*. Wiesbaden, Germany: Franz Steiner.

Berthelot, Yves. 1994. "Globalisation et regionalisation: Une mise en perspective." In *L'integration regionale dans le monde*, edited by Gemdev (Groupement d'intéret scientifique, économie mondiale, Tiers monde, Développement), 11–18. Paris: Karthala.

Best, M. H. 1990. *The New Competition: Institutions of Industrial Restructuring*. Cambridge: Polity Press.

Beteille, R. 1991. "La revolution boursiere internationale." *L'information geographique* 5: 1–10.

Blaut, J. M. 1961. "Space as Process." *Professional Geographer* 13: 1–7.

Bloch, Ernst. 1970. *A Philosophy of the Future*. New York: Herder and Herder.

Bloch, Marc. 1974. *Apologie pour rhistoire ou metier d'historien*. Paris: Clin.

Boeke, J. H. 1953. *Economics and Economic Policy of Dual Societies, as Exemplified by Indonesia*. Haarlem: H. D. Tjeenk Willink and Zoon N. V.

Bohm, David. 1957. *Causality and Chance in Modern Physics*. New York: D. Van Nostrand Company.

Böhme, G. 1987. "Die Technostrukturen in der Gesellschaft." In *Technik und sozialer Wandel*, edited by B. Lurz, 53–65. Frankfurt: Campus.

Boismenu, Gerard. 1993. "Polycentrisme dissymetrique et strategie defensive dans la transformation du rapport salarial." Seminaire analyse du systeme monde et de l'economie mondiale. Gemdev (Groupement d'intéret scientifique, économie mondiale, Tiers monde, Développement). Paris: 4 et 5 Fevrier.

Bollnow, O. Friedrich. 1969. *Hombre y espacio*. Barcelona: Labor.

Borelli, Silvia H. Simoes. 1992. "Memoria e temporalidade: Dialogo entre Walter Benjamin e Henri Bergson." *Margem—Fauldade de Ciencias Socias da PUC-SP*, 1: 79–90.

Bosi, Alfredo. 1992. *Dialetica da colonização*. 3rd ed. São Paulo: Companhia das Letras.

Boudeville, Jacques. 1964. *Les espaces economiques*. 2nd ed. Paris: Presses universitaires de France.

Boudon, Pierre. 1971. "Sabre un status del objeto: Diferir el objeto del objeto." In *Los objetos: Comunicaciones*, 95–127. Buenos Aires: Editorial Tiempo Contemporaneo.

Boundas, Constantin V., ed. 1993. *The Deleuze Reader*. New York: Columbia University Press.

Braudel, Fernand. 1979a. *Civilisation materielle. Economie et capitalisme, Xv-Xviii~ siecle, 1. Les structures du quotidien: le possible e l'impossible*. Paris: Armand Collin.

Braudel, Fernand. 1979b. *Le temps du monde*. Paris: Armand Collin.

Braudel, Fernand. 1982. *La Méditerranée et le monde méditerranéen a l'epoque de Philippe fl* (1949). 2 vols. 5th ed. Paris: Armand Collin.

Braun, Ingo, and Bernward Joerges. 1992. "Techniques du quotidien et macro-systèmes techniques." In *Sociologie des techniques de la vie quotidienne*, edited by Alain Gras, Jeorges Gras, and Victor Scardigli, 69–86. Paris: Harmattan.

Brender, Anton. 1977. *Socialisme et cybernetique*. Paris: Calmann-Levy.

Brentano, Franz. 1935. *Psicología*. Madrid: Revista de Occidente.

Breton, Philippe. 1991. *Historia da informatica* (1987). São Paulo: Unesp.

Breton, Stanislas. 1968. "Reflexion philosophique et humanisme technique." In *Civilisation technique et humanisme*, 111–48. Paris: Beauchesne.

Brie, Christian de. 1993. "Des democraties sans voix." In *Le Monde Diplomatique: Les frontieres de l'economie globale. Maniere de voir* 18 (mai-juin-juillet): 27–29.

Britton, Stephen. 1990. "The Role of Services in Production." *Progress in Human Geography* 14, no. 4: 529–46.

Broek, Jan M. O., and John N. Webb. 1968. *A Geography of Mankind.* New York: McGraw Hill.

Bruneau, Michel. 1989. "Les geographes et la tropicalite." In *Les enjeux de la tropicalite*, edited by M. Bruneau and D. Dory, 67–81. Paris: Masson.

Brunet, Roger. 1962. *Le croquis de la geographie regionale et economique.* Paris: Sedes.

Brunet, Roger, and Olivier Dollfus. 1990. *Mandes nouveaux.* Vol. 1, Geographie Universelle, edited by R. Brunet. Paris: Hachette-Redus.

Brunhes, Jean. 1947. *La geographie humaine.* Abridged edition. Paris: Presses universitaires de France.

Brzezinski. Zbigniew. 1976. *Between Two Ages: America's Role in the Technetronic Era* (1970). New York: Penguin Books.

Buchsenschutz, Olivier. 1987. "Archeologie, typologie, technologie." *Techniques et cultures* 9 (jan.–juin): 17–26.

Busino, Giovanni. 1991. "Du naturel et de l'artificiel dans les sciences sociales." *Revue Europeenne des Sciences Sociales*, no. 29 (91): 65–80.

Buttimer, Anne. 1976. "Grasping the Dynamism of Lifeworld." *Annals of the Association of American Geographers* 66, no. 2 (June): 227–92.

Calvino, Italo. 1991. *Seis propostas para o próximo milênio* (1988). São Paulo: Companhia das Letras.

Candido, Antonio. 1977. *Os Parceiros do rio Bonito.* 4th ed. São Paulo: Duas Cidades.

Canguilhem, Georges. 1955. *Formation du concept de reflexe.* Paris: Presses universitaires de France.

Carneiro Leão, Emmanuel. 1987. "Os desafios da informatização." In *A maquina e seu avesso*, edited by Emmanuel Carneiro Leão, Marcio Tavares d'Amaral, Muniz Sodré, and Francisco Antonio Doria, 1–23. Rio de Janeiro: Francisco Alves.

Carneiro Leão, Emmanuel, Marcio Tavares d'Amaral, Muniz Sodré, and Francisco Antonio Doria, eds. 1987. *A maquina e seu avesso.* Rio de Janeiro: Francisco Alves.

Carreras, Carles. 1993. "O novo mapa da Europa." In *Fim de século e globalização*, edited by Milton Santos, 129–38. São Paulo, Hucitec-Anpur.

Cassirer, Ernst. 1965. *The Philosophy of Symbolic Forms* (1953). New Haven, CT: Yale University Press.

Cassirer, Ernst. 1974. *The Logic of Humanities.* New Haven, CT: Yale University Press.

Célis, Raphael. 1992. "De la ville marchande à l'espace-temps." In *Congres de la Societe Beige de Philosophic: Le temps et l'espace*, edited by R Alexander, 91–108. Bruxelles: Ousia.

Chesnais , Francois. 1994. *La mondialisation du capital.* Paris: Syros.

Chesneaux, Jean. 1983. *De la modernite.* Paris: Maspero/La Decouverte.

Chevalier, Michel. 1832. "Exposition du systeme de La Mediterrannee." *Le Globe,* 12 janvier.

Cicciolella, Pablo. 1993. *Hacia un capitalismo sin fronteras? O la historia recien comienza.* Actas del II Seminario Latinoamericano de Geografía Crítica realizado del 26 al 30 de noviembre de 1990. Buenos Aires: Facultad de Filosofía y Letras, Instituto de Geografía, Universidad de Buenos Aires.

Cicciolella, Pablo. 1994. "Descontrução/Reconstrução do territorio no ambito dos processes de globalização e integração: Os casos do Mercosul e do Corredor Andino." In *Território: Globalização e Fragmentação,* edited by Milton Santos, Maria Adelia Aparecida de Souza, and Maria Laura Silveira, 296–307. São Paulo: Hucitec-Anpur.

Claval, Paul, 1993. *La geographie au temps de la chute des murs: Essais et etudes.* Paris: L'Hannattan.

Cohen, Stephen S. 1994. "Speaking Freely." *Foreign Affairs* 73, no. 4 (July–August): 194–97.

Cohen, Yves. 1994. "Le xx siecle commence en 1990: Sciences, techniques, action." *Alliage: Pour penser les techniques* 20–21: 88–104.

Collingwood, Robin George. 1946. *The Idea of History.* Oxford: Clarendon.

Cooke, Philip. 1992. "Global Localization in Computing and Communications." In *Towards Global Localization: The Computing and Telecommunications Industries in Britain and France,* edited by Philip Cooke, Frank Moulaert, Erik Swyngedouw, Oliver Weinstein, and Peter Wells, 200–14. London: University College of London Press.

Cooke, Philip, and Peter Wells. 1992. "Globalization and Its Management in Computing and Communications." In *Towards Global Localization: The Computing and Telecommunications Industries in Britain and France,* edited by Philip Cooke, Frank Moulaert, Erik Swyngedouw, Oliver Weinstein, and Peter Wells, 61–78. London: University College of London Press.

Coriat, Benjamin. 1982. *L'atelier et le chronometre* (1979). Paris: Editions Christian Bourgois.

Corm, Georges. 1993. *Le nouveau desordre economique mondial: Aux racines des echecs du developpement.* Paris: La Decouverte.

Correa, Ana Maria G., Alejandra Lavalle, Miriam Ambrosio, Alicia Laurin, and Maria Nelida Martinez. 1993. *El big-bang de inversiones en Chimpay.* Neuque, Argentina: Universidad Nacional del Comahue.

Correa, Roberto Lobato. 1993. "Redes, fluxos e territorios: Uma introdução." In *Anais do 3." Simposio Nacional de Geografia Urbana,* 31–32. Rio de Janeiro: Ufrj/Agb/Ibge.

Correa, Roberto Lobato. 1994. "Territorialidade e corporação: Um exemplo." In *Território: Globalização e Fragmentação,* edited by Milton

Santos, Maria Adelia Aparecida de Souza, and Maria Laura Silveira, 51–56. São Paulo: Hucitec-Anpur.

Cunill, Pedro. 1994. "A banalizaição das paisagens culturais." Conferencia na Universidade de Salamanca (Espanha), 25 de junho.

Curien, Nicolas. 1988. "D'une problematique generate des reseaux a l'analyse economique du transport des informations." In *Reseaux territoriaux*, edited by Gabriel Dupuy, 211–28. Caen, France: Paradigme.

Cuvillier, Armand. 1973. *Introduccion a la sociologia*. Buenos Aires: La Pleyade.

Daghini, Giairo. 1983. "Babel-Metropole." *Change internationale* 1: 23–26.

Damiani, Amelia Luisa. 1994. "O lugar e a produição do cotidiano." Encontro Internacional: Lugar, Formação Socioespacial, Mundo, Anpege (Associação Nacional de Pesquisa e Pos Graduação em Geografia), Universidade de São Paulo, 8 a 10 de setembro.

Darby, H. C. 1957. "The Relations of Geography and History." In *Geography in the Twentieth Century*, edited by Griffith Taylor, 640–45. New York: Philosophical Library.

Dardel, Eric. 1952. *L'homme et la terre: Nature de la realite geographique*. Paris: Presses universitaires de France.

Debray, Regis. 1991. *Cours de mediologie generate*. Paris: Gallimard.

De Britto, Luis Navarro. 1986. *Política e espaço regional*. São Paolo: Nobel.

Defarges, Philippe Moreau. 1993. *La mondialisation, vers la fin des frontieres?* Paris: Ifri-Dunod.

De Jong, Gerben. 1962. *Chorological Differentiation as the Fundamental Principle of Geography*. Groningen: J. B. Wolters.

De Spinoza, Benedictus. 1910. *Spinoza's Short treatise on God, Man and His Wellbeing*. New York: A. C. and Black.

Delcourt, Jacques. 1992. "Globalisation de l'economie et progres social: L'etat social a l'heure de la mondialisation." *Futuribles* 164: 3–34.

Demangeon, A. 1942. *Problemes de geographie humaine*. Paris: Armand Collin.

Demoule, Jean Paul. 1994. "Sans mode d'emploi, l'archeologie des objets techniques." *Alliage: Pour penser les techniques*. 20–21: 15–27.

Dessauer, Friedrich. 1964. *Discusion sobre la tecnica* (1956). Madrid: Rialp.

Diano, Carlo. 1994. *Forme et evenement: Principles pour une interpretation du monde grec*. Paris: L'Eclat.

Dias, Leila Christina. 1990. "Un indicateur de l'organisation territoriale: L'activite bane a ire et son evolution au Bresil." In *La dynamique spatiale de l'economie contemporaine*, edited by G. B. Benko, 293–308. Brussels: Editions de l'Espace Europeen.

Díaz Muñoz, Maria Angeles. 1991. "Unas notas sobre las possibilidades docentes y aplicaciones de la Geografia del Tiernpo." In *Geografias Personales*, edited by Joaquín Bosque and María Ángeles Díaz, 131–63. Alcalá de Henares: Universidad de Alcalá.

Dicken, Peter. 1992. *Global Shift: The Internationalization of Economic Activity*. London: Paul Chapman.

Dicken, Peter. 1994. "Global-Local Tensions: Forms and States in the Global Space-Economy (The Roepke Lecture in Economic Geography)." *Economic Geography* 70, no. 2 (April): 101–28.

Dicken, P., and Lloyd, P. E. 1981. *Modern Western Society: A Modern Perspective of Work, Home and Well Being*. London: Harper and Row.

Di Meo, Guy. 1991a. "La genese du territoire local: Complexite dialectique et espace-temps." *Annales de Geographie* 559: 273–94.

Di Meo, Guy. 1991b. *L'homme, la societe, l'espace*. Paris: Anthropos-Economica.

Dollfus, Olivier. 1971. *L'analyse geographique*. Paris: Presses universitaires de France.

Dorfles, Gillo. 1976. *Simbolo, Comunicacion y Consumo*. Barcelona: Lumen.

Dory, Daniel. 1989. "La civilisation: Reflexions sur les avatars d'un concept ambigue." In *Les enjeux de la tropicalite*, edited by M. Bruneau and D. Dory, 111–16. Paris: Masson.

dos Santos, Thetonio. 1993. "Quelques idees sur le systeme monde." *Points de vue sur le systeme monde*. Gemdev (Groupement d'intéret scientifique, économie mondiale, Tiers monde, Développement), *Cahier 20*, mai 1993.

dos Santos, Thetonio. 1994. "A globalização reforca as particularidades." In *Território: Globalização e Fragmentação*, edited by Milton Santos, Maria Adelia Aparecida de Souza, and Maria Laura Silveira, 72–76. São Paulo: Hucitec-Anpur.

Druet, Pierre-Philippe, Peter Kemp, and Georges Thill. 1980. *Technologies et societe*. Paris: Galilee.

Dulong, Philippe. 1993. "L'informatique: Espace et logistique." In *Les noveaux espaces de l'entreprise*, edited by Michael Savy and Pierre Veltz, 163–80. Paris: Auber/Datar.

Dupuy, G. 1991. *L'urbanisme des reseaux: Theories et methodes*. Paris: Colin.

Dupuy, Jean-Pierre. 1975. "Le culte des heures fertiles." *Projet* , no. 97.

Durand, Marie-Francoise, Jacques Lévy, and Denis Retaillé. 1992. *Le monde, espaces et systeme*. Paris: Presses de la Fondation Nationale des Sciences Politiques/Dalloz.

Durkheim, Emile. 1962. *The Rules of Sociological Method* (1938). Chicago: University of Chicago Press.

Duvignaud, Jean. 1977. *Lieux et non lieux*. Paris: Galilee.

Eaton, Ralph Monroe. 1964. *Symbolism and Truth: An Introduction to the Theory of Knowledge* (1925). New York: Dover Publications.

Eco, Umberto. 1983. *O nome da rosa* (1980). Translated by Aurora F. Bernardini and Homero F. de Andrade. Rio de Janeiro: Nova Fronteira.

Eddington, Sir Arthur. 1968. *Space, Time and Gravitation: An Outline of the General Relativity Theory* (1920). Cambridge: Cambridge University Press.

Einstein, Albert. 1905. "On the Electrodynamics of Moving Bodies." In *Annalen der Physik* 17:891–921

Einstein, Albert. 1923. *Principles of Relativity: A Collection of Original Memoires on the Special and General Theory of Relativity.* New York: Doner.

Ellias, Denise. 1996. *Meio tecnico-cientifico-informacional e urbanização na regiao metropolitana de Ribeirao Preto.* Doctoral thesis, Universidade de São Paulo.

Ellul, Jacques. 1964. *The Technological Society.* New York: Vintage Books/Random House.

Ellul, Jacques. 1977. *Le systeme technicien.* Paris: Calmann-Levy.

Ellul, Jacques. 1988. *Le bluff technologique.* Paris: Hachette.

Escolar, Marcelo. 1992. *Los lugares donde se sijo el movimiento: Diferenciacion e identificacion geografica.* Doctoral thesis, Universidad de Buenos Aires.

Escolar, Marcelo. 1996. *Critica do discurso geografico.* São Paulo: Hucitec.

Fel, A. 1978. "La geographie et les techniques." In *Histoire des Techniques*, edited by B. Gille. Paris: Encyclopedie de la Pleiade.

Ferrara, Lucrécia d'Alessio. 1989. "Desenho industrial: Objeto e valor." *Design e interiores* 12, no. 2.

Ferrara, Lucrécia d'Alessio. 1990. "Percepção ambiental: Informação e contextualização." *Sinopses* 13 (maio): xx–xx.

Ferrara, Lucrécia d'Alessio. 1993. "O mapa da mina: Informação; Espaço e lugar." In *Fim de siculo e globalização*, edited by Milton Santos, 161–71. São Paulo: Hucitec-Anpur.

Fischer, Andre. 1990. "Les effers geographiques des technologies nouvelles: Approche generate." *Notes de Recherche* 22. Paris: Institut de Geographie, Centre de Recherche sur l'Industrie et l'Amenagement.

Fischer, Gustave-Nicolas. 1980. *Espace industriel et Iiberte: L'autogestion clandestine.* Paris: Presses universitaires de France.

Focillon, Henri. 1981. *Vie des formes* (1943). 7th ed. Paris: Presses universitaires de France.

Fouquin, Michel 1993. "Regional and World-Wide Dimensions of Globalization." Document du travail 93–4. *Seminar on Development Aid and Foreign Investment. Beijing June 28–July 1.*

Frampton, Kenneth. 1985. "Hacia un regionalismo critico: Seic puntos para una arquitectura de resistencia." In *La Posmodernidad*, edited by Hal Foster, 37–58. Buenos Aires: Kairos.

Freeman, T. W. 1961. *A Hundred Years of Geography.* London: Gerald Duckworth.

Friedmann, Georges. 1949. "Les technocrates et la civilisation technici-enne." In *Industrialisation et technocratie*, edited by Georges Gur-vitch, 43–62. Paris: A. Colin.

Friedmann, Georges. 1966. *7 etudes sur l'homme et la technique*. Paris: Denoel-Gonthier.

Friedmann, John. 1963. "Regional Economic Policy for Developing Areas." *Papers and Proceedings of the Regional Science Association* 11: 41–61.

Funtowicz, Silvio, and Jerome R. Ravetz. 1993. *Epistemologia politica: Ciencia con la gente*. Buenos Aires: Centro Editor de America Latina.

Ganne, Bernard. 1993. "L'industrialisation et la reprise des Pme." In *Naissance de nouvelles campagnes*, edited by B. Kayser, 105–18. Paris: L'Aube/Datar.

García Ballesteros, Aurora, ed. 1992. *Geografía y humanismo*. Barcelona: Oikos/Tau.

Garelli, Stéphane, and Madeleine Linard de Guertechin. 1995. "La com-petitivite mondiale: *World Competitiveness Report* de l'I. M.D. et du World Economic Forum." *Futuribles* 198 (mai): 57–81.

Gaudin, Thierry. 1978. *L'ecoute des silences: Les institutions contre l'innovation?* Paris: Union Generale des Editions.

Gauthier, Yves. 1989. *La crise mondiale de 1973 a nos jours*. Paris: Complexe.

Geiger, Pedro P. 1993. "Mapa do mundo pos-moderno." In *Fim de seculo e globalização*, edited by Milton Santos, 104–6. São Paulo: Hucitec.

Gellner, Ernest. 1989. "A psicanalise enquanto instituição social." *Folha de S. Paulo,* 23 September.

Gellner, Ernest. 1992. *El arado: La espada y el libro, la estructura de la historia humana* (1988). Mexico City: Fondo de Cultura Económica.

George, Pierre. 1968. *L'action humaine*. Paris: Presses universitaires de France.

George, Pierre, ed. 1970. *Dictionnaire de la geographie*. Paris: Presses universitaires de France.

George, Pierre. 1974. *Vere des techniques: Constructions on destructions*. Paris: Presses universitaires de France.

Gertel, Sergio. 1993. "Globalização e meio tecnico-cientifico: O nexo in-formacional." *Fim de Seculo e Globalização*, edited by Milton Santos, 188–200. São Paulo: Hucitec.

Giddens, Anthony. 1978. *Novas regras do metodo sociologico: Uma critica positiva dos sociologos*. Rio de Janeiro: Zahar.

Giddens, Anthony. 1984a. *The Constitution of Society*. London: Polity Press/Basil Blackwell.

Giddens, Anthony. 1984b. *Sociologia: Uma breve porem critica introdução* (1982). Translated by Alberto Oliva and Lis Alberto Cerqueira. Rio de Janeiro: Zahar.

Giddens, Anthony. 1987. *La constitution de la societe* (1984). Paris: Presses universitaires de France.

Giddens, Anthony. 1991. *As consequencias da modernidade.* São Paulo: Unesp.

Gille, Bertrand. 1978. *Histoire des techniques.* Paris: Encyclopedie de La Pleaide: 1978.

Gille, Bertrand. 1981. "Pour un musee de la science et de la technique." *Milieux* 6 (juin–sept.): 24–27.

Gille, Laurent. 1987. "Les reseaux prives face aux reseaux intégrés publics." *Reseaux Prives: Actes des 9 journees internationales de l'IDATE* 30 (nov.): 122–29.

Goblot, J. J. 1967. "Pour une approche theorique des facts de civilisation." *La Pensee* 133: 134–36.

Godelier, Maurice. 1966. "Systme, structure et contradiction dans *Le Capital.*" *Temps Modernes* 246 (nov.).

Godelier, Maurice. 1972. *Rationality and Irrationality in Economics.* London: New Left Books.

Godelier, Maurice. 1974. *Rationalite et irrationalite en economie.* 2 vols. Paris: Francois Maspero.

Goffman, Erving. 1961. *Encounters.* Indianapolis, IN: Bobbs-Merrill.

Goldfinger, Charles. 1986. *La geofinance.* Paris: Le Seuil.

Goldmann, Lucien. 1967. *Origem da dialetica: A comunidade humana e o universo em Kant.* Translated by Haraldo Santiago. Rio de Janeiro: Paz e Terra.

Goldmann, Lucien. 1970. *Marxisme et sciences humaines.* Paris: Gallimard.

Gorz, André. 1964. *Historia y enajenacion.* Translated by Julieta Campos. Mexico City: Fondo de Cultura Economica.

Gould, Peter R. 1970. "Tanzania 1920–1963: The Spatial Impress of the Modernization Process." *World Politics* 22: 147–70.

Gourou, Pierre. 1973. *Pour une geographie humaine.* Paris: Flammarion.

Graham, Julie. 1993. "Firm and State Strategy in a Multipolar World: The Changing Geography of Machine Tool Production and Trade." In *Trading Industries, Trading Regions,* edited by Helzi Noponen, Julie Graham, and Ann R. Markusen, 140–74. New York: Guilford Press.

Granstedt, Ingmar. 1980. *Impasse industrielle.* Paris: Seuil.

Gras, Alain. 1992. "Le bonheur, produit surgelc." In *Technologies du quotidien: La complainte du progres,* edited by Alain Gras and Caroline Moricot, 12–31. Paris: Autrement.

Gras, Alain. 1993. *Grandeur et dependance: Sociologie des macrosystemes techniques.* Paris: Presses universitaires de France

Gras, Alain, Bernward Joerges, and Victor Scardigli. 1992. *Sociologie d'techniques de la vie quotidienne.* Paris: L'Harmattan.

Grataloup, Christian. 1975. "La géographie aux champs." *Espace Temps* 1, no. 1: 26–28.

Gross, Bertram M. 1971. "Planning in an Era of Social Revolution." *Public Administration Review* 31, no. 3 (May–June): 259–97.

Groupe de Lisbonne. 1995. *Limites a la competitivite: pour un noveau contrat mondial.* Paris: La Decouverte.

Guénon, René. 1945. *La crise du monde moderne.* Paris: Gallimard.

Guigou, Jean-Louis. 1995. *Une ambition pour le territoire: Amenager le temps et l'espace.* Paris: l'Aube/Datar.

Guillaume, Marc. 1978. *Eloge du desordre.* Paris: Gallimard.

Gurvitch, Georges. 1969. *A vocação atual da sociologia.* Lisbon: Editora Cosmos .

Gurvitch, Georges. 1971. *Dialectica y sociologia* (1968). Madrid: Alianza Editorial.

Habermas, Jürgen. 1971. *Legitimation Crisis.* Translated by Thomas McCarthy. Boston: Beacon Press.

Habermas, Jürgen. 1973. *La technique et la science comme "ideologie"* (1968). Translated by Jean-Rene L'Admiral. Paris: Gallimard.

Habermas, Jürgen. 1987. *Theorie de l'agir communicationnel,* vol. 1, *Rationalite de l'agir et rationalization de la societe,* Translated by J. M. Ferry (1981). Paris: Fayard.

Hägerstrand, Torsten. 1969. "What about People in Regional Science?" *Papers of the Regional Science Association* 24: 7–21.

Hägerstrand, Torsten. 1973. "The Domain of Human Geography." In *Directions in Geography,* edited by R. J. Chorley, 65–87. London: Methuen.

Hägerstrand, Torsten. 1985. "Time-Geography: Focus on the Corporeality of Man." In *The Science and Praxis of Complexity,* edited by Shūhei Aida, 193–216. Tokyo: United Nations University.

Hägerstrand, Torsten. 1989. "Reflections on 'What about People in Regional Science?'" *Papers of the Regional Science Association* 66: 1–6.

Hägerstrand, Torsten. 1991a. "Que hay acerca de las personas en la ciencia regional?" Universidad Alcala de Henares. *Serie Geografica* 1: 93–110.

Hägerstrand, Torsten. 1991b. "Reflexiones sobre 'Que hay acerca de las personas en la ciencia regional?'" Universidad Alcala de Henares. *Serie Geografica* 1: 111–18.

Halévy, Daniel. 1948. *Essai sur l'acceleration de l'histoire.* Paris: Les Iles d'Or.

Hall, P., and P. Preston. 1988. *The Carrier Wave: New Information Technology and the Geography of Innovation, 1846–2003.* London: Unwin Hyman.

Hamilton, David. 1973. *Technology: Man and the Environment.* London: Faber and Faber.

Harvey, David. 1967. "Models of the Evolution of Spatial Patterns in Human Geography." In *Models in Geography,* edited by R. J. Chorley and Peter Hagett, 549–608. London: Methuen.

Harvey, David. 1989. "From Managerialism to Enterpreneuralism: The Transformation in Urban Governance in Late Capitalism." *Geografiska Annaler: Series B, Human Geography* 71, no. 1: 3–17.

Harvey, David. 1993. "From Space to Place and Back Again: Reflections on the Condition of Post-Modernity." In *Mapping the Futures: Local Culture, Global Change*, edited by J. Bird, 3–29. London: Routledge.

Hasbaert, Rogério. 1995. *Gauchos no nordeste*. Doctoral thesis, Universidade de São Paulo.

Hawley, Amos. 1950. *Human Ecology: A Theory of Community Structure*. New York: Ronald Press.

Hegel, G. W. F. 1966. *Texts and Commentary: The Preface to Phenomenology*. Translated and edited by Walter Kaufmann. New York: Anchor Books.

Hegel, G. W. F. 2010. *The Science of Logic*. Translated and edited by George di Giovanni. New York: Cambridge University Press.

Heidegger, Martin. 1992. *Que e uma coisa?* Translated by Carlos Morujão (1962). Lisbon: Edicoes 70.

Heller, Ágnes. 1982. *La revolucion de la vida cotidiana*. Barcelona: Peninsula.

Hepworth, Mark E. 1989. *Geography of the Information Economy*. London: Belharen Press.

Hériard, Bertrand. 1994. "De l'ambiguite de la passion technique: L'exemple d'Edison." *Alliage: Pour penser les techniques* 20–21: 143–51.

Herrera, Almicar. 1977. "Ressources naturelles." In *Technologie et dependance*, edited by Candido Mendes. Paris: Seuil.

Hewitt, Kenneth, and F. Kenneth Hare. 1973. *Man and Environment: Conceptual Frameworks*. Commission on College Geography, Resource Paper 20. Washington, DC: American Association of Geographers.

Hiernaux-Nicolas, Daniel. 1994. "Tempo, espaco e apropriação social do territorio: Rumo a fragmentação da mundialização?" In *Território: Globalização e Fragmentação*, edited by Milton Santos, Maria Adelia Aparecida de Souza, and Maria Laura Silveira, 85–101. São Paulo: Hucitec-Anpur.

Hindess, Barry. 1987. "Rationality and the Characterization of Modern Society." In *Max Weber: Rationality and Modernity*, edited by Scott Lash and Sam Whimster, 137–53. London: Allen and Unwin.

Hirschman, Albert. 1958. *The Strategy of Economic Development*. New Haven, CT: Yale University Press.

Hirst, Paul, and Grahame Thompson, 1996, *Globalization in Question: The International Economy and the Possibilities of Governance*. Cambridge: Polity Press.

Hobbes, Thomas. 1841. *The English Works of Thomas Hobbes, Volume 2*, edited by William Molesworth. London: John Bohn.

Horkheimer, Max. 1974. *Eclipse of Reason* (1947). New York: Seabury Press.

Horkheimer, Max. 1976. *Eclipse da razao*. Rio de Janeiro: Editorial Labor do Brasil.

Horning, Karl H. 1992. "Le temps de la technique et le quotidien du temps." In *Sociologie des techniques et vie quotidienne*, edited by A. Gras, B. Joerges, and V. Scardigli, 45–49. Paris: L'Harmattan.

Hottois, Gilbert. 1994. "Gilbert Simondon: Entre les interfaces techniques et symboliques." In *Ordre biologique, ordre technologique*, edited by Franck Tinland, 72–95. Paris: Champ Vallon.

Hughes, Tom P. 1980. *Networks of Power: The Electrification of Western Society*. Baltimore, MD: Johns Hopkins University Press.

Hughes, Tom P., and Renate Maynz. 1988. *The Development of Large Technical Systems*. Frankfurt: Campus.

Humbert, Marc. 1991. "Perdre pour gagner? Technique ou culture, technique et culture." *Espaces Temps* 45 (1), 53–61.

Husserl, Edmund. 1959. *Fenomenologia de la conciencia del tiempo inmanente*. Buenos Aires: Editorial Nova.

Husserl, Edmund. 1975. *La crise de l'humanite europeenne et la philosophie* (1935). Paris: La Pensee Sauvage.

Ianni, Octavio. 1992. *Sociedade global*. Rio de Janeiro: Civilização Brasileira.

Ianni, Octavio. 1993. "Nação e globalização." In *Fim de seculo e globalização*, edited by Milton Santos, 66–74. São Paulo: Hucitec-Anpur.

Isachenko, A. G. 1975. "Landscape as a Subject of Human Impact." *Soviet Geography* 16, no. 10: 631–43.

Isard, Walter. 1956. *Location and Space Economics*. Cambridge, MA: MIT Press.

Jacob, François. 1970. *La logique du virant*. Paris: Gallimard.

Jacques, Elliott. 1982. *The Form of Time*. New York: Crane Russak/ Heinemann.

Jacques, Elliott. 1984. *La forma del tiempo*. Buenos Aires: Paidos.

Jaeggi, Urs. 1968. *Ordnung und Chaos: Der Strukturalismus als Methode und Mode*. Frankfurt am Main: Suhrkamp.

Jaeggi, Urs. 1969. *Orden y çãos: El estructuralismo como metodo y coma moda*. Caracas: Monte Avila Editores.

Jakubowsky, Franz. 1971. *Les superstructures ideologiques dans la conception materialiste de l'histoire*. Paris: Ecudes et Documentation Internationales.

James, William. 1950. *Principles of Psychology* (1890). London: Dover.

Janicaud, Dominique. 1985. *La puissance du rationnel*. Paris: Gallimard.

Jay, Martin. 1984. *Marxism and Totality: The Adventures of a Concept from Lukacs to Habermas*. Los Angeles: University of California Press.

Joerges, Bernward. 1988. "Large Technical Systems: Concepts and Issues." In *The Development of Large Technical Systems*, edited by Renate Maynz and Thomas P. Hughes, 9–36. Frankfurt: Campus.

Johnson, E. A. J. 1970. *The Organization of Space in Developing Countries*. Cambridge, MA: Harvard University Press.

Johnson, James H. 1956. "The Geography of the Skyscraper." *Journal of Geography* 55, no. 8: 379–87.

Johnston, R. J., and P. J. Taylor, eds. 1986. *A World in Crisis? Geographical Perspectives*. Oxford: Basil Blackwell.

Jung, C. G. 1984. *Sincronicidade*. Petropolis, Brazil: Vozes.

Junqueira, Claudette B. 1994. "A rede dos lugares." ANPEGE (Associação Nacional de Pesquisa e Pos Graduação em Geografia) Conference, University of São Paulo, 8–10 September.

Kant, Immanuel. 1802. *Physische Geographie*. Königsberg: Bey Göbbels and Unzer.

Kant, Immanuel. 1999. *Crítica da Razão Pura*. São Paulo: Editora Nova Cultural.

Karpik, Lucien. 1972. "Le capitalisme technologique." *Science: Rationalite et Industrie. Sociologie du travail* 14 (1) (jan.-mars): 2–34.

Kayser, Bernard. 1993. "Des campagnes vivantes." In *Naissance de nouvelles campagnes*, edited by Bernard Kayser, 7–21. Paris: L'Aube/Datar.

Kayser, B., and A. Brun. 1993. *La place de l'espace rural dans une politique d'aménagement du territoire*. 6 juillet (mimeografado).

Kébabdjian. Gérard 1994. *L'economie mondiale enjeux nouveaux: Nouvelles theories*. Paris: Seuil.

Kende, Pierce. 1971. *L'abondance est-elle possible? Essai sur les limites de la croissance*. Paris: Gallimard.

King, Anthony D. 1990. *Global Cities, Post-Imperialism and the Internationalization of London*. London: Routledge.

Kolars, John F., and John D. Nysten. 1974. *Human Geography: Spatial Design in World Society*. New York: McGraw-Hill.

Korsch, Karl. 1967. *Karl Marx*. Ariel: Barcelona.

Kosík, Karel. 1967. *Dialetica de lo concreto: Estudio sobre los problemas del hombre y el mundo*. Mexico City: Grijalbo.

Koyré, Alexandre. 1957. *From the Closed World to the Infinite Universe*. Baltimore, MD: John Hopkins University Press, 1957.

Koyré, Alexandre. 1979. *Do mundo fechado ao universo infinito*. Translated by D. M. Garschagen. São Paulo: Forense-EDUSP.

Krampen, M. 1979. *Meaning in the Urban Environment*. London: Pion.

Krugman, Paul. 1994. "Competitiveness: A Dangerous Obsession." *Foreign Affairs* 73 (March–April): 28–44.

Kubler, George. 1973. *Formes du temps: remarques sur l'histoire des choses*. Paris: Editions du Champ Libre.

Kusmin, Vsevolod. 1974. "Systemic Quality." *Social Sciences* 4: 64–77.

Laborit, Henri. 1971. *L'homme et la ville.* Paris: Flammarion.

Laborit, Henri. 1987. *Dieu ne joue pas aux des.* Paris: Grasset.

Labriola, Antonio. 1947. "Del materialismo storico" (1896). In *La concezione materialistica della storia.* Laterza, Italy: Bari.

Laclau, Ernesto. 1990. *New Reflections on the Revolution of our Time.* London: Verso.

Ladriere, J. 1968. "Technique et eschatologie terrestre." In *Civilisation technique et humanisme,* 211–43. Paris: Beauchesne.

Lagopoulos, A. P. 1993. "Postmodernism, Geography, and the Social Semiotics of Space." *Environment and Planning D: Society and Space* 11: 255–78.

Laidi, Zaki. 1992. "Sens et puissance dans le systeme international." In *L'ordre mondial relache: Sens et puissance apres la guerre froide,* edited by Zaki Laïdi, 13–44. Paris: Berg/Presses de la Fondation Nationale de Sciences Politiques.

Lambert, Denis-Clair. 1979. *Le mimetisme technologique du tiers-monde.* Paris: Economica.

Landes, D. S. 1992. "Petite histoire de la ponctualite." In *Technologies du quotidien,* edited by A. Gras and C. Monicot, 94–103. Paris: Autrement.

Lanvin, Bruno. 1988. "Services et nouvelles strategics industrielles." *Revue Tiers Monde, July: 9,* 949–60.

Laski, Harold. 1948. *The American democracy.* New York: Viking Press.

Laszlo, Erwin. 1992. "Changing Realities of Contemporary Leadership." *Futures* 24, no. 2 (March): 167–72.

Latour, Bruno. 1987. *Science in Action: How to Follow Scientists and Engineers through Society.* Cambridge, MA: Harvard University Press.

Latour, Bruno. 1989. *La science en action.* Paris: La Decouverte.

Latour, Bruno. 1991. *Nous n'avons iamais ete modernes: Essai d'anthropologie symetrique.* Paris: La Decouverte.

Latour, Bruno. 1992. *Aramis, ou, L'amour des techniques.* Paris: La Decouverte.

Le Lannou, Maurice. 1949. *La geographic humaine.* Paris: Flammarion.

Lecourt, Dominique. 1974. *Pour une critique de l'epistemologie: Bachelard. Canguilhem, Foucault.* Paris: F. Maspero.

Ledrut, Raymond. 1984. *La forme et le sens dans la societe.* Paris: Librairie des Meridiens.

Lee, Roger. 1991. "Book Review: Iain Wallace; *The Global Economic System.*" *Transactions of the Institute of British Geography* 16: 242–43.

Leecew, Sander E. van der. 1994. "La dynarniquc des innovations." *Alliage: Pour penser les techniques.* 20–21: 28–42.

Lefebvre, Henri. 1949. "Les conditions sociales de l'industrialisation." In *Industrialisation et technocratie*, edited by Georges Gurvitch, 118–42. Paris: A. Colin.

Lefebvre, Henri. 1953. "Perspectives de la sociologie rurale." *Cahiers de sociologie*, 14: 122–40

Lefebvre, Henri. 1958. *Critique de la vie quotidienne*, vol. 1, *Introduction*. Paris: L'Arche.

Lefebvre, Henri. 1971. *Vers le cybernanthrope, contre les technocrates*. Paris: Denod-Gonthier.

Leibniz, G. W. 1994. *Systeme noveau de la nature et de la communication des substances* (1695). Paris: Flammarion.

Leiss, William. 1972. *The Domination of Nature*. New York: G. Braziller.

Leite, Maria Angela Faggin Pereira. 1994. *Destruição e descontrução? Questoes da paisagem e tendencias de regionalização*. São Paulo: Hucitec-FAPESP.

Leroi-Gourhan, André. 1945. *Milieu et techniques*. Paris: Albin Michel.

Lespes, Louis. 1980. "La propagation inegale des techniques." In *Le point critique*, edited by Charles Moraze, 59–76. Paris: Presses universitaires de France.

Lévy, Jacques. 1994. *L'espace legitime: Sur la dimension geographique de la fonction publique*. Paris: Presses de la Fondation Nationale des Sciences Politiques.

Lewin, K. 1934. "Der Richtungs Begriff in der Psychologie." *Der spezielle und allgemeine hodologische Raum. Psychologische Forschung* 19, no. 1: 249–99.

Ley, David. 1979. "Social Geography and the Taken-for-Granted World." *Philosophy in Geography*. Springer: Dordrect.

Li Carrillo, Victor. 1968. "*Estructuralismo y antihumanismo*." In *Cuaderno del Instituto de Filologia Andres Bello*. Caracas: Universidad Central de Venezuela, Facultad de Humanidades y Educación.

Lipietz, Alain. 1978. "La dimension regionale du developpement du tertiaire." *Travaux et recherches de prospective*, no. 75. Paris: La Documentation Francaise.

Lloyd, P. J. 1993. "Global Integration." *The Australian Economic Review* 26, no. 1: 35–48.

Lo, Fu-chen. 1991. *Current Global Adjustment and Shifting Techno-Economic Paradigm on the World-City System*. Tokyo: United Nations University.

Lojkine, Jean. 1992. *La revolution informationnelle*. Paris: Presses universitaires de France.

Lowenthal, David. 1975. "Past Time, Present Place: Landscape and Memory." *The Geographical Review* 65, no. 1 (Jan.): 1–36.

Lu, Martin. 1984. *Os grandes projetos da Amazonia: Integração nacional e (sub)desenvolvimento regional?* São Paulo: Fipe/FEA-USP.

Luijpen, William. 1966. *Phenomenology and Humanism.* Pittsburgh, PA: Duquesne University Press.

Lukács, G. 1972. *History and Class Consciousness: Studies in Marxist Dialectics.* Boston: MIT Press.

Lwoff, Andre. 1969. *L'ordre biologique.* Paris: Marabout Universite.

Mackenzie, Donald, and Judy Wajcman, eds. 1985. *The Social Shaping of Technology.* Philadelphia: Open University Press/Milton Keynes.

Maffesoli, Michel. 1989. "Toquio cria o barraco pos-moderno." *Folha de S. Paulo,* 12 February, 1.

Malraux, André. 1951. *Lês Voix du Silence.* Paris: La Galerie De La Pleiade.

Mamigonian, Armen. 1994. "A America Latina ca economia mundial: O caso brasileiro." Paper presented at the Fourth Meeting of Latin American Geographers, Havana, Cuba.

Mandel, Ernest. 1980. *Long Waves of Capitalist Development: The Marxist Interpretation.* Cambridge: Cambridge University Press.

Mannheim, Karl. 1935. *Man and Society in an Age of Reconstruction.* New York: Harcourt, Brace.

Marcel, Gabriel. 1965. *Being and Having: An Existential Diary* (1949). New York: Harper and Row.

Margolin, Jean-Louis. 1991. "Maillage mondial, espaces nationaux, histoire." *Espacestemps* 45–46, 95–102.

Markus, Gyocgy. 1973. *Marxismo y "antropologia"* (1971). Barcelona: Geijalbo.

Marx, Karl. 1904. *A Contribution to the Critique of Political Economy.* New York: International Library Publishing Company.

Marx, Karl. 1906. *Capital: A Critique of Political Economy.* New York: Modern Library.

Marx, Karl. 1956. *Capital Volume 2.* Translated by I. Lasker. Moscow: Progress Publishers.

Marx, Karl. 1974. *The Economic and Philosophical Manuscripts.* Translated by Gregor Benton. Moscow: Progress Publishers.

Marx, K., and F. Engels. 1947. *The German Ideology.* New York: International Publishers.

Masini, Jean. 1988. "Prospective methodologique pour une etude prospective de l'avenir du Ticrs-Mondc." *Cahier du GEMDEV* 8 (oct.): 101–17.

Masuda, Yonesi. 1982. *A sociedade da informação.* Rio de Janeiro: Rio.

Mattelart, Armand. 1992. *La communication monde: Histoire des idees et des strategies.* Paris: La Decouverte.

Mattos, Carlos A. de. 1990. "Reestructuracion social, grupos economicos y desterritorializacion dcl capital: El caso de los paises del cono sur." In *Revolucion Technologica y Reestructuracion Productiva: Impactos y*

Desafíos Territoriales, edited by F. A. Llorens, C. A. de Mattos, and R. J. Fuchs, 205–40. Santiago de Chile: Ilpes-Universidad Catolica.

Maurel, J Bosque. 1994. Globalização e regionalização da Europa, da Europa dos Estados a Europa das regiões. In *Território, globalização e fragmentação*, edited by Milton Santos. São Paulo: Hucitec/Anpur.

Mauss, Marcel. 1947. *Manuel d'etnographie*. Paris: Payot.

McBride, Sean. 1986. "Foreword." In *The Myth of the Information Revolution: The Social and Ethical Implications of Communication Technology*, edited by M. Traber. London: Sage.

McConnell, J. E. 1982. "The Internationalization Process and Spatial Form: Research Problems and Prospects." *Environment and Planning A* vol. 14, no. 12: 1633–44.

Meliujin, Serafin T. 1963. *Dialetica del desarrollo en la natureza inorganica*. Mexico: Juan Grijalbo.

Meløe, Jakob. 1973. "Aktøren og Hans Verden." *Norsk Filosofisk Tidskrift B* 8, no. 2: 133–43.

Merleau-Ponty, Maurice. 1994. *Phenomenologie de la perception* (1945). Paris: Gallimard.

Messer, August. 1929. *Filosofia y educacion* [Weltanschaung und Erziehung]. Madrid: Publicaciones de la Revista de Pedagogía.

Messer, August. 1932. *La estimativa o la filosofia de los valores en la actualidad*. Madrid: Revista de Occidente.

Michalet, Charles-Albert. 1994. "Globalisation, attractivite et polirique industrielle." *Cahier du* GEMDEV 20: 129–49.

Miquel, Cristian, and Guy Ménard. 1988. *Les ruses de la technique: Le symbolisme des techniques a travers l'histoire*. Montreal: Meridiens-Klincksieck.

Mitcham, Carl. 1989. *Que es la filosofia de las tecnologias?* Barcelona: Anthropos.

Mlinar, Zdravko. 1990. "Territorial Identities: Between Individualization and Globalization." In *Globality versus Locality*, edited by A. Kuknski. Warsaw: University of Warsaw.

Moles, Abraham. 1971a. "Objeto y comunicacion." In *Los objetos*, 9–35. Buenos Aires: Editorial Tiempo Contemporaneo.

Moles, Abraham. 1971b. "Teoria de la complejidade y civilizacion industrial." In *Los objetos*, 77–94. Buenos Aires: Editorial Tiempo Contemporaneo.

Moles, Abraham. 1972. *Theorie des objets*. Paris: Editions Universitaires.

Moles, Abraham. 1973. "Funcoes sociais do objeto." In *Rumos de uma cultura tecnologica*, 197–224. São Paulo, Perspectiva.

Moles, Abraham. 1974. "Phenomenologie de l'acrion." In *Les sciences de l'action*. Paris: Hachette.

Moles, Abraham A., and Elisabeth Rohmer. 1983. *Teoria estructural de la comunicacion y sociedad*. Mexico: Trillas.

Monod, Jacques. 1970. *Le hazard et la necessite: Essai sur la philosophie de la biologic moderne*. Paris: Seuil.

Monod, Jacques. 1974. *Chance and Necessity: An Essay on the Natural Philosophy of Modern Biology*. Glasgow: Collins/Fontana Books.

Monteiro, Carlos Augusto F. 1991. *Clima e excepcionalismo*. Florianópolis, Brazil: Editora da Ufst.

Moraes, Antonio Carlos Robert, and Wanderley Messias da Costa. 1984. *A valorização do espaco*. São Paulo: Hucitec.

Moreira, Ruy. 1995. "O tempo ea forma: a sociedade e suas formas de espaço no temp." *O espaço do geografo* 4, no. x: 8–10.

Morgan, Kevin. 1992. "Digital Highways: The New Telecommunications Era." *Geoforum* 23, no. 3: 317–32.

Morgenstern, Irvin. 1960. *The Dimensional Structure of Time*. New York: Philosophical Library.

Morin, Edgar. 1965. *Introduction a une politique de l'homme*. Paris: Seuil.

Morin, Edgar. 1972. "Le retour de l'evenement." *Communications* 18: 6–20.

Morin, Edgar. 1990. "L'homme domine-t-il sa planete?" In *La pensee, aujourd'hui*, 2: 44–45.

Morrill, R. 1965. "Waves of Spatial Diffusion." *Journal of Regional Science* 8, no. 1: 1–8.

Mumford, Lewis. 1963. *Technics and Civilization* (1934). New York: Harcourt, Brace and World.

Musso, Pierre. 1994. *Communique demain nouvelles technologies de l'information et de la communication*. Paris: L'Aube/Datar.

Myrdal, Gunnar. 1957. *Economic Theory and Underdeveloped Regions*. New York: Harper and Row.

Naville, Pierre. 1963. *Vers l'automatisme social?* Paris: Gallimard.

Neves, Gervásio R. 1994. "Territorialidade, desterritorialidade, novas territorialidades: Algumas notas." In *Território: Globalização e Fragmentação*, edited by Milton Santos, Maria Adelia Aparecida de Souza, and Maria Laura Silveira, 270–82. São Paulo: Hucitec-Anpur.

Nora, Pierre. 1974. "O retorno do fato." In *Historia: Novas problemas*, edited by Jacques Le Goff and Pierra Nora, 179–93. Rio de Janeiro: Francisco Alves.

Nordau, Max. 1968. *Degeneration* (1892). New York: Fertig.

Nze-Nguema, Fidele Pierre. 1989. *Modernite tiers-mythe et bouchemisphere*. Paris: Publisud.

O'Brien, Richard. 1992. *The End of Geography? Global Financial Integration*. London: Pinter.

Ó hUalacháin, Breandán. 1994. "Foreign Banking in the American Urban System of Financial Organization." *Economic Geography* 70, no. 3 (July): 206–28.

Ollman, Bertell. 1971. *Alienation: Marx's Conception of Man in Capitalist Society.* Cambridge: Cambridge University Press.

Ominami, C. 1986. *Le tiers-monde dans la crise.* Paris: La Decouverte.

Ortega y Gasset, José. 1947. "Meditacion de la tecnica" (1939). In *Obras completas*, vol. 5, *Ensimismamiento y alteracion*, xx–xx. Madrid: Revista de Ocidente.

Ortiz, Renato. 1994. *Mimdialização e cultura.* São Paulo: Brasiliense.

Paché, Gilles. 1990. "L'enterprise eclatee representation economique de l'espace productif." In *Communications et territoires*, edited by Henry Bakis, 83–92. Paris: La Documentation Francaise.

Pagés, Max, Michel Bonetti, Vincent de Gaulejac, and Daniel Descendre. 1979. *L'emprise de l'organisation.* Paris: Presses universitaires de France.

Paré, Suzanne. 1982. *Informatique et geographie.* Paris: Presses universitaires de France.

Parkes, Don, and Nigel Thrift. 1980. *Time, Spaces and Places: A Chrono-geographic Perspective.* Chichester: John Wiley and Sons.

Parrochia, Daniel. 1993. *Philosophie des reseaux.* Paris: Presses universitaires de France.

Parsons, Talcott, and E. A. Shils. 1952. *Toward a General Theory of Action.* Cambridge, MA: Harvard Untvcrsity Press.

Pascallon, Pierre. 1986. *Réflexions sur le développement.* Clermont-Ferrand: Faculté des sciences économiques.

Passet, René. 1979. *L'economique et le vivant.* Paris: Grasset.

Pastré, Olivier. 1983. *L'informatisation et l'emploi.* Paris: La Decouverte/ Maspero.

Paul, Leslie. 1961. *Persons and Perception.* London: Faber and Faber.

Pauwels, Louis. 1977. *Crencas e duvidas.* Rio de Janeiro: Civilização Brasileira.

Paviani, Aldo, and Nielsen de Paula Pires. 1993. "Apropriação de recursos e a gestão externas de territorios: As novas configurações e mapeamentos." In *Fim de seculo e globalização*, edited by Milton Santos, 119–28. São Paulo: Hucitec-Anpur.

Peet, Richard. 1991. *Global Capitalism: Theories of Societal Development.* London: Routledge.

Peirce, C. S. 1960. *Collected Papers.* Cambridge, MA: Harvard University Press.

Perrin, Jacques. 1988. *Comment naissent les techniques: La production suciale des techniques.* Paris: Publisud.

Perroux, Francois. 1961. *L'economie du xx siecle.* Paris: Presses universitaires de France.

Perroux, Francois. 1962. *L'economie des jeunes nations.* Paris: Presses universitaires de France.

Petit, Jean-Luc. 1990. "L'action intentionnelle: La theorie de Davidson est-elle vraiment intentionaliste?" In *Raisons pratiques 1: Les fornes de l'action,* edited by Patrick Pharo and Louis Quéré, 71–84. Paris: Editions de l'Ecole de Hautes Etudes en Sciences Sociales.

Petit, Jean-Luc. 1991. "La constitution de l'evenement social." In *L'evenement en perspective,* 9–38. Paris: Editions de l'Ecole des Hautes Etudes en Sciences Sociales.

Petrella, Riccardo. 1989. "La mondialisation de la technologic et de l'economie: Une (hypo)these prospective." *Futuribles* 135 (Sept.): 3–25.

Petrella, Riccardo. 1995. "Critique de la competitivite." *Futuribles* 198 (May): 71–80.

Picciotto, Sol. 1991. "The Internationalisation of the State." *Capital and Class* 43 (spring): 43–63.

Pickles, John. 1985. *Phenomenology, Science and Geography: Spatiality and the Human Sciences.* Cambridge: Cambridge University Press.

Pinaud, Christian. 1988. "Trans Intercom. pac. Petit abécédaire de la commutation." In *Reseaux territoriaux,* edited by G. Dupuy, 69–104. Caen, France: Paradigme.

Pinch, T. J., and W. E. Bijker. 1987. "The Social Construction of Facts Artifacts: Or How Sociology of Science and the Sociology of Technology Might Benefit Each Other." In *The Social Construction of Technological Systems,* edited by Wiebe E. Bijker, Thomase Parke Hughes, Trevor Pinch, et al., 18–50. Cambridge, MA: MIT Press.

Pinchemel, Philippe, and Geneviève Pinchemel. 1994. *La face de la terre: Elements de geographie* (1988). 3rd ed. Paris: Armand Colin.

Poche, B. 1975. Mode de production et structures urbaines. *Espaces et Sociétés, 16,* 15–30.

Polanyi, Karl. 1957. *The Great Transformation: The Political And Economic Origins of Our Time* (1944). New York: Rinehart.

Postman, Neil. 1992. *Technopoly: The Surrender of Culture to Technology.* New York: Vintage Books.

Prades, Jacques, ed. 1992. *La technoscience: Les fractures des discours.* Paris: L'Harmattan.

Pred, Allan R. 1966. *The Spatial Dynamics of United States Urban Industrial Growth 1800–1914: Interpretative and Theoretical Essays.* Cambridge, MA: MIT Press.

Prestowitz Jr., Clyde V. 1994. "Playing to Win." *Foreign Affairs* 73, no. 4 (July–August): 186–89.

Queau, Philippe. 1987. "Des vies de forme." *Milieux* 30: 4–11.

Quéré, Louis. 1990. "Agir dans l'espace public: L'intentionalite des actions comme phenomene social." In *Raisons pratiques 1: Les formes de l'action*, edited by Patrick Pharo and Louis Quéré, 85–112. Paris: Editions de l'Ecole de Hautes Etudes en Sciences Sociales.

Raffestin, Claude. 1979. "Du pausage a l'espace ou les signes de la geographie." *Herodote* 9 (jan.-mar.): 90–104.

Raffestin, Claude. 1980. *Pour une geographie du pouvoir.* Paris: Litec.

Ramonet, Ignacio. 1993. "Mondialisation et ségrégations." *Les frontieres de l'économie globale: Maniere de voir* 18, nos. 6–7 (May-June-July). https://www.monde-diplomatique.fr/mav/18/RAMONET/55000.

Randolph, Rainer.1990. "Configucação e organização territorial: Analise da espacialidade e temporalidade." *Cadernos do Ippur* 4, no. 1 (dez.): 9–34.

Reboratti, Carlos E. 1993. "La geografia en la escuela secundaria: De inventario intranscendente a herramienta de comprension." *Geographikos: Una revista de geografia* 3, no. 4: 7–32.

Relph, Edward. 1976. *Place and Placelessness.* London: Pion.

Remy, Jean. 1991. "Comentaire: G. Dupuy, *L'urbanisme des reseaux: Theories et methodes." Espaces et societes* 72: 167–71.

Remy, Jean, and Liliane Voyé. 1981. *Ville, ordre et violence: Fonnes spatiales et transition sociale.* Paris: Presses universitaires de France.

Retaillé, Denis. 1992. "La transaction economique." In *Le monde, espaces et systemes*, edited by M. F. Durand, J. Lévy, and D. Retaillé, 83–127. Paris: Fondacion Nationale des Sciences Politiques/Dalloz.

Ribeill, Georges. 1988. "Au temps de la revolution ferroviaire: L'utopique reseau." In *Reseaux territoriaux*, edited by G. Dupuy, 51–66. Caen, France: Paradigme.

Ribeiro, Ana Clara Torres. 1991. "Materia e espirito: O poder (des) organizador dos meios de comunicação." In *Brasil: Territorio da desigualdade*, edited by R. Piquet and A. C. T. Ribeiro, 44–55. Rio de Janeiro: Zahar.

Ricci, François. 1974. "Structure logique du paragraphe I du *Capital.*" In *Logique de Marx*, edited by Jacques d'Hondt, 105–33. Paris: Presses universitaires de France.

Richta, Radovan. 1968. *La civilisation au carrefour.* Paris: Anthropos.

Richta, Radovan. 1972. *Economia socialista e revolução tecnologica.* Rio de Janeiro: Paz e Terra.

Ricoeur, Paul. 1986. *Du texte a l'action: Essais d'hermeneutique.* Paris: Seuil.

Ridell, J. Barry. 1970. *The Spatial Dynamics of Modernization in Sierra Leone.* Evanston, IL: Northwestern University Press.

Rieu, Alain-Marc. 1987. "La pensee et son double: Penser l'informatique et pensee informatique." *Milieux* 30: 44–53.

Rimbaud, Placide. 1973. *Societe rurale et urbanisation* (1969). Paris: Seuil.

Ritchot, Gilles. 1991. *Etudes de geographic structurale*. Quebec: Centre de Recherches en Amenagement et en Developpement, Universite Laval.

Riu, Federico. 1966. *Ontologia del siglo xx*. Caracas: Universidad Central de Venezuela.

Riu, Federico. 1968. *Historia y totalidad*. Caracas: Monte Avila Editores.

Robin, Jacques. 1993. "Mutation technologique: Stagnation de la pensee." *Les frontieres de l'economie globale: Maniere de voir* 18 (mai): 72–74.

Roca, Pierre-Jean. 1989. "Les geographes tropicalistes et la technique." In *Les enjeux de la tropicalite*, edited by M. Bruneau and D. Dory, 119–27. Paris: Masson.

Rodrigues Garcia, José Luiz. 1994. "Nuestros magnificos pasados." In La Espera, *El Mundo* (Madrid), 9 abril.

Rogers, Everitt M. 1962. *Diffusion of Innovation:* New York, Free Press.

Rose, J. 1974. *The Cybernetic Revolution*. London: Paul Elek/Scientific Books.

Rose, J. 1978. *La revolucion cibernetica*. Mexico City: Fondo de Cultura Econcomica.

Rosnay, Joel de. 1975. *Le macroscope: Vers une vision globale*. Paris: Seuil.

Rossi-Landi, F. 1968. *Il linguaggio come lavoro e coma mercato*. Milano: Bompiani.

Rotenstreich, Nathan. 1985. *Reflection and Action*. Dordrecht, Netherlands: Martiners Nijhoff Publishers.

Roux, Jean-Michel. 1980. *Territoire sans lieux: La banalisation planifiee des regions*. Paris: Dunod/Bordas.

Russell, Bertrand. 1945. *A History of Western Philosophy*. New York: Simon and Schuster.

Russell, Bertrand. 1966. *Human Knowledge: Its Scope and Limits*. New York: George Allen/Unwin.

Russell, Bertrand. 1974. ABC *da relatividade*. Rio de Janeiro: Paz e Terra.

Rybczynski, Witold. 1983. *Taming the Tiger: The Struggle to Control Technology*. New York: Viking Press/Penguin Books.

Salomon, Jean Jacques. 1982. *Promethee enchaine: La resistance au changement technique*. Paris: Pergamon.

Salsbury, Stephen. 1988. "The Emergence of an Early Large-Scale Technical System: The American Railroad Network." In *The Development of Large Technological Systems*, edited by R. Maynz and T. P. Hughes, 37–68. Frankfurt: Campus.

Sánchez, Joan-Eugeni. 1991. *Espacio, economia y sociedad*. Madrid: Siglo Veintiuno.

Sanguin, Andre-Louis. 1977. *La geographie politique*. Paris: Presses universitaires de France.

Santos, Milton. 1971a. "Analyse regionale et amenagement de l'espace." Revue *Tiers monde* 12, 45 (janv.-mars): 199–203.

Santos, Milton. 1971b. *Le métier de géographe en pays sous-développé.* Paris: Ophrys.

Santos, Milton, ed. 1972. *Modernisations et espaces derives.* Special issue, *Revue tiers monde* 50 (abr.-jun). Paris: Presses universitaires de France.

Santos, Milton. 1975. "Space and Domination: A Marxist Approach." *International Social Sciences Journal* 27, no. 2: 346–63.

Santos, Milton. 1977. "Society and Space: Social Formation as Theory and Method." *Antipode* 9, no. 1 (fev.): 3–13.

Santos, Milton. 1978. *O trabalho do geografo no terceiro mundo* (1971). São Paulo: Hucitec.

Santos, Milton. 1979. *O espaco dividido.* Rio de Janeiro: Francisco Alves.

Santos, Milton. 1984. "The Rediscovery and the Remodeling of the Planet in the Technico-Scientific Period and New Roles of Sciences." *International Social Science Journal* 36, no. 4.

Santos, Milton. 1991a. "Meio ambiente construido e flexibilidade tropical." *Revista de arquitetum e urbanismo* 38 (out.–nov.): 73–80.

Santos, Milton. 1991b. *Pensando o espaco do homem* (1982). 3rd ed. São Paulo: Hucitec.

Santos, Milton. 1992. *Espaco e metodo* (1985). 3rd ed. São Paulo: Nobel.

Santos, Milton. 1993a. *A urbanização Brasileira.* São Paulo: Hucitec.

Santos, Milton. 1993b. "Sistema internacional de credito: Conecito e desenvolvimento." *Instabilidade econômico, moeda e finanças, 41–60.* São Paulo: Hucitec.

Santos, Milton. 1994. *Por una economia politica da cidade.* São Paulo: Hucitec-Editora PUC-SP.

Santos, Milton. 1996a. *Metamorfoses do espaco habitado* (1988). 4th ed. São Paulo: Hucitec.

Santos, Milton. 1996b. *O espaco do cidadao* (1987). 3rd ed. São Paulo: Nobel.

Santos, Milton. 1996c. *Por una geografia nova* (1978). 4th ed. São Paulo: Hucitec.

Santos, Milton. 1996d. *Tecnica, espaco, tempo: Globalização e meio tecnico-cientifico-informacional* (1994). 2nd ed. São Paulo: Hucitec.

Sartre, Jean-Paul. 1938. *La Nausée.* Paris: Éditions Gallimard.

Sartre, Jean-Paul. 1960. *Critique de la raison dialectique.* Paris: Nrf-Gallimard.

Sartre, Jean-Paul. 1968. *Search for a Method* (1960). New York: Vintage.

Sartre, Jean-Paul. 1969. *L'imagination* (1936). Paris: Presses universitaires de France.

Sartre, Jean-Paul. 1970. *Critica de la razon dialetica.* Buenos Aires: Losada.

Sauer, Carl O. 1925. "Morphology of Landscape." *Publications in Geography* 22: 19–53.

Sauer, Carl O. 1963. *Land and Life: Selected Writings of Carl Sauer.* Berkeley: J. Lenghley.

Savy, Michel, and Pierre Veltz. 1993. "Amenager le territoire dans un monde ouvert." In *Les nouveaux espaces de l'entreprise*, edited by Michel Savy and Pierre Veltz, 181–94. Paris: L'Aube/Datar.

Scardigli, Victor. 1983. "Electronique, informatique et modes de vie." *Futuribles* 2000 (avril): 23–33.

Schaff, Adam. 1992. *A sociedade informatica* (1990). 3rd ed. São Paulo: UNESP-Brasiliense.

Schaltenbrand, Georges. 1973. "Conciencia, sucesion e infinito." In *La mente y el tiempo*, 21–46. Caracas: Monte Avila.

Scharping, Rudolf. 1994. "Rule-Based Competition." *Foreign Affairs* 73, no. 4 (July–August): 192–94.

Schiller, Herbert I. 1986. "The Erosion of National Sovereignity by the World Business System" *The Myth of Information Revolution*, edited by M. Traber, 21–34. London: Sage.

Schon, Donald A. 1973. *Beyond the Stable State: Public and Private Learning in a Changing Society* (1971). Harmondsworth: Penguin Books.

Schumpeter, Joseph A. 1969. *The Theory of Economic Development* (1911). Cambridge, MA: Oxford University Press.

Schutz, Alfred. 1967. *The Phenomenology of the Social World.* Translated by George Walsh and Frederic Lehnert. Evanston, IL: Northwestern University Press.

Schutz, Alfred. 1987a. *Le chercheur et le quotidien. phenomenologie des sciences sociales.* Paris: Meridiens Klincksieck, 1987.

Schutz, Alfred. 1987b. "Sens commun et interpretation scientifique de l'action humaine" ["Common-Sense and Scientific Interpretation of Human Action" (1953)]. In Alfred Schutz, *Le chercheur et le quotidien*, 7–63. Paris: Meridiens Klincksieck.

Schutz, Alfred. 1987c. "Sur les realites multiples" ["On Multiple Realities" (1945)]. In Alfred Schutz, *Le chercheur et le quotidien*, 103–67. Paris: Meridiens Klincksieck.

Seamon, D. 1982. "Philosophical Direction in Behavioral Geography with an Emphasis on the Phenomenological Contribution." Paper presented at the Annual Meeting of the Association of American Geographers, San Antonio, Texas.

Séris, Jean-Pierre. 1994. *La technique.* Paris: Presses universitaires de France.

Serres, Michel. 1990. "Entrevista a Bernardo Carvalho." *Folha de S. Paulo,* 21 abril.

Siegfried, Andre. 1955. *Aspects du xxe siecle.* Paris: Hachette.

Sigaud, François. 1981. "Pourquoi les geographcs s'interessentils a peu pres a tout sauf aux techniques?" *L'espace geographique* 4: 291–93.

Sigaud, François. 1991. "Apercus sur l'histoire de la technologie en tant que science humaine." In "Histoire des techniques et comprehension de l'innovation," special issue, *Économie et sociologie rurales: Actes et communications* 6: 67–79.

Silva, Armando Correa da. 1993. "O mercado mundial ea alocação de capital e trabalho." In *Fim de seculo e globalização*, edited by Milton Santos, 75–82. São Paulo: Hucitec-Anpur.

Silveira, Maria Laura. 1993. "Totalidade e fragmentação: O espaco global, o lugar e a questao metodologica, um exemplo argentino." In *Fim de seculo e globalização*, edited by Milton Santos, 201–9. São Paulo: Hucitec-Anpur.

Silveira, Maria Laura. 1994. "Os novos conteudos da regionalização: Lugares modernizados e lugares letargicos no pianalto nordpatagonico argentino." *Finisterra* 29, no. 58: 65–83.

Silver, Hillary. 1992. "A New Urban and Regional Hierarchy?" Paper presented at "Impacts of Modernization: Restructuring and the End of Bipolarity," Los Angeles, California. *International Journal of Urban and Regional Research* 16, no. 4 (Dec.): 651–53.

Simmel, Georg. 1903. "Soziologie des Raumes." *Jahrbuch fur Gesetzgebung, Verwaltung und Volkswirtschaft im Deutschen Reich* 1, no. 1: 27–71.

Simmel, Georg. 1980. *Essays on Interpretation in Social Science.* Translated by Guy Oakes. Totowa, NJ: Rowman and Littlefield.

Simondon, Gilbert. 1989. *Du mode d'existence des obiets techniques* (1958). Paris: Aubier.

Slater, David. 1995. "Challenging Western Visions of the Global: The Geopolitics of Theory and North-South Relations." *The European Journal of Development Research* 7, no. 2 (Dec.): 366–88.

Smith, C. T. 1965. "Historical Geography: Current Trends and Prospects." In *Frontiers in Geographical Teaching*, edited by Richard J. Chorley and Peter Hagett, 118–43. London: Methuen.

Smith, Neil. 1979. "Geography, Science and Post-Positivist Modes of Explanation." *Progress in Human Geography* 3, no. 3 (Sept.): 356–83.

Smith, Neil. 1984. *Uneven Development: Nature, Capital and Production of Space.* Oxford: Basil Blackwell.

Smith, Neil. 1988. *Desenvolvimento desigual.* Rio de Janeiro: Bertrand Brasil.

Sodré, Muniz. 1988. *O terreiro ea ciclade: A forma social negro-brasileira.* Petropolis, Brazil: Vozes.

Soja, Edward W. 1968. *The Geography of Modernization in Kenya.* Syracuse, NY: Syracuse University Press.

Soja, Edward W. 1971. *The Political Organization of Space.* Washington, DC: Association of American Geographers.

Soja, Edward W. 1993. *Geografias pos-modernas a reafirmação do espaco na teoria social crítica* (1989). Rio de Janeiro: Zahar.

Sorel, Georges. 1947. *Les illusions du progres.* Paris: Marcel Riviere.

Sorokin, Pitirim. 1964. *Comment la civilisation se transforme.* Paris: Marcel Riviere.

Sorre, Max. 1948. "La notion de genre de vie et sa valeur actuelle." In *Annales de geographie* 57: 97–108, 193–204.

Sottsass, Ettore. 1991. "On the Nature of Metropolises." *Terrazzo, Architecture and Design* 6: 38–40, Milano.

Souza, Maria Adélia Aparecida de. 1994. *A identidade da metropole.* São Paulo: Hucitec-EDUSP.

Souza, Maria Adélia Aparecida de. 1995. "Razao global/Razao local/Razao clandestina/Razao migrante: Reflexoes sobre a cidadania e o migrante; Relendo (sempre) e homenageando Milton Santos." *Boletim Gaucho de Geografia* 20: 64–67.

Steil, Benn. 1994. "Careless Arithmetic." *Foreign Affairs* 73, no. 4 (July–August): 197.

Stern, Richard Martin. 1973. *The Tower.* New York: David McKay.

Stiegler, Bernard. 1994. *La technique et le temps*, vol. 1, *La faute d'Epimethee.* Paris: Galilee.

Subirats, Eduardo. 1988. *A flore o cristal: Ensaios sabre arte e arquitetura modernas* (1986). São Paulo: Nobel.

Subirats, Eduardo. 1989. *A cultura como espetaculo.* São Paulo: Nobel.

Swedeberg, Richard. 1990. "International Financial Networks and Institutions." *Current Sociology* 38, nos. 2–3: 259–81.

Szilasi, Wilhelm. 1973. *Introduccion a la fenomenologia de Husserl* (1954). Buenos Aires: Amorrortu.

Tarde, Gabriel. 1921. *Les lois de l'imitation: Étude sociologique.* Paris: Felix Akan.

Targowski, Andrew S. 1990. "Strategies and Architecture of the Electronic Global Village." *Information Society* 7, no. 3: 187–202.

Tavares d'Amaral, Marcio. 1987. "Impacto cultural da informatização na sociedade." In *A maquina e seu avesso*, edited by Emmanuel Carneiro Leão, Marcio Tavares d'Amaral, Muniz Sodré, and Francisco Antonio Doria, 25–42. Rio de Janeiro: Francisco Alves.

Taylor, M. J., and N. J. Thrift. 1982. "Industrial Linkage and the Segmented Economy: Some Theoretical Problems." *Environment and Planning A* 14: 1601–13.

Thévenot, Laurent. 1994. "Objets en societe ou suivre les choses dans tous leurs etats." *Alliage: Pour penser les techniques* 20–21: 74–87.

Thurow, Lester C. 1994. "Microchips, Not Potato Chips." *Foreign Affairs* 73, no. 4 (July–August): 189–92.

Tinland, Franck. 1994. "Le site de la technique: eclairages theoriqucs et enjeux pratiqucs." In *Ordre biologique, ordre technologique*, edited by Franck Tinland, 23–44. Paris: Champ Vallon.

Tornqvist, Gunnar. 1968. *Flows of Information and the Location of Economic Activities. Human Geography* 30, Lund Studies in Geography, Series B. Lund, Sweden: C. W. K.-Gleerup.

Tornqvist, Gunnar. 1970. *Contact Systems and Regional Development.* Lund, Sweden: C. W. K.-Gleerup.

Tornqvist, Gunnar. 1973. *Systems of Cities and Information Flows.* Lund, Sweden: C. W. K.-Gleerup.

Tornqvist, Gunnar. 1990. "La geographie de l'innovation." In *La géographie de la créativité et de l'innovation*, edited by Michel Chevalier. Paris: Publications du Departement de Geographie de l'Universite de Paris-Sorbonne.

Traber, Miche. 1986. "Introduction." In *The Myth of Information Revolution*, edited by M. Traber, 1–6. London: Sage.

Tran-Duc-Thao. 1971. *Fenomenologia y materialismo dialectico.* Buenos Aires: Nueva Vision.

Tsuru, Shigeto. 1961. "Has Capitalism Changed?" In *Has Capitalism Changed?*, edited by Tsuru Shigeto, 1–66. Tokyo: Iwanami Shoten.

Ullman, Edward L. 1973. "Ecology and Spatial Analysis: A Comment on the James D. Clarkson Article." *Annals of the Association of American Geographers* 63, no. 2 (June): 272–74.

Uribe Ortega, Graciela, and Silvana Levi Df. Lopez. 1993. "Globalização e fragmentação: O papel da cultura e da informação." In *Fim de seculo e globalização*, edited by Milton Santos, 172–87. São Paulo: Hucitec-Anpur.

Usher, Abbott P. 1954. *A History of Mechanical Inventions* (1929). Cambridge, MA: Harvard University Press.

Valéry, Paul. 1922. Oeuvres, La Plêiade, vol. I. Paris: Gallimard.

Van Lier, Henri. 1971. "Objeto y estética." In *Los Objetos: Comunicaciones*. Buenos Aires: Tiempo Contemporáneo.

Vattimo, Gianni. 1992. *The Transparent Society.* Baltimore, MD: Johns Hopkins University Press.

Veblen, Thorstein. 1932. *The Theory of Business Enterprise* (1904). 3rd ed. New York: New American Library.

Veltz, Pierre. 1993. "Logiques d'entreprise et territoires: Les nouvelles regles du jcu." In *Les nouveaux espaces de l'entreprise*, edited by Michel Savy and Pierre Veltz, 47–80. Paris: L'Aube.

Vilhena, Vasco de Magalhaes. 1979. *Progresso: Historia breve de uma ideia.* Lisbon: Editorial Caminho.

Virilio, Paul. 1977. *Vitesse et politique: Essai de dromologie.* Paris: Editions Galilee.

Virilio, Paul. 1984. *L'espace critique.* Paris: Christian Bourgeois.

Von Uexhüll, Thure. 1979. "Ais Mitteilung und Formung," *Praxis der Psychotherapie.* 18: 137–150.

Wagner, Philip L. 1960. *The Human Use of the Earth*. Glencoe, IL: Free Press.

Walker, Richard. 1978. "Two Sources of Uneven Development under Advanced Capitalism: Spatial Differentiation and Capital Mobility." *Review of Radical Political Economics* 10, no. 3: 26–27.

Warf, Barney. 1989. "Telecommunications and the Globalization of Financial Services." *Professional Geographer* 41, no. 3: 257–71.

Warneryd, Olof. 1968. *Interdependence in Urban Systems*. Gothenburg, Sweden: Regionkonsult Akticbolag.

Watkin, E. I. 1950. *A Philosophy of Form*. London: Sheed and Ward.

Weber, Max. 1958. *The Protestant Ethic and the Spirit of Capitalism* (1905). New York: Charles Scribner's Sons.

Weber, Max. 1969. *Economica y sociedad: Esbozo de sociologia comprensiva* (1922). Mexico City: Fondo de Cultura Economica.

Weber, Max. 1971. *Economie et societe*. Paris: Pion.

Weissberg, Daniel. 1990. "Les marches de l'informatique." *L'information geographique* 54, no. 3: 103–7.

Werlen, Benno. 1993. *Society, Action and Space: An Alternative Human Geography* (1988). London: Routledge.

White, Lancelot Law. 1974. *The Universe of Experience*. New York: Harper and Row.

Whitehead, Alfred North. 1919. *An Enquiry Concerning the Principles of Natural Knowledge*. Cambridge, MA: Cambridge University Press.

Whitehead, Alfred North. 1938. *Modes of Thought*. London: Macmillan.

Whitehead, Alfred North. 1971. *The Concept of Nature*. Cambridge: Cambridge University Press.

Whitehead, Alfred North. 1997 [1925]. *Science and the Modern World*. New York: Free Press.

Whiteman, John L. 1990. "Globalisation and Strategic Trade Policy: Some Implications for the Australian Information Technology Industry." *Prometheus* 8, no. 1: 35–49.

Whitrow, G. J. 1993. *Tempo na nistoria: Concepcoes do tempo da prehistoria aos nossos dias* (1988). Rio de Janeiro: Zahar.

Whittlesey, Derwent. 1929. "Sequent Occupance." *Annals of the Association of American Geographers* 19, no. 3: 162–65.

Wiener, Norbert. 1948. *Cybernetics: Or control and communication in the animal and the machine*. Cambridge, MA: MIT Press.

Winner, Langdon. 1980. "Do Artifacts Have Politics?" *Daedalus, Modern Technology: Problem or Opporunity?* 109, no. 1: 126–36.

Wittgenstein, Ludwig. 1961. *Tractatus logico-philosophicus*. London: Routledge and Kegan Paul.

Woeikof, A. 1901. "De L'influence de l'Homme sur la Terre." *Annales de Géographie* 50: 97–114.

Zimmermann, Jean-Benoit. 1988. "Les complexes industriels transnationalises: Problematique pour l'analyse des strategies d'industrialisation l'fans les pays en developpement." *Cahiers du* GEMDEV 8 (oct.): 119–27.

Index

competition, 126, 136, 140, 143, 148–49, 209, 233; fluidity and, 187; norms and, 154, 171; places and, 168; surplus value and, 230–31; technical networks and, 186; territorial groups and, 180

configurations: geographic, 35, 43, 78, 185, 222

content, 5–8, 14, 221, 223; capitalist, 209; content-form and, 59–66, 77–78; context and, 57; events and 93, 96; history and, 74, 82, 87, 105; information and, 143, 149, 154–55; networks and, 177–78, 185, 195; rationality and, 199; region and, 166–67; temporal, 100; technical, 22, 24, 29, 35, 43, 51, 146–47, 173–74; universality and, 128

context, 33, 232; action and, 151; events and, 97; expansion of, 172, 190, 207; momentary convergence and, 133; objects and, 57–60, 100; symbols and, 79–80; technique and, 115, 119–20

consciousness, 38, 47–49, 53–54, 219, 225, 228

content-form, 5–7, 21, 61–62, 64, 66, 77–78, 191

cooperation, 30, 194, 217, 221, 235; division of labor and, 156, 172–73, 190, 207, 223, 231; density and, 118, market-driven, 147

copresence, 108, 175, 219–20, 235

corporations, 98, 133, 164–65, 183, 232–33; competition and, 141; as deciders, 47; labor and, 87; nature and, 131; normalization and, 155; technical systems and, 121, 129; transnational, 136

cybernetics, 270. See also informatics

Debray, Regis 74, 115

density, 14; capital and, 171, 222; communicational (see Berger, Gaston); of the event, 167; informational, 148, 174–75, 186, 209; population, 89, 118; social, 219; technical, 174–75, 186, 209

deregulation, 120, 137, 141, 188

deterritorialization, 42, 125, 164, 172, 226, 230, 234–35. See also reterritorialization

dialectic, 66; social, 65, 78; of territory, 186

Diano, Carlo, 55, 61, 93, 98

Dicken, Peter, 133, 136, 140, 165

distance, 15, 30, 153, 156, 159, 162, 218–19; communication and, 132, 134, functional, 50

division of labor, 70, 81–82, 84–85, 150, 156; alienation and, 150; cities and, 209, 219, 222–23; context and, 172–73; hegemonic systems and, 11, 156; international, 83, 104, 106, 159, 166; interpretation of, 87; interurban, 195; networks and, 231; places and, 8; population density and, 117–18; social, 88, 90, 190, 207; specialization of places and, 168; territorial, 5, 83, 85–86, 89–90, 146, 163, 183–86, 207. See also Horkheimer, Max; labor

Durkheim, Émile, 14, 42–44, 51, 89, 107, 118

economy, 121, 156, 168, 170, 189, 194; capital and, 33, globalization and, 103, 165; labor and, 89; world, 83, 103, 125, 145, 180. See also systems: financial

Eddington, Arthur, 92, 98, 104–5

Einstein, Albert, 29, 52, 105

Ellul, Jacques: on norms, 155; on regionalism, 190; on technical systems, 115–16, 119; on technique, 18, 59, 122, 127

Engels, Friedrich, 46, 221

environment, 5, 40, 46, 100, 150, 173, 175, 227; built, 89–90, 169, 211, 216, 222; business, 154; change and, 83; geographic, 8, 18–19, 223; humans and, 13, 21, 171, 225; immediate, 124; material, 199; natural, 18, 20; nature and, 161; society and, 15, 18, 73; technical, 116; techniques and, 125, 127. See also milieu

epistemology, 61; geographical, 7, 25–26, 70, 200–201, 239n3; of modernity, 57. See also Latour, Bruno; Serres, Michel

epochs, 30–31, 39, 57, 206

events, 1, 6, 8, 87, 90–108, 205–6; acceleration and, 162, 166–67, 226–27; causality and, 49–51; geographic space and, 55; information and, 146; momentary convergence and, 130, 132, 134–35; objects and, 82; particularity and, 77; quasi-objects and, 61; social geography and, 57; solidarity, 175,

184; space-time and, 29; techniques and, 115; totality and, 70

everyday, the, 216, 220, 235; discourse and, 152; geographic content of, 6, 221; place and, 8

extension, 24, 30, 42, 45, 76; events and, 95–97, 99, 108; geographical, 107; horizontal, 199; of territory, 159, 190; time and, 88, 95. *See also* Séris, Jean-Pierre; succession

Fel, André, 15, 17–18

Ferrara, Lucrécia d'Alessio, 40, 145

finance, 84, 121, 133, 137–38, 140, 173, 183. *See also* globalization; systems: financial

Fischer, Gustave-Nicolas, 59, 178, 202

fixes, 173, 189, 200

flexibility, 171, 204; of technical systems, 118; tropical, 223

flows, 8, 102, 144, 172–73, 187–89, 196, 202; capital and, 162; circulation and, 182; events as, 98; fixtures and, 34–35; functional integration and, 193; information and, 200; machines and, 113; networks and, 133; norms and, 154; spatial arrangements and regulatory, 194; spatial systems and, 146. *See also* horizontalities; verticalities

Focillon, Henri, 36, 39, 92, 99

form, 43, 59–62, 78; money, 137, 203; as norm, 234; objects and, 19, 40, 79, 100, 144, 205; of regions, 166; roughness and, 89; social, 44; space and, 7, 24; totality and, 75, 77; urban, 170. *See also* content-form

Gaudin, Thierry, 19, 118

geographic milieu, 7, 20–21, 25, 174; contemporary, 157–58, 161; objects and, 40, 78; rationalization and, 198, 202; technology and, 119

geographic space, 5–6, 29–31, 34, 45, 51–52, 55 57–58; cities and, 156; contemporary, 161, 173; epistemology of, 61, 70; the everyday and, 221; flows and, 102; globalization and, 124; networks and, 179; planning and, 15; objects and, 41, 43, 60; rationality and, 198–202, 206–7; technical phenomena and,

17–18, 23; techniques and, 111, 239n3; time and, 30

geographic studies, 16, 27

geography, 2–4, 7–8, 24, 26–29, 34–35, 43–45, 70, 101, 191; competition and, 168; epistemology and, 20–21, 25, 63, 239n3; event and, 99; the everyday and, 175; of flows and fixes, 173, 194; globalization and, 133; horizontality and verticality and, 192; human, 41, 89, 93; *long durée* and, 181; of movement, 28; networks and, 177, 188; objects and, 37, 41–42, 44, 58, 61; of popular culture, 220; of production, 176, 194; retrospective, 64; simultaneity of temporalities and, 102; situation and, 96; of skyscrapers, 169; social, 49–50; space and, 49, 52, 191; technical milieu and, 158; technique and, 15, 17, 25; of time, 27, 56, 108; totality and, 69, 84

George, Pierre, 16, 63, 117, 178

Giddens, Anthony, 46–47, 52, 131–32, 220

Gille, Bertrand, 15, 115

globalization, 6, 103–5, 131–33, 171, 174, 209–10, 240n1; contemporary, 23; corporality and, 47, 215–16; empirical universality and, 70; global business and, 136–38, 141, 164–66; horizontalities and, 176; networks and, 184, 189–90, 203, 223, 232, 234; technical systems and, 126, 161, 169, 207; technique and, 32, 116, 123; time and, 181–82, 231; unicity and, 124. See also *mundialização*

Goblot, J. J., 75, 78

Godelier, Maurice, 61, 76, 153, 198, 212

Goldmann, Lucien, 72, 95, 104

governments, 47, 87, 154, 164–65, 205, 232

Gras, Joerges, 174, 179, 203, 206

Guillaume, Marc, 154, 203

Gurvitch, Georges, 3, 23, 73

Habermas, Jürgen, 48, 149, 198–200, 204, 216–17

Hägerstrand, Torsten, 3, 27, 29, 56, 61, 108, 181

Halévy, Daniel, 122, 206

Harvey, David, 27, 168

Hegel, G. W. F., 58, 74–75

Pagès, Max, 46, 140, 150, 155
Parkes, Don, 28–29, 169. *See also* Thrift, Nigel
Parsons, Talcott, 45, 51
particularity, 6, 76–77, 87, 103, 216
periodization, 3, 28, 111, 113. *See also* milieu, technical systems
Pickles, John, 44, 56
planetary intelligence, 8, 124. *See also* networks
power, 60–61, 128; centers of, 155; events and, 97–98; information and, 121–22; local, 210, 224; networks and, 184–86, 189; techno-logical, 22, 126; territorial organization and, 85–86
practico-inert, 89, 218, 227. *See also* Sartre, Jean-Paul
Prades, Jacques, 19, 144
praxis, 46, 152, 175, 204, 217, 220, 226
production, 73; areas, 197; capital and, 170; centers of, 189; circulation and, 182, 186, 226; cities and, 173; of commodities, 41; complexity of, 173; of consciousness, 219, 225; division of labor and, 82, 90; industrial, 71, 107, 197; information and, 140, 221; of geographic space, 23; global, 39, 135; of globalization, 141; events and, 97, 99, 107; flexibility and, 171; fluidity and, 188–89; of history, 228; history of, 26, 33; human, 35; intentionality and, 54; of irrationality, 209–10; of knowledge, 56, 59; local, 33, 185–86, 210; the market and, 208; mass, 187, 112–13; of material, 17, 144, 141; of meaning, 173; means of, 65, 101, 147, 161; methods of, 16; modes of, 39, 63, 84, 86–88; movement of, 7; networks and, 137, 179, 231; of norms, 120, 232; of objects, 19; of operational concepts, 26; of order, 46, 190; organ-ization of, 95–96, 176; of people, 152, 225; of place, 170; of planetary intelligence, 8, 124; politics and, 140; process of, 64, 83, 136, 182, 185, 194–95, 234; of rationality, 210–12; of reality, 6; relations of, 36; respatialization and 162; of rigidity, 115, 171; scientific, 14; of social systems, 216; social, 121; of space, 101; of the technical-scientific-informational

milieu, 160, 171; technical objects and, 143–45, 160; technique and, 16–17, 31–32, 147, 176, 197, 239n1; technology and, 19, 119; territory and, 190; of things, 54; totality and, 73, 183; of scarcity, 210, 212; science and, 116; spaces of, 209; of space, 101; standard-ization of, 33; stages of 158; symbolic, 41; of verticalities, 8; of world history, 112
proximity, 108, 218–20, 223
psychosphere, 5, 173–75
purpose, 37, 46, 48, 51, 147

railroads, 22, 113–15, 117, 122, 199, 202, 239n3
rationality: 5–9, 198–99, 201–2, 204–5, 207–10, 224, 229; artificiality and, 122; counter-, 174, 211–12; division of labor and, 219; instru-mental, 123, 148–49; globalization and, 137, 194–95, 235; objects and, 145; the psycho-sphere and, 173–74; rational action and, 48, 56; of space, 5, 8, 199–200; technical systems and, 119–20; technique and, 217
rational space, 148, 198–99, 205–7, 230
real, the, 3–4, 6, 70, 135; ideology and, 79; social facts and, 43; technology and, 63; totality and, 72
resources, 25, 83–84, 124–25, 162–64, 191; cities and, 209–10, 222, 225, 233; events and, 81, 94, 106; global business and, 136; nature and, 131, 134; networks and, 182, 184–85; technical, 174; techniques and, 118–19, 147
region, 166–67, 233–34; centrifugal forces and, 196, 208; events and, 91, 97; global business and, 136, 145, 152, 159, 172; geography and, 5, 17, 69, 71, 87–88; integration and, 176, 184–185, 190–191, 193–94; resources and, 163–64, 166–167; solidarity events and, 106–107, 127
Relph, Edward, 100, 169
regulation, 173, 232–33; colonization and, 23; events and, 95; global markets and, 137, 156; informatics and, 120–21; networks and, 162, 179, 182, 184, 186; urban systems and, 208–9, 211. *See also* deregulation
reterritorialization, 125, 235

succession, 24, 115; axis of, 102, 221. See also
coexistence; extension; Séris, Jean-Pierre

symbols, 37, 59, 78–80, 145, 182, 216–17

systems: communication, 16, 132; economic,
27, 118; financial, 84, 131, 133, 137–39; hegemonic, 58, 118, 127, 147; macro-, 188, 209;
micro-, 117, 171; productive, 23

systems of objects, 5, 36–37, 58, 60–62, 153,
193–94, 230; information and, 144; norms
and, 188; production and, 41, 45; rationality
and, 201; technical objects and, 146; time
and, 102; universality and, 128; value and,
100. *See also* Baudrillard, Jean; geographic
space

systems of actions, 5, 35–36, 45, 60–62, 153, 193,
230; information and, 144; norms and, 188;
rationality and, 201; technical systems and,
120, 150; time and, 102. *See also* geographic
space

technical objects, 17–22, 40–41, 61, 142–47,
171; artificiality and, 119–20; landscape
and, 63; networks and, 189; order and, 156;
perfect objects and, 76; rationality and, 48,
159–61, 209, 224; space and, 30, 35; technical
density and, 175; technical-scientific milieu
and, 200, 230; technique and, 32, 204;
time and, 181; trans-individuality and, 218;
universality and, 128

technical systems, 8, 14, 115–21, 191; contemporary, 143, 147–48, 150, 152–53, 203;
milieu and, 158–60, 206; objects and,
230; succession of, 21–22, 111; unicity and,
123–26, 131. *See also* universality

technique, 5–8, 13–19, 21–27, 30–33, 61, 230,
239n3; action and, 46, 48; contemporary,
142–43, 145, 147–50, 229; globalization
and, 70, 152–53; finance and, 137; flows and,
169–74, 188; hegemonic, 140; integration and, 193; milieu and, 157–58, 160–62;
networks and, 179, 186, 190; objects and, 57,
59, 100; production and, 176, 197; rationality and, 199–202, 204–6, 208–11, 216–218;
technical systems and, 111–16, 118–20, 122;

technical unicity and, 124–32, 135; totality
and, 76; universality of, 38; urban systems
and, 222, 224

technology, 13–25, 169, 204, 207; action and,
48, 56; communications, 133; division of
labor and, 87; global business and, 126, 128,
165; hypertely and, 200, 207; materiality
and, 63–64; objects and, 146, 230; science
and, 162, 173–74; technique and, 160; technical systems and, 112–13, 116–17, 119–21,
148, 154; time and, 30–33, 106; totality and,
76–77, 83

technosphere, 5, 173–75, 224

temporality, 6, 86–87, 102, 181, 206, 211

temporalization, 6, 86, 107

territory, 29, 103, 163–66, 172–74, 230, 232–35;
action and, 56; finance and, 85; global
markets and, 155–56, 161; information and,
107, 111, 195; national, 87, 89, 96–97; networks and, 176–79, 181–86, 190; productive
systems and, 199–200, 202–4; rationality
and, 8, 123, 125–26, 142, 153, 207; technical
objects and, 19, 23, 159; technical systems
and, 147–48, 169–70, 188; technique and,
13–15, 17, 21, 32–33; technology and, 119;
urban, 211, 219–20, 222

territorial configuration, 35, 43, 62, 73, 185, 201

territoriality, 108, 151, 164, 166, 218, 227

time: external, 88, 221; fast and slow, 181–82;
internal, 88, 221; measure of, 29, 86, 131; of
place, 33, 88; real, 28, 121, 131–32, 138, 150,
230; as succession, 102; of the world, 87–88,
151

time-space, 28, 31. *See* also space-time

things, 58–60, 89; convergence and, 131, 134,
151; events and, 93–95, 101, 104; integration
and, 192; intentionality and, 53–55; movement of, 16; objects and, 36–37, 39, 41–46,
147, 194; the present and, 74–75, 78–80;
rationality and, 200–201; rational space
and, 204–5, 207; time and, 24; totality and,
71–72; value and, 82–83, 158

Thrift, Nigel, 28–29, 169, 184. *See also* Taylor,
M. J.

tools, 37, 112, 114, 120, 210; place and, 168; social frameworks and, 24; technique and, 118

totality, 4, 6–8, 25–26, 69–79, 181, 183–84; division of labor and, 81, 87; events and, 91, 103–6; normalization and, 155; objects and, 37, 135, 161; place and, 178; power and, 96–98; praxis and, 217; proximity and, 219; resources and, 83–84; technical systems and, 120, 148

totalization, 6–7, 73–74, 78, 106, 153

transportation, 16–17, 33, 104; public, 146

Ullman, Edward, 27, 29

unicities, 124; technical, 124, 127–28; of technique, 169, 239n2; of time, 130, 135, 137, 139, 141

universalism, 127, 161

universality, 6, 104, 217, 234; empirical, 70; the particular and, 77 (*see also* particularity); technical systems and, 135, 143; of technique, 32, 38, 128–29

urbanization, 173, 200–201, 208–9

urban space, 170, 211

Usher, Abbott, 19, 199

Valéry, Paul, 108, 224

value, 75, 82–84, 203; of currency, 96; of events, 94; exchange, 51, 162, 209; of form and content, 60; objects and, 41, 45, 58, 62, 66, 99–101, 187; places and, 170; relative, 24; of space, 182–83, 187, 218; surplus, 135, 139–41, 144, 150, 171–72, 186, 231; systems and, 178; technical, 19; of technique, 205; universal law of, 84, 136

Van Lier, Henri, 37, 59

Veblen, Thorstein, 24, 206

vectors, 96–97, 142, 161, 190, 222; cultural, 234; diachrony and, 102; events and, 57, 84, 91; hegemonic, 231; urban space and, 211; verticalities and, 176, 195–96

Veltz, Pierre, 165, 184–85

verticalities, 108, 176, 192–97, 231

Vilhena, Vasco de Magalhães. *See* Magalhães Vilhena, Vasco de

virtuality, 60, 119; forms as, 89; of nature, 116; of places, 168, 182, 234; space and, 218, 234; technique as, 33

Warf, Barney, 132, 165

Weber, Max, 48, 198, 207, 212, 216

Werlen, Benno, 49–52, 205, 218, 220

Winner, Langdon, 20, 204

Wittgenstein, Ludwig, 71–72, 104

Whitehead, Alfred North, 49; on events, 91–92, 95, 99–100, 103–105; on knowledge, 65, 116; on objects, 57, 61, 82; on the present, 74–75

work, 202; action and, 48; hegemonic, 144; local, 185–86; nature and, 46, 158; networks, 231; objects and, 36, 42, 57, 59, 100, 147; productivity and, 167; technical objects and, 63–64, 143, 159; technical systems and, 153; technique and, 18, 30–31, 33; urban systems and, 211, 222–23

worldization. See *mundialização*

world system, 69, 216. *See also* Braudel, Fernand

world-totality, 69–70, 98

World War II, 1, 117, 126, 133, 160, 166, 181

www.ingramcontent.com/pod-product-compliance
Lightning Source LLC
Chambersburg PA
CBHW071733270326
41928CB00013B/2657